SCIENCE AND RELIGION IN ISLAM

SCIENCE AND RELIGION IN ISLAM

S R Ali

MD PUBLICATIONS PVT LTD
NEW DELHI
www.mdppl.com

Published by :

MD Publications Pvt Ltd
"MD House", 11, Darya Ganj,
New Delhi-110 002
Phone : +91-11-45355555
E-mail : contact@mdppl.com
Website : www.mdppl.com

ISBN : 978-81-7533-290-4

Published and Printed by Mr. Pranav Gupta on behalf of MD Publications Pvt Ltd at Printext, New Delhi.

Preface

Religion is a powerful force throughout the Arab world—but perhaps nowhere more so than here. The common explanation is that the Egyptian people, rich and poor alike, turned to God after everything else failed: the mess of the government's socialist experiment in the 1960s; the downfall of Gamal Abdel Nasser's Arab nationalism; the military debacle of the 1967 war with Israel; poverty; inept government—the list goes on.

The relationship between true science and Islam is a matter of extreme controversy. In the Muslim world, many believe that modern science was first developed in the Muslim world rather than in Europe and Western countries, that "all the wealth of knowledge in the world has actually emanated from Muslim civilization," and what people call "the scientific method" is actually "the Islamic method". The development of scientific thought and knowledge has caused differing reactions among Muslims. In the Muslim world today, most of the focus on the relation between Islam and science involves scientific interpretations of the Quran (and sometimes the Sunna) that claim to show these sources make prescient statements about the nature of the universe, biological development and other phenomena later confirmed by scientific research, and proof of the divine origin of the Qur'an. This effort has been criticized by some scientists and philosophers as containing logical fallacies, being unscientific, likely to be disproven by evolving scientific theories.

Seeking knowledge is obligatory in Islam for every Muslim, man and woman. The main sources of Islam, the Quran and the Sunnah (Prophet Muhammad's traditions), encourage Muslims to seek knowledge and be scholars, since this is the best way for people to know Allah (God), to appreciate His wondrous creations and be thankful for them.

Muslims have always been eager to seek knowledge, both religious and secular, and within a few years of Muhammad's mission, a great civilization sprang up and flourished. The outcome is shown in the spread of Islamic universities; Al-Zaytunah in Tunis and Al-Azhar in Cairo go back more than 1,000 years and are the oldest existing universities in the world. Indeed, they were the models for the first European universities, such as Bologna, Heidelberg, and the Sorbonne. Even the familiar academic cap and gown originated at Al-Azhar University.

Muslims made great advances in many different fields, such as geography, physics, chemistry, mathematics, medicine, pharmacology, architecture, linguistics and astronomy. Algebra and the Arabic numerals were introduced to the world by Muslim scholars. The astrolabe, the quadrant, and other navigational devices and maps were developed by Muslim scholars and played an important role in world progress, most notably in Europe's age of exploration.

I am very grateful to Mr. Pranav Gupta, Director of MD Publications Pvt Ltd, New Delhi, for his kind cooperation and support for this book.

S R Ali

CONTENTS

1

Historical Islamic Views of Science

Charles Darwin, in the 19th century put forward a theory that man came into being through a long process of evolution and not all of a sudden in one stroke as stated in the Bible. He concluded that the evolutionary process which produced man in his present form probably took millions of years. The second main point in Darwin's theory is that man evolved from lower forms of animal life. In the beginning there existed only small types of animals which during the course of time were followed by larger and larger ones. Eventually one of these kinds of animals developed into man as we know him but it has now become extinct although it can be maintained that a better form of that animal, the missing linkage is represented by the monkey.

This theory is based on the fact that ancient human skeletons which have been unearthed in various places show remarkable differences from one age to another in the size or structure of the bones or skull. This is taken to indicate that there has been a slow development and progress of the species from era to era. It is also argued that the embryo in the womb, at different stages of its development, successively resembles a number of lower animals such as a rabbit, fish or something else. This is taken to furnish ground for the conclusion that the stages which the embryo passes through represent, so to say, the stages which man has passed through from a lower animal to that of a human being.

A further argument advanced in support of the theory of evolution is that there are a number of similarities which seem to indicate that man and these lower animals are one and the same thing and that the structure of the human body is not an exclusive feature of the human species as it has evolved from the bodies and structures such as those shared by the apes. The second point in Darwin's theory was that man and apes developed from a common link which is now extinct. The basis of the argument is that certain kinds of monkeys have a striking resemblance to man. Darwin surmised that in this chain one link is missing as indicated by the gulf which should not have otherwise existed between man and the apes on one side, and the apes and animals on the other. Since there is a remarkable degree of similarity between man and the apes, and since, on the other hand, a gulf seems to separate the apes from other animals, it appears that some link has disappeared which bridged this gulf—the link from which man and the apes have evolved during the process of time.

Haeckel, after Darwin, was of the opinion that the missing link was an animal which he called Lipotylu which has become extinct leaving no trace behind it. If this animal, or its remains, could be found then the missing link which breaks the chain of continuity would come to hand and leave no vagueness or uncertainty about the theory of evolution. Thinkers of this kind believe that the gorilla and chimpanzee stand in the line of human ancestry. Darwin's theory was subjected to criticism by many thinkers who pointed out that the wide gulf separating man from the apes precluded a common ancestry for both. In these differences, however, Huxley found further support for the theory of evolution. He pointed out that the difference found between different kinds of monkeys was greater than the one found between man and the apes. In spite of the wide differences between varieties of monkeys, all were taken and accepted as monkeys.

Huxley argued that when differences between different species of monkeys were so wide then why could not man have also traveled a long way from the ape during the course of time? He concluded, therefore, that this gulf did not stand against evolution but on the other hand tended to support it. More recent research which is supported by Professor Jones and Professor Osborne tends to conclude that although man has developed through an evolutionary process he branched off from other animals at a much earlier period; and during that time he developed on independent exclusive lines as compared with other animals. In other words, man did not branch off from some kind of ape, as Darwin believed, but a long time before that during the development of animal life.

Archaeologists and anthropologists have found that human civilization has passed through very distinct stages. In the Stone Age man took his first step towards culture and civilization. Since that time he had evolved into a state of only the most rudimentary human existence and, in contrast with other forms of animal life, he did not have the advantage of claws and fangs, he used stones as weapons for offense and defense. Then came the Bronze Age when man made use of this metal. This was followed by the Iron Age. As a result of excavations archaeologists are agreed that all the stages of his life man have been a bearer of culture of one kind or another.

On the Creation of Man

First refer to the following passage from the Holy Quran:

What is the matter with you that you hope not for greatness and wisdom from Allah? And He has created you in different forms and different conditions. See you not how Allah has created seven heavens in perfect harmony, and has placed the moon, therein a light and made the sun a lamp? And Allah has caused you to grow out of the earth as a good growth. Then will He cause you to return, thereto, and He will bring you forth a new bringing forth. (71:14-19)

A close paraphrase of this passage would be:

O you human beings! What is the matter with you that you fail to understand that Allah does not do anything unless there is wisdom and purpose underlying it? You yourselves are not ready to accept the assumption that you do things with no aim or purpose in view. Why do you therefore assume that Allah, the Most Wise and All Knowing do things without purpose? Why do you jump to the thoughtless conclusion that He created man with no purpose in view? Why do you fail to grasp the evident truth that your creation has not been the result of a sudden meaningless impulse? It was the result of wise planning and deliberate execution in a succession of stages from one point to another. Do you not see that Allah has created the seven heavens in perfect harmony with each other and similarly the sun and the moon? Also the earth was one of the stages through which you passed in a process of slow growth to the point of perfection?

This is the description of the origin and emergence of man given in the Quran. The law of evolution working in the universe which Europe claims to have discovered was clearly defined in the Holy Quran more than fourteen hundred years ago that man was not created in an instant in the form in which he is today. God did not make a model of clay and breathed life into it to become the first man. No! Man has reached his present stage after passing through many intermediary stages. Man originated from and on this earth—Allah caused you to grow out of the earth as a good growth.

It is particularly distressing to note, however, that the present day popular Muslim belief has lost sight of the two crucial points that man's creation and emergence did not take place in an instant. He was created from the earth and on the earth. Popular Muslim belief has come to have it that man was created in paradise from where he was put down on earth. It is also believed by a large section of Muslims that God has a bag of souls which, from time to time, He releases singly to become human beings. In view of the prevalence of such foolish fancies that the popular Muslim mind, through some irony, is peculiarly bent upon holding views contrary to the clear teachings of the Holy Quran.

The Quran tells us that the creation of man took place in gradual stages, the underlying wisdom being that through this slow development defects should be eliminated from his constitution and nature. The gross ignorance of the views held by some Muslim religious leaders may be gagged from the following. Maulvi Syed Sarwar Shah, a prominent member of the Ahmadiyya Movement and companion of the Promised Messiah, used to relate that one of his teachers once said that the explanation for one man being handsome and another ugly, and yet another middling, is that at the time God decided to make man. He awarded a contract to the angels for carrying out the job fixing a daily quota which had to be fulfilled. The angels started kneading the clay well and shaping from it nice and handsome figures. They worked steadily, without hurry, until noon giving careful attention to each piece.

After a while they found that they were lagging behind the quota fixed and began to work only with the idea of completing it. They ceased paying careful artistic attention to their work with the result that the beings formed during the first spell of their work were very attractive while those formed in the early part of the afternoon were middling. As the afternoon wore on the angels realized with dismay that they were still lagging far behind the quota for the day so they threw all care to the wind. They hurriedly shaped a figure from the clay with a finger-poke to make the mouth and two pokes to make the eyes. No wonder these ungainly dented figures could not be compared with those made during the first spell of work. This example shows how, through ignorance, unwarranted beliefs among Muslims, Christians, Jews and others have turned beautiful truths into distressing caricatures and spurious myths.

First Stage

The next point revealed by the Quran in connection with the creation of man is that the first stage was a condition of non-existence and a controversial subject. The view of the Arya Samajists is that matter, from which the universe has been shaped, is eternal. God did no more than to bring the soul to matter together into a close relationship and so man was created. This belief is repudiated by the Quran which teaches that matter is not eternal but it is a creation of God and that man was created. God says in the Holy Quran:

Does not man remember that we created him before, when he was naught? (19:68)

Human birth now takes place from the seed of the male. This verse refers to the first original creation of the species, or the first man. It should be carefully noted that the Quran does not say that existence was created from non-existence. It says that prior to the stage when matter and other things came into being; there was a stage when nothing existed. We say that a chair can be made from a piece of wood; or we say that a chain can be made from a piece of iron. Here we have matter in one form which can be utilized to make another article. Atheists often raise the objection that it is not possible to shape out anything from nothing. This, however, is not what is meant by the Quran. What is meant is that prior to the creation of the universe there was a stage when nothing existed. Then come creation and the creation of man. God has not given knowledge to man as to how this came about, possibly because it is beyond the comprehension of man to grasp. If man could visualize how creation took place then he would be in a position to create man himself.

Second Stage

It appears from the Holy Quran that the second stage in the creation of man was a state of existence when the human body was there but the brain or its active faculties which distinguish a human being from the lower animals were not operative and active as they came to be later. There was, so to say, a human body which was not yet a human being or, in other words, there was the physical human body minus the evolved and perfected human brain or mind. We are not in a position to say whether in this state he was a kind of rock formation or a kind of plant. We can say, however, that he was not yet an animal.

The Quran says: There has certainly come upon man a period of time when he was not a thing spoken of. In other words, there has been a stage in the history of man when it was not madhkur, i.e., it was not aware of itself. lacked consciousness at the time and was not capable of recognition. He was a form of being without consciousness and intelligence, not aware of himself or of other things.

Third Stage

The third stage in the evolution of man was reached when he attained to a state of being where the production of the species began to take place through the seed of the male planted in the body of the female through sexual intercourse. From this point onwards occurs the almost infinite variety of individual human temperaments. Among animals there are varieties not characterized by sex. God says in the Quran that a stage came in the course of the evolution of man when he developed into an animal characterized by sex, divided into males and females, when his procreation began to take place through the seed of the male which is a characteristic of the higher forms of animal life. His procreation began to occur from a nutratin amshajin, from the male sperm drop embracing a combination of a number of elements. God says in the Holy Quran:

Indeed: We have created man from a mingled sperm-drop that we might try him, so we made him hearing, seeing. From this stage his procreation began to be compounded from many elements because his role in the universe was to be many sided which necessitated that he should possess a wide range of qualities.

Fourth Stage

The fourth stage came when the human brain reached perfection and characterized by a highly developed form of awareness and intelligence. From having the capacity of hearing and seeing which are qualities also to be found in the lower animals, he became capable of exercising his intelligence to a point where, through a sustained spirit of inquiry and search, inference and invention came within the range of his faculties. Here he raised one very distinct step higher than the other forms of animal life, an animal capable of sustained thought and speech.

These links in the chain of the evolution of man are the initial links of the various stages. The intervening periods between the emergence of these links have not been clearly brought out by the Quran for it is not a scientific treatise on the subject. The Quran refers to these matters which were necessary for bringing out a point of moral spiritual truth, leaving the filling in of the gaps to the human mind. We glean from other passages in the Quran that there are also other links in the chain of human evolution:

And Allah created you from dust, then from a sperm-drop, then he made you pairs.

Elsewhere the Quran says: 'And Allah caused you to grow from the earth, a good growth ', while here it is said: 'Allah created you from dust, then from a sperm-drop'. The remaining links have been omitted, till He made you pairs. i.e., a being capable of living in social units the point from which emerges what we call civilization and culture, with a system and order of life. The meaning of Azwaj used in the Arabic text of the verse which I have just quoted does not mean division into male and female because that point has already been covered in the mention of creation by a sperm-drop. Then he made you pairs, coming after sperm-drop has to be interpreted to mean something beyond the emergence of sex.

In Arabic the word zauj also means kind, variety or

complimentary groups; and this is the meaning implied here. When the human mind fully developed and a variety of temperaments emerged, individuals began to evince leanings towards or away from certain other individuals. This gave rise to the emergence of social units on this or that basis such as family groups or combination of certain individuals well disposed towards each other. The evolution of man may be summed up by saying that at first man was only a clod of earth or some kind of rock formation. After some intermediary stages which the Quran has not mentioned, man reached a stage where he became a kind of animal growth divided into male and female and procreating through sexual intercourse.

Again the Quran leaves out some intermediary stages until man emerges as a social being divided into several groups as a result of which there sprung up a variety of mental, physical or economic affiliations. This is the point where the story of human civilization begins. Among the stages of the evolution of man is when water mingled with the particular dust, clod of earth or rocky substance. This mingling of the dry clod with water which resulted in a kind of life being born in it is mentioned in the Quran:

And we made from water every living thing... (21:31)

He who has made perfect everything He has created and He began the creation of man from clay. (32:8)

The word in the Arabic text for clay is teen which means earth mixed with a quantity of water which becomes adhesive. According to the Quran, therefore, human life originated in a substance which was a mixture of earth and water which, in the course of time, developed into man. In the fore-going verses we are told that an early initial stage in the evolution of man was when he was given a particular form from wet earth. That was followed by a stage when man began to be procreated through function of the sex organs of the male and female of his species. In the words of the Holy Quran:

Then He made His progeny from an extract of an insignificant fluid. (32:9)

Did we not create you from an insignificant fluid, and we placed it in a safe place? (77:22)

These verses indicate very clearly that man's origin in dry earth or rock was one stage from which step by step he passed through a stage when it was mixed with water causing the development of a rudimentary form of life which later on began to procreate through the functioning of the sex organs which had developed in the male and female. All these stages represent different periods of time the duration of which can at best be only vaguely conjectured or imagined.

The Holy Quran mentions a general principle with regard to the creation of man:

And that with thy Lord is the final judgment; and that it is He Who makes people laugh and makes them weep; and it is he who causes death and gives life; and that He creates the pairs, male and female, from a sperm-drop when it is emitted; and that it is for Him to bring forth the second creation. (53:43-48)

From these verses of the Quran emerge the following conclusions:

- The material from which man has been created is not eternal. It was created by God.
- Man's creation involved an evolutionary process extending over a long period of time. He was not created in a moment.
- Man was created from an origin of his own species. It is not correct that he evolved from a species of monkeys or apes which is the theory advanced by Darwin.
- One of the evolutionary stages through which he passed was something akin to stone or rock.
- He next passed through a stage of animal life but intelligence had not yet developed in him although he moved about, ate and drank like other animals.
- He became an intelligent being able to speak and communicate.

- In his final stage he devised a system of life and started on the road to civilization and culture. Instead of each individual living for himself, as is the case with other and lower animals, he began to work in co-operation with others of his species evolving a system and law of life.

The Origin of Life

The Quran provides a clear cut answer to the question: At what point did life begin? In this section, I shall set forth the verses of the Quran in which it is stated that the origins of life are aquatic. The first verse also refers to the formation of the universe:

Do not the Unbelievers see that the heavens and the earth were joined together, then we clove them asunder and we got every living thing out of water? [21:30]

The notion of 'getting something out of something else' does not give rise to any doubts. The phrase can equally mean that every living thing was made of water (as its essential component) or that every living thing originated in water. Life is in fact of aquatic origin and water is the living component of all living cells. Without water, life is not possible. When the possibility of life on another planet is discussed, the first question is:

Is there a sufficient quantity of water to support life?

Modern data leads us to think that the oldest living beings probably belonged from the vegetable kingdom: Algae have been found that date from the pre-Cambrian period, the time of the oldest known lands. Organisms belonging to the animal kingdom probably appeared slightly later: They too came from the sea. The words translated here as 'water' is in fact 'ma', which means both water in the sky and water in the sea, or any kind of liquid. In the first meaning, water is the element necessary to all vegetable life:

[God is the One Who] sent water down from the sky and thereby we brought forth pairs of plants each separate from the other. [20:53]

This is the first reference to a 'pair' of vegetables; we shall cause to return to this notion later. In the second meaning, which refers to any kind of liquid, the words are used in its indeterminate form to designate the substance at the basis of the formation of all animal life.

God created every animal from water. [24:45]

Thus, the statement in the Quran on the origins of life whether referring to life in general, the element that gives birth to the plants in the soil, or the seed of animals are all strictly in accordance with modern scientific data. None of the myths on the origins of life that abounded at the time the Quran was communicated to man are mentioned in the text.

There is some that trouble you, and would pervert the gospel of Christ. But though we, or an angel from heaven, preach any other gospel unto you than that which we have preached unto you, let him be accursed. Galatians 1:7-8

Only thirty years after the crucifixion of Jesus Christ, the Holy Spirit moved the Apostle Paul to warn the churches of Galatia of variant doctrines of "other Gospels." The warning was not superfluous. By the seventh century A.D., much of the church was dominated by an unbiblical papal system, and it's accompanying unbiblical doctrines. Throughout the Middle East the Gnostic cultists promulgated counterfeit scriptures containing a counterfeit gospel, a counterfeit Christ, and a counterfeit God. It was in this world, that the religion of Islam was born.

In 610 A.D. Muhammad Ibn Abdullah reported that the angel Gabriel visited him with commands to preach religious and social reforms. While meditating on Mt. Hira, he received the first of many revelations which would eventually develop into the Quran and the second largest religion on earth. Needless to say, not everyone was or is overjoyed about this. Like every other religion, Islam had its detractors from its very birth and like every other religion, Islam has its defenders. This chapter is a summary critique of some common Muslim defences, and the orthodoxy of those defences with regard to the Quran. I argue that in their zeal to defend their faith, Muslims sometimes deny fundamental Quranic teachings.

The Qualifiers

It rarely makes for dazzling prose to begin one's monograph with qualifiers yet I think qualifiers are necessary. Now, some content. . .

The Arguments

Christian apologist William Lane Craig opened a recent book with an interesting statement: "Probably no chapter in the history of the cosmological argument is as significant or as universally ignored as that of the Arabic theologians and philosophers....the contribution of these Islamic thinkers is virtually ignored in western anthologies and books on the subject." This silence, however, is not a result of any reluctance on the part of Muslims to argue for their cause. Muslim apologists have long been obeying the Quranic directive to "Invite (all) to the way of the Lord with wisdom and beautiful preaching; and argue with them in the ways that are best and most gracious." On this invitation, I will turn my attention to the intellectual defences of Islam.

Seven arguments dominate the Muslim literature used in the defence of Islam and its scriptures: (1) The beauty of the Quran, (2) Scientific details revealed in the Quran, (3) Quranic inerrancy, (4) the spread of Islam, which ties in with (5) fulfilled prophecy, (6) the Miracle of Quranic composition, and (7) the preservation of the Quran. Obviously a summary critique such as this cannot treat all seven to any proper analysis nor does it need to. The remainder of the chapter is dedicated to an examination of the two arguments which are left.

Science in the Quran

One of the main advocates of the miraculous revelation of scientific facts in the Quran' position is Maurice Bucaille. In his popular polemic, *The Bible, the Quran and Science*, Bucaille enumerates and expounds selected Biblical and Quranic texts that have relevance to creation, astronomy, the earth, the 'animal and vegetable kingdoms' and human reproduction. Over two thirds of Bucaille's "objective study of the texts" constitutes an assault on the Bible and its alleged scientific errors.

Important as that is, *this* chapter is focusing on the claims regarding the *Quran* and its relation to science. Bucaille opens our discussion with some biographical pontifications:

I had to stop and ask myself: If a man was the author of the Quran, how could he have written facts in the Seventh century A.D. that today are shown to be in keeping with modern scientific knowledge?....What human explanation can there be to this observation? In my opinion there is no explanation; there is no special reason why an inhabitant of the Arabian Peninsula should....have had scientific knowledge on certain subjects that was ten centuries ahead of our own.

In their monograph on embryology, the Islamic Information & Da'wah Centre International people answer Dr. Bucailles rhetorical question:

All of this goes to show that the Quran could not have been the product of the mind of Muhammad....or any other human being living in the 7th century. How could he access information that will not be discovered until the 18th-20th century? How could he or anyone else study the human embryo in its very early stages without using a microscope? But then the Quran must be from God as it claims.

Other Muslim publications espouse the same position: incredible scientific facts are revealed in the Quran centuries before they were discovered by scientists and this is a sure sign of divine revelation. Bucaille maintains that there are no discrepancies between the Quran and genuine science. In spite of this impressive list, there remains a problem inherent in the "scientific argument" a problem epitomized in these verses.

Maurice Bucaille introduces the problem for us in his "Animal and Vegetable Kingdoms" section with a very revealing paragraph:

> It will become clear that numerous translations of these passages in the Quran, made by men of letters, must be deemed inaccurate by the scientist. The same holds true for commentaries made by those who do not possess the scientific knowledge necessary for an understanding of the text.

The significance of his hermeneutical principle is profound. He argues explicitly here and elsewhere, that scientific phraseology must be used in translating the Quran even though the literal text suggests something else. He acknowledges that older and contemporary commentators and Arabic scholars disagree with the rendering that he advocates. Bucaille blatantly advocates a type of eisigisis over the orthodox method of exegesis. This is a prevailing problem wherever a translator is first and foremost a scientist, or an apologist, and forces their reading on the text. It is no wonder then that one finds scientific details in some translations of the Quran. First our scientist describes or translates a text using scientific language, then he stands back in amazement, surprised at the striking parallels he has found.

In spite of this crippling defect, one may still accept these parallels. I am willing to grant that if the Quran revealed detailed scientific facts to the seventh century Arabians, we have something which did not originate with man. Both Bucaille and Keith Moore draw very concise interpretations from very vague references. Phrases such as "...could refer to..." and "...Is it possible..." are prevalent in their literature. And, necessarily so. It is also worth noting that there are 'unscientific' passages in the Quran that are dismissed as folklore, or allegorized. And no passage is any more specific in scientific detail than the writings of Euclid, for example, the atomists or the Pythagoreans.

It must be noted that even if this unorthodox method of translating the Quran was allowable, we are still only left with *Bucaille's* conclusion not the conclusion found in the paper on Dr. Moore. Bucaille states that "All of this go to show that the

Quran could not have been the product of the mind of Muhammad....or any other human being living in the 7th century." If detailed evidence were seen, we could safely conclude that Muhammad did not write it. But *logically* speaking, that only tells us that the Quran would be the product of some superhuman intelligence and that does not lead one to conclude that the information is from *God*. The Quran speaks of jinns, angels, and a deceiver named Satan. All have been around for many centuries, learning and observing. All have super human intelligence and interestingly, Muhammad had plaguing doubts at first that it *was* Satan deceiving him. Certainly, this is not compatible with orthodox Islam but then again, neither is the hermeneutic that give us the "scientific revelation".

Quranic Inerrancy

Key to any understanding of the Quranic position on inerrancy is, of course, knowledge of the claims which the Quran makes for itself. And the claim which it makes for itself is very clear: "Will they not then meditate upon the Quran? Had it been other than Allah they would have found therein much discrepancy" (4:82). Surah 41:42 says in part that "No falsehood can approach [the Quran] from before or behind it." Muslims understand by these texts that "Here God challenges people to find an error in the Quran. If it contains errors then it cannot be from God." Muslims allow for error in *interpretation*, but not error in *content*. With this in mind, we take up the challenge, and look for error not playing on the wording of any text, but on its content.

There are two kinds of inaccuracies which are usually brought up by scholars critiquing the Quran: 'internal' and 'external' contradictions within the text, and incongruencies and anachronisms between the Quran and earlier documents. There are a number of examples of apparent contradictions within the Quran. Aside from the type mentioned in note 22 of this chapter, we also see simple things like the discrepancy between six and eight day creation accounts, the creation of man out of water or clay etc. However there are possible interpretations that can deal with these problems, and therefore I will not spend any time on them.

The majority of alleged errors occur in the area of history. Those familiar with the culture and education of seventh century Arabians notice that there tends to be massive "time compression" in the narration of events. The *content* of stories was regarded as more important than the *chronology* of the accounts. In Surah 28:35-42 for example, we see Pharaoh commanding Haman (a Persian ruler born about a thousand years later) to build a tower that closely resembles the Biblical account of the tower of Babal (which was erected hundreds of years before) all in the time of Moses.

The standard method of analyzing historical documents is to accept the older documents as authoritative, unless there is strong evidence of corruption. This brings us to the heart of the issue. When compared with the ancient writings of the Bible, Josephus, and Biblical Archaeology, there are vast areas of disagreement. The standard method for Muslim apologists - understandably - has been to deny the accuracy of these ancient texts, and to assert the reliability of the newer text - the Quran. Generally the Muslim apologists appeal to the "higher criticism" which was very much in vogue (in the last century), pseudo-scholastic groups such as the Jesus Seminar, and the generic nobody-really-believes-the-Bible-is-accurate-anymore type arguments.

The object of this chapter is not to critique the validity of this manoeuvre as a tool of historical analysis. Rather, I raise a more fundamental question for Muslims. Can a Muslim hold that the Bible is corrupted - *and* still hold an orthodox interpretation of the Quran? I say you can not - and the reason is simple. The Quran is very clear about a number of facts. Allow me to list them. Fact one: God's Word cannot contain err, and cannot change. Allah is said to preserve the Quran in Surah 15:9; 41:41-42; 85:21-22; 56:77-78 and later the words of Allah are said to be unalterable: "there is none that can alter the Words (and Decrees) of Allah..." and "...none can change

His Words..." Let's stop here for a moment. If the Quran is true, then what Allah inspires cannot change, and cannot be corrupted. So we ask the obvious question: are the Torah and the Gospels said to be inspired? Any Muslim, who knows the Quran, knows the answer.

Surah 3:3 tells us that Allah "...sent down to thee (step by step), in truth, the Book, Confirming what went before it; And he sent down the Torah and the Gospels." Typical of every mention of the Torah and the Gospels, there is no word about textual corruption. Surahs 3:7, 21, 23, 48, 84, 65, 93, 184, 199; 4:44, 51, 136; 5:15, 43-49, 57-59, 66-69, 113; 6:91, 154; 10:37; 11:17; 16:43; 17:2; 20:133; 21:7, 33; 23:49; 26:196; 32:23; 41:42-45; 46:10-12; 54:43; 57:27; 80:11-16; and 87:18-19 all confirm, rather than repudiate the Torah and Gospels. Surah 5:43-49 for example starts off with a revealing passage:

But why do they come to thee for decision, when they have Torah before them? Therein is the plain command of Allah; yet even after that they would turn away.

It is plain that the author of the Quran believed the text of the Torah was fine in the seventh century. The same fact is echoed in the following verses, while verses 66 and 68-69 make it crystal clear that the problem with the Jews was their refusal to "stand fast by the Torah, The Gospel, and all the revelation that has come to you from the Lord." Verse fifteen records that they "pass over" the truths of Allah. The Quran commands the Jews to remedy their misunderstandings by a study of the Torah: "Bring the Torah and study it, if ye be men of truth." Further evidence of the integrity of the text is found in Surahs 16:43; 21:7; and 46:10, 12 where Muhammad's detractors are told to "ask of those who possess the Message" as a confirmation of the Quran. This point cannot be overstressed, but I will stop short of flogging it to death.

For a Muslim to be in accordance with the Quran in his theology, he cannot maintain that the Torah and the Scriptures are corrupted - unless the corruption took place after the Quran was written. Muslims must make a distinction between ignorance of, and rebellion against the Quran and the Bible, and corruption of the Quran and Bible. Already in the days of Muhammad, there was "a section who distorts the book with their tongues," - when it comes to the Quran, Muslims are quick to point out that false teaching is not to be equated with textual corruption. A consistent interpretation of the Quran requires that the texts used to support textual corruption in the Bible must be treated in the same way.

The Muslim is not given a pleasant choice either way. The one fork in the road leads to historical inaccuracies between revelations - the three books that the Quran says are inspired by God. The other allows a Muslim to account for the differences between the revelations - but it leaves him with an equally serious dilemma. It gives him a Quran which says the Word of God is uncorrupted, yet Muslims are belying that revelation in their zeal to defend that revelation. It leaves the Muslim with a god that cannot preserve his word from interpolations and errors. Furthermore, the apologist who holds to the corruption of previous inspiration is left without a theological court of appeal when he is faced with allegations of textual corruption within the Quran itself.

And there are such allegations. He can't announce that God's revelation is incorruptible - for he defends that revelation by maintaining that God's Word was corrupted. Clearly, this argument is not in accordance with the Quran. Clearly, it is not orthodox. This short chapter has only concentrated on two out of seven arguments the two unorthodox ones. The 'scientific proofs' require an unorthodox translation of the Quran and the 'corruption' position on inerrancy requires an unorthodox treatment of the Quran. If Muslims wish to defend an orthodox faith honestly, they need to reconsider one argument - and forget the other. Does this critique offer solutions for these problems?

Some Qualifiers

This chapter argues a point which requires a considerable degree of care, tact, honesty and a few other rare virtues hence, the qualifiers - three of them. The first comment I feel obliged to make, is something which I hope will be evidence itself throughout the paper: I am writing a constructive critique. It can be brushed aside as anti-Islamic rhetoric, and nothing will be gained. Or, they can be seriously considered, and solutions, if there are any, can be sought out, and defective arguments remedied.

The second qualifier is about Muslim apologetics itself, and my methodology. With the many factions and divisions within Islam regarding doctrine and practice, it would not be surprising to find many differing defences for the many differing doctrines. In my research on Muslim apologetics, I found exactly this—many different defences— in fact, even conflicting defences. To avoid critiquing some radical fringe, or freelancing apologist of Islam, I limit myself to examining the most popular arguments which are shared by many Muslims, from many different schools of thought.

Lastly, I also have tried to avoid erroneous criticisms by reading the entire Quran, comparing relevant difficult passages between eight different translations, and referring to commentaries where possible. This chapter does not extract allegorical or esoteric interpretations of the texts referred to. I assume the perspicuity of the majority of the Quran, and hold that the best interpreter of the Quran is the Quran itself. I allow the text to speak for itself, and where I disagree with Abdullah Yusuf Ali's comments, I provide reasons. In Christianity, if someone has a differencing opinion, we allow the Bible to be the judge as God's Word, and avoid appealing to the authority of scholars to settle disputes as scholars can be wrong, and often differ with each other. There is a common and very simple saying when someone espouses an unheard of, or otherwise dubious position: "Chapter and verse?" I apply the same hermeneutic to the Quran, as Muslims hold it to be the very word of Allah. It is my prayer that any error in exègesis will not be a result of carelessness.

Chronology and History Problems

"Muhammad supposed Imran or Amran to be the father of the Virgin Mary -Mary and Elizabeth to be sisters; who, with Jesus, John, and Zacharias, make up the family of Imran. It is difficult to avoid the conclusion that Muhammad is guilty of the anachronism of confounding Miriam with the Virgin Mary. On the other hand is the difficulty of conceiving that as the sequence of time and fact is observed with tolerable accuracy in regard to the main features of Jewish and Christian History, he should have fallen into so serious an error, or have so inadvertently adopted, as Mr. Muir supposes, the phraseology of his Jewish informants (amongst whom the only well-known Mary (Mirian) was the daughter of Imran and the sister of Moses) as to have overlooked the discrepancy in their respective dates. But it is possible that Muhammad believed, as some Muslim writers assert, that Miriam's soul and body were miraculously preserved till the time of Jesus in order to become Mary his mother. Certainly the Talmudists fabled that the Angel of Death and the worm of corruption had no power over Mirian."

Surah 20:90-100 records a Samaritan helping the Israelites build the golden calf. The Samaritans only came into existence after about 600 B.C. when Israel and Judah were taken into captivity. Not the time of the Exodus. Commentators understand that Surah 18:89-98 refers to Alexander the Great. The passage records that he was a devout Muslim and lived to a ripe old age—history records that he was a polytheist and died young. In Surah 11:42-43 "Noah's (unnamed) son is said to have refused to take refuge in the ark while the flood waters were rising, and despite his father's plea, chose rather to flee to a mountaintop, from which he was swept away by a wave. Gen 6-7 indicates that Noah had only three sons, and that they all entered the ark. Gen. 10 gives the line of descendants from each."

Surah 12:11-20 records that "Joseph did not go seeking his brother up at Dothan (As Gen 37 records), but rather the brothers, having already plotted his death, persuaded Jacob to let him go with them simply for fun and sport. Having gotten him into their power, they put him down into a well with water in it (rather than a dry pit). Nor was it they who sold him to the passing merchantmen, but rather a chance wayfarer who had come to the well to draw water. He sold the boy to the merchants "for a few dirhams" (rather than the substantial price of twenty shekels of silver, as Gen. 37:28 states.)"

Contrast Surah 26:55-60 with Exodus 1:9 and Surah 2:57, 61 with Exodus and Numbers. The Quran records that "During the exodus, the Israelites became tired of manna and demanded vegetables from the soil. After scolding them, Moses said, Get down to Egypt, for you shall have what you asked.' They proceeded to do so: 'and they returned with wrath from God.' Ancient history is very clear that "while discontented Israelites spoke of returning to Egypt, none of them actually did so. . . .In this connection, it is stated v. 61: They disbelieved the signs of God, and slew the Prophets unjustly; this, for they rebelled and transgressed.'" The Bible records no prophets being killed prior to Moses.

Problems with Prophecy

History is replete with examples of men claiming to be prophets. Generally they have promoted conflicting and erroneous doctrines and proclamations. The result, from earliest times has been a real mess. Deuteronomy 18:21-22 gives us the litmus test for judging true and false prophets:

> And if thou say in thine heart, "how shall we know the word which the Lord hath not spoken?" When a prophet speaketh in the name of the Lord, if the thing follows not, nor come to pass, that is the thing which the Lord hath not spoken, but the prophet hath spoken it presumptuously: thou shalt not be afraid of him.

Since God spoke these words, many prophets have come. And the test has been applied many times. From the ancient prophets of Baal, to the more modern Bab, Bahaullah, Joseph Smith, Brigham Young, 'Rev.' Moon and the current 'Christian' prophecy pundits—all have three things in common. All promise success for their followers, those who claim to be prophets all maintain that their coming was foretold in the Bible, and all have made miscellaneous prophecies about the future, which have not come to pass.

The success of Islam's expansion has already been given a brief treatment in note four of this chapter. The only thing that I want to add here, is a point on pragmatism. Every man with any kind of intelligence invariably predicts the success of his followers for one good reason—he can't lose. Simply put, if the prophecy comes true, and the religion or cult survives and grows, the prophecy is touted as proof of his success. If the prophecy ends up failing, "then we never hear of his promises because they, along with his movement, are forgotten."

How about Biblical prophecy regarding Muhammad? Muslims usually cite Surah 7:157 as clear Quranic support for such a prophecy: "Those who follow the Apostle, the unlettered Prophet, Whom they find mentioned in their own Scriptures, in the Torah and the Gospel..." This of course presents a profound problem for Muslim apologists.

As has been documented earlier in this chapter, Muslim apologists maintain that the Bible is corrupted. Typical of those advocating corruption, there is no specific reference to what portions, percentage or degree the text is corrupted. This leaves them in an awkward position when they do want to cite Scripture to support their claims. If Muslim apologists accept the arguments of "higher criticism" to support the alleged corruption of the Biblical text, then they must provide justification for the integrity and purity of any text that they do cite.

The absurdities and arbitrary assertions which inevitably result without such a governing principle can be seen in Maulana Ataullah Kaleem's Hazrat *Muhammad (SAW) in the Bible.* After announcing that John 16:7 teaches us that the "Comforter" is Muhammad, he uses this text to demonstrate textual corruption in John 14:26 where the Comforter is clearly identified as the Holy Ghost. And in the very verse used as proof that

Muhammad was mentioned—John 16:7—Muslim apologists maintain that there has to be corruption. No one informs us what would motivate first century Christians to remove a reference to a man named Ahmed of whom they had never heard.

Leaving this problem aside, we will examine the other key texts used in support of their position—all which can be accounted by any serious student of the Bible with very little difficulty. Before listing them, I will reduce their number. The many references to verses outside of the Torah and Gospels are of no value to an orthodox Muslim apologist, as the Quran says specifically that the passage will be found in the Torah or Gospels. This leaves us with Genesis 21:13 & 18, Matthew 5:17-18, 21:43-46 and Mark 8:27-30 in conjunction with Deuteronomy 18:15-19; Deuteronomy 33:2; and the passages relying on textual corruption in John.

The passages in John are too trivial a point to dwell on—it would be more consistent and logical to say the text is missing than to rely on a corrupted text for support. In spite of the in-depth articles written on the two passages in Deuteronomy, all make a significant error which destroys their position. The Deuteronomy 33:2 passage reads as follows:

And he said the Lord came from Sinai, and rose up from Seir unto them; he shined forth from mount Paran, and he came with ten thousands of saints: from his right hand went a fiery law for them.

Muslims argue that this is a prophecy regarding the march of Muhammad and ten thousand of his men on Mecca. There is very simple problem with this. The entire context of the passage and the tense of the verb clearly reveal that this is a record of something which has past—as in history, not prophecy. Whatever commentators say about the passage, they always understand it to be what it plainly is, and that, is history. One can of course maintain that the verb tenses, grammar and context are all corrupted. But then the apologist must be asked where the evidence is for such detailed know-ledge of the corruption, and furthermore, why the passage is cited if it's in such "rough shape."

Deuteronomy 18: 15-19 presents similar problems for those who would like it to speak of Muhammad. It reads as follows:

The Lord thy God will raise up unto thee a Prophet from the midst of thee, of thy brethren, like unto me; unto him ye shall hearken. According to all that thou desiredst of the Lord thy God in Horeb in the day of the assembly, saying, Let me not hear again the voice of the Lord my God, neither let me see this great fire any more, that I die not. And the Lord said unto me, They have well spoken that which they have spoken. I will raise them up a Prophet from among their brethren, like unto thee, and will put my words in his mouth; and he shall speak unto them all that I shall command him.

Typically the apologist follows the pattern of Ahmed Deedat who catalogues alleged dissimilarities between Jesus and Moses, and similarities between Moses and Muham-mad. It must be noted at the outset, that a degree of simi-larity and dissimilarity can always be found between any two people. For example, both Jean Chrétien (the Prime Minister of Canada) and I have the same father in Noah, both grew up in Canada, both have some similarities in religious heritage, both drive cars, both went to university, both have been active in politics, etc. etc. In spite of this there are numerous dissimilarities. I need not list them. What must be key to our brief discussion, are two things: major similarities, and fulfilment of this passage.

Let's discuss the second one first. Looking to verse 15, is Muhammad from their midst—of their brethren? The answer is simple. In spite of appeals to Genesis, where it is clear that Muslims and Jews had the same father in Abraham, the immediate context makes it very clear that the "brethren" are Jews. The Jews are given the rules on Kingship, and are told that the King was to be of their brethren, and not a stranger. History makes it clear that God himself appointed the first three kings—Jews—as were all the rest. No Muslims ever reigned over Israel.

Muslims say that Christ was not a lawgiver—Jesus said he was: John 13:34. Deedat holds that Christ didn't claim to be a prophet—Jesus said he was: Luke 13:33. Jesus also spoke words which His Father gave Him: John 12:49. Like Moses, he was Jewish; left great wealth to deliver Israel; both left Egypt to minister to their people; he was literate; worked miracles; and spoke directly to God. This last is a key characteristic of Moses—specifically mentioned in Scripture as his great distinguishing mark:

And there arose not a prophet since in Israel like unto Moses, whom the Lord knew face to face, In all the signs and the wonders, which the Lord sent him to do in the land of Egypt, to Pharaoh, and to all his servants, and to all his land, and in all that mighty hand, and in all the great terror which Moses showed in the sight of all Israel.

Yes, there were similarities between Moses and other prophets. But the Scriptures make it clear that Jesus was ultimately the best expositor of Scripture, and that his rebuke of the Jews was legitimate:

Do not think that I will accuse, you to the Father: there is one that accuseth you, even Moses, in whom ye trust. For had ye believed Moses, ye would have believed me: for he wrote of me. But if ye believe not his writings, how shall ye believe my words? - John 5:45-47

The Roman Empire was terminally ill by the end of the second century A.D. It had used its skills in administration, engineering, and military strategy to dominate a region spanning three continents. But its heart was weakened by the rise of an absolutist monarchy led, all too frequently, by weak, ineffectual emperors. Slowly, the Roman armies abandoned the most distant outposts and could not prevent the Vandals, Goths, and Huns from penetrating the inner-most parts of the Empire. The Goths sacked major Greek cities in 268, gave the same treatment to Rome in 410, and in 476 deposed the last Western Roman Emperor. Deprived of Roman law and economy, much of the region plunged into disorder and poverty.

Lost from the scene was a significant portion of classical Greek science, including Ptolemy's astronomy, Euclid's mathematics, Galen's anatomy, and Aristotle's naturalistic writings. But it hardly could be said that nothing was going on in these "Dark Ages," as some are inclined to characterize the next few hundred years. In particular, the establishment of monasteries in the sixth century provided a means for religious training. Literacy improved because instruction depended on readings from the Bible, commentaries, and works of the church Fathers. Monasteries also provided access to the relatively scant classical works available in Latin. Through the writings of Augustine (354-430), scholars were especially familiar with Plato's *Timaeus*. This work lent itself to Christian interpretation because it argued that the Universe had a first cause—an eternal self-mover—that created motion and order.

Further, because Plato's god was good, he created a world that was good for us, the creature. Unlike the Christian God, this self-mover was not a personal god; he did not love man, he was not omnipotent, and he was not the object of worship. However, Plato's arguments for a Creator-God, combined with biblically based expectations of seeing God's handiwork in creation, encouraged medieval theologians to affirm the fundamental intelligibility of God's creation. Although Augustine frowned upon the systematic study of nature, the concept of nature's basic orderliness provided an important key to the development of modern science.

During this same period, Arabic-Islamic science had reached tremendous heights. It led the world in mathematics, physics, optics, astronomy, and medicine. The stability and wealth brought by the spread of Islamic power in the seventh and eighth centuries fostered patronage of higher learning. In 762, al-Mansur established Baghdad as his new capital, and "cultivated a religious climate that was relatively intellectual, secularized, and tolerant". Over the next few generations, Arab scholars enhanced their own knowledge with medicine from Persia, mathematics from India and China, and the classical Greek heritage preserved in Byzantium. Much emphasis was given to knowledge that had special utility for Islamic culture. For example, the Chinese abacus, and the Hindu system of numbers and place-valued decimal notation, was used to advance trigonometry and Ptolemy's astronomy. These, in turn, could be used to determine the direction to Mecca and the times of prayer for any town in the Muslim world.

Crucial to the development of Arabic science was a massive translation program begun by Hunayn ibn Ishaq (808-73), a member of the Nestorian Christian sect. Arabs filled their numerous libraries with tens- or hundreds-of-thousands of books, whereas the Sorbonne in Paris could boast of a paltry two thousand as late as the fourteenth century. Despite this clear superiority, why did modern science arise in Western Europe, and not in the Islamic world? Some Muslim leaders, like some of their counterparts in early medieval Europe, had a low regard for the study of nature. Academic pursuits were tolerated, but learning was divided into traditional studies based on the Quran, and "foreign" studies based on knowledge obtained from the Greeks. Although there were Arabic rationalists, there were also those who saw in this rationalism a threat to the authority of the holy writings.

A conservative reaction in the late tenth century, together with a decline in peace and prosperity, impeded further scientific advance in the Muslim world. According to the emerging Islamic orthodoxy, man was not a fully rational creature, and no room was allowed for a purely rational investigation of God's creation. It was in this very early period of decline that the baton of science began to pass gradually into the hands of the Europeans, especially those who came into contact with the wealth of Islamic knowledge in Spain. Perhaps the next most significant event was the fall of Muslim-held Toledo in 1085. Many important Arabic and classical works from its vast library were translated into Latin.

Within a century, these had begun to filter into centers of learning all over Europe. They arrived at a time when scholars such as Anselm (1033-1109) already were reviving the role of reason in faith. Their arrival coincided also with the development of the university as a legal entity with political and intellectual autonomy. No similar institution appeared in the Arabic world until the twentieth century due, in part, to the orthodox Muslim concept of nature and reason. Religious constraints also played a role in late medieval Europe, but an academic world committed to the biblical views of man's rationality and freedom of choice provided a fertile ground for the rise of modern science.

Origin of the Decimal System

A common claim from the Muslim side is:

Should I remind you that the numbers you use (1,2,3, ...) are Arabic? Algebra, Algorithm, and many other mathe-matical words are also Arabic. If you like Math and Science, you should thank the Quran for bringing them to you, because there is no other scripture that has given to science more than the Quran did.

Let us investigate these claims. The Arabic numerals are more properly called Hindu-Arabic numerals because they did not originate in Arabia but originated with the Hindus as early as 200 B.C. The system was adopted by the Arabs by about A.D. 800 at the very earliest. They brought it to Spain about 900. It was brought to the rest of Europe about 1100...

Very few Arabs at the time of Mohammad could read or write or know arithmetic. Mohammad himself said we are a nation that does not know how to write or to do arithmetics (nahnu 'omah la takteb wa la tahseb).

It is the Jewish prisoners of war in early Islam that taught the early Muslims how to read and write etc. and in return they received their freedom. The Arabs used the local tradesmen, architects and scholars of the conquered countries and learned their skills from them. The scientific measure of the Arabs at the time of Mohammad is best reflected in the Hadith and the Quran. After this quick overview let us now be more specific in regard to the above claims:

Should I remind you that the numbers you use (1, 2, 3 ...) are Arabic.

They Arabic symbols for the digits do look different from the Western way of writing them. Just look at the verse numbers in an Arabic Quran. The way of writing them (i.e. the symbols themselves) are obviously not the same, so they are not "Arabic", therefore I guess the claim refers probably to the way of manipulating them, i.e. the positional number system. (The Greeks and Hebrews had signs for numbers long before the Arabs.) Assuming the positional number system is meant and not the symbols for the digits, I have to sadly pop this illusion as well since even that is not from the Arabs.

Algebra, Algorithm, and many other mathematical words are also Arabic. Algebra and Algorithm, I agree. But I am not so sure if you can add "MANY others" to this list as claimed. (But then exaggeration is a very Arabic thing also.) If you like Math and Science, You should thank the Quran for bringing them to you, because there is no other scripture that has given to Science more than the Quran did. Would you mind showing us where exactly the Quran did bring math to us? I have not found that yet. Please quote exact passages which explain those mathematical concepts you seem to allude to.

The Arabs kept learning from the local scholars until they began to reinterpret the Quran. But thank God for a man called Ghazali he squashed the new approach and put Islamic thinking hundred of years back because the new approach contradicted the hadith. If it was not for Imam Ghazali the Muslims not the Americans would have been the technological masters of this planet. The words Algebra and Algorithm come from the Arabic, no question. But e.g. the word Arithmetics comes from the Greek word Arithmos meaning number. So, there are terms coming from one language and other terms coming from other languages, and then what exactly are we to conclude from this? Also ponder this one: The word "computer" is English and that is used all over the world even though the first computers were built by the German engineer Konrad Zuse between 1930 and 1942. But it was the Americans who first built them on a large scale and distributed them, so that the English word became the standard word used for it in many languages.

In a similar way, the Arabs have taken over the work others have done [the Greeks and the Indians] and mainly have disseminated it and the Arabic name for it has stuck. The positional number system was developed fully by the Hindu Indians in the 4th-6th century and adapted by the Arabs only in the 9-10th century. Somehow many people still believe it was the Arabs who invented it while they only made it known world wide after they have taken it over from the Hindus. There is even a public inscription using the positional number system in India from the year 576, which shows that by this time it was in public use and not only used by the scholars in their studies. And you know that 576 is before the revelation of the Quran.

Let me quote in excerpts from Carl B. Boyer, "History of Mathematics", (a standard reference book):

During the first century of the Arabic conquests there had been political and intellectual confusion ... The Arabs were at first without intellectual interest, and they had little culture, beyond a language, to impose on the peoples they conquered. ... But by 750 the Arabs were ready to have history repeat itself, for the conquerors became eager to absorb the learning of the civilizations they had overrun. By 766 we learn that an astronomical-mathematical work, known to the Arabs as the "Sindhind", was brought to Baghdad from India. ... A few years later, perhaps about 775, the Siddhanta was translated into Arabic, and it was not long afterward (ca. 780) that Ptolemy's astrological "Tetrabiblos" was translated into Arabic from the Greek ...

The first century of the Muslim empire had been devoid of scientific achievement. This period had been, in fact, perhaps the nadir in the development of mathematics, for the Arabs had not yet achieved intellectual drive, and concern for learning in the other parts of the world had pretty much faded. Had it not been for the sudden cultural awakening in Islam during the second half of the eighth century, consider-ably more of the ancient science and mathematics would have been lost. To Baghdad at that time were called scholars from Syria, Iran, and Mesopotamia, including Jews and Nestorian Christians; under three great Abbasid patrons of learning — al-Mansur, Haroun al-Rashid, and al-Mamun — the city became a new Alexandria. During the reign of the second of these calliphs... part of Euclid was translated....

Mohammed ibn-Musa al-Khwarizmi, who died sometime before 850, wrote more than a half dozen astronomical and mathematical works, of which the earliest were probably based on the Sindhind derived from India. Besides ... [he] wrote two books on arithmetic and algebra which played very important roles in the history of mathematics. ... In this work, based presumably on an Arabic translation of Brahmagupta, al-Khwarizmi gave so full an account of the Hindu numerals that he probably is respon-sible for the widespread but false impression that our system of numeration is Arabic in origin. Al-Khwarizmi made no claim to originality in connection with the system, the Hindu source if which he assumed as a matter of course...

Through his arithmetic, al-Khwarizmi's name has become a common English word; through the title of his most important book, Al-jabr wa'l muqabalah, he has supplied us with an even more popular household term. From this title has come the word "algebra", for it is from this book that Europe later learned the branch of mathematics bearing this name. Diophantus sometimes is called "the father of algebra", but this title more appropriately belongs to al-Khwarizmi. It is true that in two respects the work of al-Khwarizmi represented retrogression from that of Diaophantus.

First, it is on a far more elementary level than that found in the Diophantine problems and, second, the algebra of al-Khwarizmi is thoroughly retorical, with none of the syncopation found in the Greek Arthmetica or in Brahma-gupta's work.

Even numbers were written out in words rather than symbols! It is quite unlikely that al-Khwarizmi knew of the work of Diophantus, but he must have been familiar with at least the astronomical and computational portions of Brahmagupta; yet neither al-Khwarizmi nor other Arabic scholars made use of syncopation or of negative numbers.

2

Different Views of Science from Modern Islam

Many people feel that in fact there is no such thing as the Islamic problem of science. They say science is science, whatever it happens to be, and Islam has always encouraged knowledge, *al-ilm* in Arabic, and therefore we should encourage science and what's the problem? There's no problem. But the problem is there because ever since children began to learn Lavoiser's Law that water is composed of oxygen and hydrogen, in many Islamic countries they came home that evening and stopped saying their prayers. There is no country in the Islamic World which has not been witness in one way or another, to the impact, in fact, of the study of Western Science upon the ideological system of its youth. Parallel with that however, because science is related first of all to prestige, and secondly, to power, and thirdly, without science the solution of certain problems within Islamic society is difficult, from all kinds of political backgrounds and regimes, all the way from revolutionary regimes to monarchies, all governments the way from semi-democracies to totalitarian regimes, all spend their money in teaching their young Western science. And therefore we are dealing with a subject which is quite central to the concerns of the Islamic world. In the last twenty years this subject has begun to attract some of the best minds in the Islamic world to the various dimensions of this problem.

2

Different Views of Science from Modern Islam

Many people feel that in fact there is no such thing as the Islamic problem of science. They say science is science, whatever it happens to be, and Islam has always encouraged knowledge, *al-ilm* in Arabic, and therefore we should encourage science and what's the problem? -there's no problem. But the problem is there because ever since children began to learn Lavoiser's Law that water is composed of oxygen and hydrogen, in many Islamic countries they came home that evening and stopped saying their prayers. There is no country in the Islamic World which has not been witness in one way or another, to the impact, in fact, of the study of Western Science upon the ideological system of its youth. Parallel with that however, because science is related first of all to prestige, and secondly, to power, and thirdly, without science the solution of certain problems within Islamic society is difficult, from all kinds of political backgrounds and regimes, all the way from revolutionary regimes to monarchies, all governments the way from semi-democracies to totalitarian regimes, all spend their money in teaching their young Western science. And therefore we are dealing with a subject which is quite central to the concerns of the Islamic world. In the last twenty years this subject has begun to attract some of the best minds in the Islamic world to the various dimensions of this problem.

And therefore want to begin by first of all by expressing for you, (making things easier, categorizing it a bit), three main positions which exist in the Islamic world today as far as the relationship between Islam and modern science is concerned, before delving a bit more deeply into what my own view is. First of all, is the position that many people reiterate. many of you, who would not have had much of a chance to study the philosophical implications of either your own tradition, that is Islam, nor of Western science, believe that one studies science and then one says prayers, loves God and obeys the laws of the Shariah, and that there is really no problem.

This position itself is not something new. It is something that was inculcated in many circles of the Islamic world during the past century and going back historically, it was the position taken up by Jamaluddin Al-Afghani who migrated to Egypt and called himself Al-Afghani. The famous reformer, a rather maverick, of the nineteenth century was at once a philosopher, political figure, Pan-Islamist and anti-Caliphate organizer. Nobody knows exactly what his political positions were, but he was certainly a very influential person in the nineteenth century, and was responsible, directly, and indirectly, through his student Mohammed Abduh, for the so-called reforms that took place in the 1880's and 1890's of the Christian era, that is the beginning of the fourteenth century of the Islamic era, in Egypt. Jamaluddin has been claimed, interestingly enough, by both modernists and anti-modernists forces like the Ikhwan-ul-Muslameen in Egypt during the early decades of this century.

Jamaluddin was interested in Western science, though he had very little knowledge [of it], and he was also very much interested in the revival of the Islamic world. The character of Jamaluddin's argument is absolutely crucial to the understanding of what I am talking about. He came up with view that science *per se* is what has made the West powerful and great. And the West is dominating over the Islamic world because it has this power in its pocket. And since this is being allowed, this is being done; there must be something very positive about this science, that science itself is good, because it gives power. This was the first part of his argument. Secondly, he argued, science came from the Islamic world originally and therefore Islamic science is really responsible for the West's possession of science and the West's domination of the Islamic world itself.

And therefore, all the Muslims have to do is to reclaim this science for themselves in order to reach the glories of their past and become a powerful and great civilization. This is the gist of a rather extensive argument given by Jamaluddin Afghani which equates, in fact, Islamic science with Western science. Secondly, it equates the power of the West with the power of science. To some extent this is true, but not completely so. And thirdly, it believes that acquisition of this science of the West [by the Muslims] is, no more no less, than the Muslims claiming their own property which has somehow been taken over by another continent and [the Muslims] just want back what is really their own. Now this point of view had a great deal of impact upon the Islamic world, upon the modernist circles, and in order to understand what is going on in the Islamic world today it is important to see what consequences flow from this.

There are some Christians and non-Christian Western people present which is fine, which is a way to understand another civilization's struggle to look at the major problems that it has. But my lecture is really tailored to the internal problems of the Islamic world, as far as science is concerned. The modernists in the Islamic world ar] one of three important groups that came into being in the nineteenth century. The other two being those who are now being dubbed as the fundamentalists, a term which I do not like at all but which is now very prevalent, and third, those who believe in some kind of Mahdiism, some kind of apocalyptic interference of God. These two groups I shall not be dealing with at the present moment. The most important group for us to consider are the modernists.

The modernists took on this thesis of Jamaluddin, and during the last century and a half, they have carried the banner of a kind of rationalism within the Islamic world which will accord well with the simple equation of science with Islamic science and with the Islamic idea of knowledge, *al-ilm*. Interestingly, as a consequence of this, the Islamic world during this one hundred and fifty year period produced very few historians of science and very few philosophers of science. It produced a very large number of scientists and engineers, some of whom very brilliant and studying in the best institutions of the world like here, but it produced practically no major philosopher and historian of science until just a few decades ago. This problem was just left aside because it was uninteresting and irrelevant, and all the debate that was being carried out in the West itself about the impact of science upon religion, upon the philosophy of science, [about] what this kind of knowing meant, these were circumvented, more or less, in the Islamic educational system.

There were a few exceptions. Kamal Ataturk came into power in Turkey. Though in many ways a brutal soldier, he saved Turkey from extinction. We know what he did to Islam in Turkey. But he had a certain intuition, certain visions of things. The first thing that he did was to say that in order for Turkey to stand on its feet as a modern "secular" state, what it has to do is [to] learn about the history of Western science. So when the program for the doctorate degree in the history of science headed by the late George Sarton, scholar and historian of science, was established at Harvard University which was the first program in this country, Ataturk sent the first student to study the history of science anywhere in America, to Harvard. The first person to enter the PhD program in the history of science at Harvard University is a Turk, Aideen Saeeli. He is still alive, [and] is the doyen of the Turkish historians of science.

There were exceptions but by and large, the modernists forces within the Islamic world, decided to neglect and overlook the consequences of Western science, either philosophical or religious and felt that Islam could handle the matter much better than Christianity. They felt that there was something wrong with Christianity as it buckled under the pressures of modern science and rationalism in the nineteenth century, and this would not happen to Islam. Certain Western thinkers, in fact, followed this trend of thought. One of the most rabidly anti-Christian, [and] anti-religion philosophers of France in the nineteenth century, Ernst Renan, who was known as sort of the grandfather of rationalism in nineteenth century French philosophy, wrote a book which is now a classical book on Averroes, (Ibn-Rushd), and which has been reprinted now after 140 years in France, in which he says exactly the same kinds of things.

He says that Averroes represents rationalism which led to modern science. He represents Arabic Islamic thought and Western theology, which simply did not understand this, has always been an impediment to the rise of modern science. So a kind of psychological and, loosely speaking, philosophical alliance was created between Islamic modernist thinkers and anti-religious philosophers in the West. This is something which needs a great deal of analysis later on. Let me just pass it over. It is not central to my subject, but we must take cognizance of it. And this attitude continued, gradually proliferating from a few centers who sent [people to the] West to the modern education institutions of the Islamic world such as the *Darul Fanooni* in Iran, the University of Punjab in Punjab, the Foad I University in Cairo, Istanbul University and so forth and so on, and gradually embraced the whole body of the Islamic world.

Today, every Thursday evening when you turn on Cairo radio there are one or two very famous lecturers who are, in fact, very devout Muslims, loved by the people of Egypt, [and] the heart of their message is every single verse of the Quran which deals with either *Ta'akul* or *Taffakur*, that is intellection or knowledge or observation or *mushahida*. These verses are interpreted "scientifically", that is, as an attempt to preserve Islam through scientific support for the Islamic revelation, for the Quran itself. And this is a very strong position in the Islamic world today. Therefore [the Muslim] thinks in fact there is no problem as far as Islam and modern science are concerned.

Now this position had a reverse. The *ulema,* religious scholars of the Islamic world opposed the modernist thesis, [which] was also based on the dilution of the *Sharia,* as you have seen in Turkey, the gradual introduction of Western political and economic institutions in the Islamic world, the rise of modern nationalism, all of these things which I will no go into right now. The religious scholars of Islam whose names paradoxically enough, meant scientists, in fact, disdained science completely. And so you have this dichotomy within the Islamic world, in which the modernists refuse to study the philosophical and religious implications of the introduction of Western science in the Islamic world, and the classical traditional *ulema,* and this cut across the Islamic world, all refused to have anything to do with modern science. There are again a few exceptions.

This left a major vacuum in the intellectual life of the Islamic community for which every single Muslim sitting in this room suffers in one way or another. Many people think this was all the fault of the *ulema.* We must add to this a third element [which] is that while science was spreading in the Islamic world, there had been created within the Islamic world, a reformist puritanical movement, especially within Arabia, associated with the name of Mohammed ibn Abdul Wahab, the so-called Wahabi movement, which is still very strong in Saudi Arabia, which in fact gave rise to the country with the wedding of Nejd and Hijaz in 1926-27. Its roots lie in the eighteenth century when this man lived, and his way of thinking then proliferated into Egypt and Syria.

Similiarly the *Salafia* movement in India and other places, [also] wanted to interpret Islam in a very rational and simple manner and was opposed to "philosophical" speculation and was opposed to the whole tradition of Islamic philosophy. These movements all but went along with the more quarrelsome and troublesome dimensions of the impact of science upon the faith system and the philosophical world-view of Islam. It is interesting that the Wahabi *ulema* in the nineteenth century opposed completely any interest in modern science and technology. It is today that Saudi Arabia of course has one of the best programs for the teaching of science and technology in the Islamic world. The centers at Dhahran and other places are really quite amazing but it is a very modern transformation. In the nineteenth century, those very people stood opposed to the modernists, and the traditional Muslim ulema whether they were Shafis or Malikis or anything else, felt that as far as science was concerned, opposition was justified.

This changed one-hundred and eighty degrees in our time. Today people of that kind of background, again want nothing to do with a discussion of the philosophical implications of science, but very much identify themselves with the Al-Afghani position, that science is *al-ilm* and let's get on with it, let's not bother with its implications. This is a very important position which have traced for you rather extensively, because it is still very much alive in the Islamic world today.

The second position which is held within the Islamic world today, which is now held by a number of very interesting and eminent thinkers, is that, in fact, the problem of the confrontation of modern science with Islam is not at all an intellectual problem but rather an ethical problem. All the problems of modern science, all the way from making possible the dropping of atomic bombs on people's heads, to the creation of technologies which create the enslavement of those who receive them, the technological star wars of the last year in the Persian Gulf, all of these are not the fault of modern science, but rather of the wrong ethical application of modern science. And one must separate modern science from its ethical implications and usages in the West take it and use it in another ethical system.

As if one were to buy a Boeing 747 from California, then take it to Egypt and paint it Egypt Air, and it would become an Egyptian airplane. This is a view which exists and is rather prevalent in many places. Most of the new Islamic universities which have been established throughout the Islamic world, like the Islamic University in Malaysia, the Islamic University in Pakistan, the Umm-ul Quran University in Makkah, try to emphasize this point of view. For example, in all Saudi universities, students are taught Islamic ethics with the hope that once they begin to learn science and engineering, they will take these and integrate them within this ethical system.

Now we come to the third point of view. This was discussed for a long time by practically no one, except yours truly. But in the last twenty years, it has gained a large number of followers. And that point of view is that science has its own world-view. No science is created in a vacuum. Science arose under particular circumstances in the West with certain philosophical presumptions about the nature of reality. As soon as you say, *m, f, v,* and *a,* that is, the simple parameters of classical physics, you have chosen to look at reality from a certain point of view. There is no mass, there is no force out there like that chair or table. These are particularly abstract concepts which grew in the seventeenth century on the basis of a particular concept of space, matter and motion which Newton developed. The historians and philosophers of science in the last twenty or thirty years have shown beyond the scepter of doubt that modern science has its own world view. It is not at all value free; nor is it a purely objective science of reality irrespective of the subject you study. It is based upon the imposition of certain categories upon the study of nature, with a remarkable success in the study of certain things, and also a remarkable lack of success [in others], depending on what you are looking at.

Modern science is successful in telling you the weight and chemical structure of a red pine leaf, but it is totally irrelevant to what is the meaning of the turning of this leaf to red. The "how" has been explained in modern science, the "why" is not its concern. If you are a physics student and you ask the question, 'what is the force of gravitation?', the teacher will tell you the formula, but as to what is the nature of this force, he will tell you it is not a subject for physics. So science is very successful in certain fields, but leaves other aspects of reality aside.

This event turned to discover what is the meaning of another way of looking at nature? Had it not been for the noble support of Sir Hammond Gibb, the famous British Islamicist at Harvard University, nobody would ever have allowed me to say such a thing. At that time, it was actually blasphemy to speak of Islamic science as an independent way of looking at reality and not simply as a chapter between Aristotle and somebody else in the thirteenth century.

But now a lot of water has flown under the bridge. And this perspective is based on the idea that Western science is as much related to Western civilization as any Islamic science is related to Islamic civilization. And as science is not a value free activity, it is fruitful and possible for one civilization to learn the science of another civilisation but to do that it must be able to abstract and make its own. And the best example of that is exactly what Islam did with Greek science and what Europe did with Islamic science, which is usually called Arabic science but is really Islamic science, done by both Arabs and Persians, and also to some extent by Turks and Indians.

In both of these cases what did the Muslims do? The Muslims did not just take over Greek science and translate it into Arabic and preserve its Greek character. It was totally transformed into the part and parcel of the Islamic intellectual citadel. Any of you who have actually ever studied in depth the text of the great Muslim scientists like Alberuni or Ibn Sina or any Andulusian scientists know that you are living within the Islamic Universe. You're not living within the Greek Universe. It is true that the particular descriptions might have been taken from the works of Aristotle or a particular formula from Euclid's Elements, but the whole science is totally integrated into the Islamic point of view.

The greatest work of Algebra in the pre-modern period is by the Persian poet Omar Khayyam. When we read his book, of course, if when you get [to a] particular formula or equation you could be writing in Chinese or English and could be in any civilisation, but the impact that the whole work makes upon you makes you feel that you belong to a total intellectual universe- the Islamic Universe. And this is precisely what the West did to Islamic science. When in Toledo in the 1030's and the 1040's the translations of the books from the Arabic into Latin began which really began the scientific changes of the 12th century and again in the 15th, 16th and 17th centuries of the West, books were simply being translated from the Arabic into the Latin. The first few decades were very much like what the Islamic world was, or has been, in the last few decades. That is, actual works of, say, Ibn Sina was being read in medicine as if they were in Arabic, but since no one knew Arabic, they were in Latin. They may not have been very good translations but there they were.

It only took a century, not longer than that, for the West to make this learning their own. The head-dress of the European bishops of the middle ages was kept on whereas at many Islamic universities today, we have taken both the gown and the cap from the West. We cannot think of ourselves independently. The whole thing has been taken over and has now been made our own. There are two very good cases: One of Greek science taken over by Muslims, [and the other] of Islamic science taken over by the Latin west and later on the European West. In both cases there was a period of transmission but there was also a period of digestion, ingestion, and integration which always means also rejection.

No science has ever been integrated into any civilization without some of it also being rejected. It's like the body. If we only ate and the body did not reject anything we would die in a few days. Some of the food has to be absorbed; some of the food has to be rejected. You might say what about the case of Japan which is so successful in making Mitsubishis, modern washing machines and so forth, but we haven't seen the end of the story. Will Zen, Buddhist and Shinto Japan be the same centuries from now and at the same time the science totally Western Science translated into Japanese or will Japan gradually transform the science and technology into something Japanese? We do not know yet.

But the historical cases that we do know- all point to a period of translation, and then digestion and integration and by virtue of integration, the expulsion of something which cannot be accepted, which is not in accord with that particular world view, which is exactly what the Latin West did. The Latin West was not interested in certain aspects of Islamic science which never took hold, which never became central. And some Muslims were not interested in some types of Greek Science which never took hold in Islamic soil. This is also a case which can be proven historically. Now, all these views which are expressed for you today are not given force in the Islamic world. There are people all the way from Abdus Salam, the only Muslim to have won the Noble Prize in physics, who was asked 'what happened to Islamic Science?' He said 'Nothing. Instead what we cultivated in Isfahan and Cordoba is now being cultivated in MIT, Caltech and at Imperial College, London. It's just a geographical translation of place'.

All the way from that position, which is really an echo of what Jamaluddin Afghani presented in a new garb by a great physicist, over to the views of the so-called "ajmalis" in England who emphasize the ethical dimension of Islamic science and who at least realize that modern science is not value-free and finally, to the position which is held by yours truly and many others in the Islamic world, and which has now given rise to the only institution, Aligarh University in India, which is trying to deal with this subject in a living fashion.

First and most powerful, is the continuous flow and absorption of western science and technology into all existing

Islamic countries to the extent that they can absorb it. In every single Islamic country, whatever political regime, whatever economic policy, whatever attitude towards the west they may espouse, whether they are completely pro-western or have demonstrations in the street against the west, the adoption of western science and technology goes on. Which is a very telling fact for the whole of the Islamic world? There are some places where some thought is being given to what is the consequence of this. Now there are many questions to ask here. First of all is this transfer of science and technology going on successfully? Is it not going on successfully? If it is not successful, what is it not going on successfully? And if it is, why? This is a very major issue. The whole question of the transfer of science is not really a subject for me to deal with today.

The second phenomenon that is going on today is the gradual attempt being made to study both the meaning and the history of Islamic science. In this field Muslims should really be ashamed of themselves to put it mildly. Let me give you some examples. There are now today a billion Muslims in the world. Probably in the first to the second century of the history of Islam, that is the eighth Christian century, no one knows exactly, but there were something like 20-30 million Muslims. Despite that vast Islamic empire the numbers were somewhere around there according to the demographers. It may be wrong, but it was anyway a much smaller number than the population of Muslims today.

During that 100 year period, more books in quantity, not to speak about the remarkable quality, were translated [about] the basic philosophical and scientific thought of Greek science than has been translated during a comparable 100 year period by all Muslims put together in all Islamic countries. This is really unbelievable. Not to talk about the quality, which is of a very high nature, in the early translations from Greek which made Arabic the most important scientific language in world for 700 years, whereas today, we have usually very poor quality translations into modern Islamic languages, oftentimes based on Latin knowledge of classical Arabic.

Most the history of Islamic science has been written by western scholars including the great. His one book, Introduction to the History of Science, has lead to at least 500 or 600 books in Urdu, Persian, and Malay, Arabic and other Muslim language which are sold in the streets as Islamic Science because everybody is too lazy to go do his own or her own research. Typically in such works one or two pages are just taken and culled and regurgitated and repeated and so forth and so on in a manner that is really sickening. Compared to the other civilizations of Asia, the Chinese and the Japanese and the Indian, the Muslims have not had a very good record in studying their own history of science despite the fact that this field was of great importance religiously, going back to what I said about Jamaluddin and Mohammed Abduh in the later 19th century, the rise of modernism in the Islamic world, and all of these other very powerful forces.

During the last 20-30 years, there has been a change. Gradually Muslim governments are realizing that it's very important that if you have 100 students that you have 80 of them study science and technology but it's also very important that the other twenty study the humanities and to train some people in the history of science, which although allied to science, is not really science itself. It is historical knowledge, it is linguistic knowledge, and it is philosophical knowledge. The Muslims have not yet developed their own historiography of science. This is a very important field. If you look at all the histories of science written in the west, everything ends miraculously in the thirteenth century-implying the whole of Islamic civilization came to an end in the thirteenth century.

Islamic philosophy, Islamic science, history of astronomy, history of physics, alchemy, biology, anything you study, miraculously comes to an end in the thirteenth century which coincides exactly with the termination of political contact between Islam and the West. Now Muslims always get angry at why this is so, but Western historians are completely right to study Islamic history from their own point of view. And Muslim thinkers are completely wrong in studying their own history from the point of view of western history. Many, many years ago in a statement in Pakistan 30 years ago, which has been repeated not many times, that any individual that stands in a mirror and looks at his or her own image perceives that image from the point of view of the model or the behind the mirror but we're doing this culturally, much of the Islamic world is doing this cultu-rally and that is nothing less than an insane way of looking at themselves. We should be able to look at ourselves directly and to do that we have to develop a historiography of science.

Well, that is a very brilliant period in the history of Islamic medicine and the reason you don't know anything about it is because E.G. Brown didn't write about it in his book "Arabian Medicine". That's the only reason. Because Brown was only interested in Early Islamic medicine as it influenced the great physicians in the west. Now, therefore this [question of] the historiography of Islamic science is far from being a trivial question. And it has created, in fact, a vacuum within which the integration of western science and technology is made doubly difficult in the Islamic world. That is most young Muslim students have this view which has unfortunately been abetted by Arab Nationalism. The nationalisms in the Middle East, Arabic, Persian, Turkish, are now more or less over, they are ending one way or the other. That is they're showing their bankruptcy, not completely, there are nations that still exist of course but their grand days are perhaps over.

Arab Nationalism began with a thesis, propagated by small non-Muslim minorities within the Arab world that the Islamic civilization began to go down when the Arab hegemony over Islamic civilization came to an end. That is with the Abbasids. If you look, for example, at the history of Arabic literature, everybody talks about the Ummayad and the Abbasid period and there is nothing going on for several hundred years until some poet begins to talk about the lamentations of the war in Iraq or the tragedies in Palestine. That is, of course, very gripping poetry, but what were the

Arabs doing for 700 years in between? That is totally overlooked.

There must be some Yemenese students here. Where is there a single book on the history of Arabic poetry in Yemen-one of the richest lands in the Islamic world of poetry. We don't know that there might be some local book published in Sanaa but certainly in Cambridge we know nothing about it so Arab nationalism had a lot to do with this of trying to diminish the contribution that Islamic civilization. After the Mongol invasion and the destruction of Baghdad in 1258, which coincided with the downfall of the political hegemony of the Arabs who did not regain the political hegemony, even over themselves, until the 20th century? Now, the consequence of that is, first of all, the overlooking of 700 years, not 70 years, 700 years, of Islamic intellectual history during which the Muslims were supposed to have done nothing. They were supposed to have been decadent for 700 years.

Now how can you revive a patient that has been dead for that long a time? The idea which is propagated in the West is that Muslims are very brilliant, that they did science and things like that, and then suddenly decided to turn the switch off and went to selling beads and playing with their rosaries in the bazaar for the next 700 years till Mossadegh nationalized the oil and they came back on the scene of human history are now living happily again. This, of course, is total nonsense and it brings about a scelerosis, intellectually, which is far from being trivial. They wanted to connect themselves to Al-Biruni and Khawarizmi and people like that, but this hiatus was simply too long.

This hiatus has not been created by history itself. It has been created by the study of history from the particular perspective of Western scholarship, which is perfectly within its right in its claim that Islam is interesting only till the moment that it influences the West. The great mistake is when that objective divides the history of Islam into a period of productivity and one of degeneration. In the field of history of science, that is a very important element. This leads me to the third important activity which is now going on in the Islamic World. We have studied Islamic science from our own point of view somewhat [though this study is hardly comprehensive for] it will take a long, long time to get all the relevant manuscripts. There are over three thousand manuscripts of medicine in India which have never been studied by anybody. This is [only] the tip of the iceberg.

There are thousands of manuscripts in Yemen which we don't even know about. There is a new institution being established in London which is being inaugurated at the end of next month, the *Al-Furqan* Foundation, which will be devoted to assembling Islamic manuscripts from all over the world and compiling original surveys of where the manuscripts are... places like Ethiopia for example, have treasuries of Islamic manuscripts, many of them in the sciences. The process will take a long time, but at least on the basis of what has been begun, progress can be made.

But in this field, there is now the third step of trying to further science within the Islamic world under the foundation of an Islamic logic of science. Now this is a very difficult and very tall order. It is not going something which is going to be done immediately. And we can perhaps discuss this with you during the question-answer period. It is interesting that some of the places where a great deal of the intellectual attention is being paid to the subject are not places which have been known historically as the great intellectual centers of Islamic civilization which have really always been between Lahore and Tripoli.

About nine-tenths of all famous Islamic thinkers have come from that region, Spain being the one great exception. But today, one of the places, for example, where a great deal of the work is being done is Malaysia. Normally one would think of Malaysia as a small Islamic country with only a 55% or a 57% Muslim majority. However there is, because of the interest of the government, a great deal of effort being spent in trying to understand what is the meaning of Islamic science and how can science be further explored for the basis of an Islamic view towards science. Another place is Turkey. One does not usually think of Turkey these days as being significant as a center of Islamic thought because of the secularism brought by Kamal Ataturk.

But within Turkey, despite all of this, an incredible amount of intellectual activity has been going on in the last few decades bringing things as different, as separate, as the *Naqshbandia* of Istanbul and the *Khizisists* of Istanbul University together. The most important journal which is being published in Turkey on this issue, called "Science and Technology" is not, in fact, published by secular Turks. It is published by very devout Muslims, who are extremely interested in the Islamicisty of Islamic science, and I think the Turkish will be able to make some major intellectual contributions in the future to this field.

Perhaps most interesting of all these programs is going on in Aligarh University in India. Aligarh University is of course a major Islamic university whose Islamicisty is now very much threatened, by all that is going on in India, one of the great tragedies of the last few decades. Everyday, about seven or eight people were killed just on the road. People pull you off of the car and shoot you, and you cannot do anything about it. MAAS is a unique institution founded by twenty or thirty scientists, almost all of them, scientists, physicists, chemists, biologists, and some of them very brilliant, who want to absorb, first, Islamic science, then to absorb Western science.

There is no way of establishing an Islamic science without knowing Western science well. To talk of circumventing what the West has learnt is absurd. But then the next step that has to be taken on the basis of Islamic world view and the view of nature. Whether they will succeed or not, *Allah o aalim*, 'God knows best', but mention it here as one of the most important attempts that is now being made in the Muslim world. Gradually a network is being created among young Muslim scientists who are concerned with religion and are also quite capable of dealing with the humanities.

Of course a person should never be too charmed by futurologists; otherwise you would never say *insha'llah.* Three years ago probably companies were paying fortunes to [be told] what the future of the Soviet Union was and yet nobody guessed what was going to happen. So, let's take this with a grain of salt. Only God knows. But from the point of a humble scholar of the situation, the cultural crisis created by the successful introduction of Western science and technology, successful enough to bring about rapid cultural patterns of change, is going to continue to pose major problems for the Islamic world. The best example of that is what happened in Iran. Iran had without doubt, the most advanced program for the teaching of science and technology and the largest per capita number of scientists.

It was the only country in the Muslim world where alternative technology was already beginning to be discussed, but the cultural transformation brought about by the very success of the enterprise, besides all the other political problems that were involved certainly contributed to the outcome of what happened in the late seventies. The government in Iran today, wants very much to go back to implement the very scientific programs and technological programs which were put aside during the ten years after the revolution. But I believe that the impact of the absorption of Western science and more than that, the application of technology, for science today, in the minds of Muslim governments is not separated from application of technology, they are not simply interested in pure science. Pure scientists have a lot of trouble finding money for their work; it is the applied aspect which is emphasized.

Do not think that a science museum is simply neutral in its cultural impact. It has a tremendous impact upon those who go into it. If you go into a building in which one room is full of dinosaurs, the next room is full of wires, and the third full of old trains, you are going to have a segmented view of knowledge which is going to have a deep effect upon the young person who goes there, who has been taught about *Tauhid,* about Unity, about the Unity of knowledge, about the Unity of God, the Unity of the universe. There is going to be a dichotomy created in him. You must be able to integrate knowledge.

The problem is that with the increase of success of both the teaching of science and the technology, will bring with it a cultural dislocation and philosophical questioning which have to be answered especially at a time when the Islamic world does not want to play the role of a dead duck. There is not a moment in the history of Islam, when the Muslims like the other great civilizations of Asia are trying to play the game of the West. The Islamic world wants to pull its own weight, wants to finds its own identity, and therefore this problem is going to be acute.

Secondly, a very major crisis is being set afoot by the very application of modern technology, that is the environ-mental crisis. This crisis is of course global. You cannot say, 'I am drawing a boundary around my country, I do not want the hole in the ozone zone, to make the sun shine upon my head'. You have no choice in that. Because of that, and because of the fact that Islamic countries, like Buddhist countries, like Hindu countries, will always eat from the bread crumbs of Western technology in the situation of the world today, more of an attempt is made towards the direction of alternative technologies. This began in Iran in the seventies, and thank God, is still going on a little, and [in] other places like Egypt where a little attempt to spend some of the energy of society towards alternative technology is being made. All of which also means to try to look upon science as the mother of technology in somewhat of a different way.

In his preface to Heisenberg's *Physics and Philosophy*, F. S. C. Northop made the following observation on the spread of modern science to non-Western societies:

"...modern ways are going to alter and in part destroy traditional customs and values. It is frequently assumed by native leaders of non-Western societies, and also often by their

Western advisers, that the problem of introducing modern scientific instruments and ways into Asia, the Middle East and Africa is merely that of giving the native people their political independence and then providing them with the funds and the practical instruments ... one cannot bring in the instruments of modern physics without sooner or later introducing its philosophical mentality, and this mentality, as it captures the scientifically trained youth, upsets the old familial and tribal moral loyalties."

Northrop, who made these remarks more than four decades ago, did not have to wait too long to see his predictions come true. The changes brought about by modern science in the minds and lives of people in the Muslim world have been no less profound and deep-seated than they are for people living in the western hemisphere. The crisis of legitimacy and the dissolution of traditional certainties, closely related to the scientific worldview of modern natural sciences, have a deep impact on how people in the Islamic world relate to the question of science on the one hand, and their intellectual and scientific tradition, on the other.

The wide spectrum of views on the issue range from Muslim scientists and professionals who take science to be a pure and disengaged study of natural phenomena with no hidden or explicit ideological assumptions to those who consider modern science essentially materialistic, reductionist and thus in conflict with the ethos of the religious view of the universe. Regardless of what particular position one takes in this debate, the urgency of addressing the question of (modern) science is as fresh and challenging today as it was more than a century ago for Jamal al-Din Afghani, the father of Islamic modernism in the 19th century, and his generation.

There are two important components to this debate. The first one pertains to the practical needs and concerns of Muslim countries. Keeping up with modern science and technology is the number one priority of governments in the Muslim world, as it is in fact everywhere else, and every year billions of dollars are allocated for science education, research, and transfer of technology. From Mustafa Kemal Ataturk, the founder of modern Turkey, to Mahathir Muhammad, the prime minister of Malaysia, the goal has remained the same: to fill the gap between Western and Islamic societies by empowering Muslim countries with the tools and blessings of modern science. Not only the ruling elites but also the populace at large are convinced of the intrinsic power and necessity of science and technology for this is where the superiority of the West lies in. In this sense, the Islamic world is no less pragmatic and utilitarian in its quest for power-through-technology than its European and American counterparts.

The second component of the debate over Islam and science in Muslim societies concerns the intellectual domain, which links the discussion both to modern science and its philosophical foundations and the Islamic scientific tradition as an alternative way of studying the order of nature. The philosophical foundations and, by derivation, built-in presuppositions of modern science and its historical rise in Europe have long been debated and well analyzed. Even long before the Kuhnian and post-modernist criticisms of modern science as a cultural product essentially embedded in pre-scientific assumptions and social-historical proclivities and necessities, a number of important studies showed how philosophical, cosmological, religious and metaphysical ideas played instrumental roles in the shaping of the modern scientific worldview from Galileo to Newton.

Edm und Burtt's *The Foundations of Modern Physical Sciences* and Frances A. Yates' *Giardano Bruno and The Hermetic Tradition, inter alia*, were major challenges to the 19th century view of science as studying natural phenomena from a standpoint which Thomas Nagel has aptly described as 'view from nowhere', viz., seeing the world not from a particular point in it but rather over it, hence assuming an a-historical position towards it. Therefore, there is no need to reiterate the main arguments of scientific historicism here. Rather, focus on how the Muslim world has responded to this debate and what possible positions we may expect to arise from these responses.

Scientific Universalism vs Cultural Particularism

The participation of Muslim philosophers and scholars in the debate over the historicity of modern science has added a new dimension to the debate in that the defenders of a scientific tradition rooted in Islamic metaphysics and cosmology have clearly argued for the cultural specificity and differentiation of scientific traditions. Such advocates of Islamic science as Seyyed Hossein Nasr, Naquib al-Attas, Osman Bakar, to name a few, have defended a cultural particularism of some kind against scientific universalism whereby the a-historical claims of modern scientism (and not science as such) to universal truth and validity are rejected and alternative ways of studying the order of nature are maintained against the onslaught of scientific materialism and reductionism.

This is best illustrated in the sharp contrast between the religious-sacred view of nature and the secular outlook of modern science. While the various religious traditions developed a complex cosmology and approached the world of nature as imbued with intrinsic meaning, order, and even bliss as a way of marveling at the work of the Great Artisan, modern science or rather scientism regards such meta-physical and aesthetic considerations philosophically unfounded and scientifically inconsequential for the work of the scientist. Examples abound in number to show the disparity between the two perspectives.

Bertrand Russell's celebrated essay called "A Free Man's Worship", for instance, was written as a testimonial to this view of science. If we accept, according to Russell, the scientific view of the universe as a *theory of everything*, we will be saved from the 'confusions' of both philosophy and religion at once.

"Such in outline, but even more purposeless, more void of meaning, is the world which Science presents for our belief. Amid such a world, if anywhere, our ideals henceforward must find a home. That Man is the product of causes which had no prevision of the end they were achieving; that his origin, his growth, his hopes and fears, his loves and his beliefs, are but the outcome of accidental collocations of atoms; that no fire, no heroism, no intensity of thought and feeling, can preserve an individual life beyond the grave; that all the labors of the ages, all the devotion, all the inspiration, all the noonday brightness of human genius, are destined to extinction in the vast death of the solar system, and that the whole temple of Man's achievement must inevitably be buried beneath the debris of a universe in ruins – all these things, if not quite beyond dispute, are yet so nearly certain, that no philosophy which rejects them can hope to stand".

Russell's radical scientism has lost much of its élan today. But it remains the unwritten code of the popular perceptions of science. Furthermore, the stark contrast that we see between Russell's view of science and traditional cosmologies is also to be found within the Western intellectual tradition in various controversies such as evolution versus creationism. But the contrast is sharper in the case of Islamic thought because the Islamic world has not been as exposed and vulnerable to the effects of secularization as the Judeo-Christian thought has been in the last three centuries.

It is obvious that construing modern science as a particular and not the only way of studying natural phenomena poses a serious challenge to the exclusivist and absolutist claims of modern natural sciences that reduce reality to what can be measured empirically. To better understand how this criticism applies to modern Western science, we should remember here an important distinction made in philosophy of science between the context of discovery and the context of justification. While the context of discovery refers to what the scientist actually does in her lab, the context of justification refers to how the scientist's work is interpreted and articulated in different frameworks of analysis.

Insofar as the context of discovery is concerned, we may be justified in assuming a linear historical line that connects

Ptolemy, Abu Bakr al-Razi or Nasir al-Din al-Tusi to Newton or Max Planck: the successes or failures of these scientists of different historical periods and cultural settings can be explained in terms of the accumulation of scientific know-ledge, refinement of measurement, exactitude in prediction, advancement in taxonomy, etc. What they all have in common is the continuity of the context of discovery where-by religious and cultural elements have a relatively small role to play.

The issue takes on a substantially different form when we move to the next level, i.e., the context of justification in which we attempt to understand and interpret the *meaning* of the empirical work of the scientist on the ground. Here, we are no longer in the world of 'bare facts' without suppositions notwithstanding the fact that the very concept of 'bare facts' as the building blocks of scientific procedures is open to question. Science is no longer a mirror juxtaposed against the world and the scientist the incorrigible interpreter of the reality of things.

Rather, every interpretation, extrapolation, deduction, induction, and even prediction is screened through a set of philosophical assumptions whether they are articulated explicitly or remain tacit. It is at this level of analysis that science becomes a cultural artifact bound by particular traditions, postulations, and needs. The basic tenets of modern science, which make it a secular enterprise, are all produced at the context of justification and can be accepted, questioned and/or rejected primarily on philosophical grounds.

In this sense, the multiplicity of scientific worldviews, if we may use such a term, is part and parcel of every scientific tradition in that the findings of a particular scientist or in a particular field of science are interpreted in a variety of ways that may or may not agree with other interpretations. In fact, this was the case in traditional societies where we have always multiple cosmologies both across and within specific traditions. Take the case of Islamic and Christian cosmologies. Both traditions produced elaborate cosmological schemes tightly linked to the astronomy and physics of their times, i.e., the Ptolemaic-Aristotelian astronomy.

Naturally, the cosmology of Dante's *Divine Comedy* was structured along the lines of Biblical and Christian thought whereas Islamic cosmology was the result of a deliberate attempt to reconcile Greek-Aristotelian cosmology with Quranic theology and eschatology. Yet, we still find more cases of plurality within each of these traditions. The scholastic-Thomistic view of nature is not the same as St. Francis of Asisi's mystical and poetical deliberations of nature. In the same way, certain parts of Ibn Sina's Neoplatonic cosmology or that of the Brethren of Purity is considerably different from Ibn al-'Arabi's "Five Divine Presences" and Mulla Sadra's *mundus imaginalis*.

The case for particularism and the multiplicity of interpretations within and across various cultural traditions does not lead to parochialism. It is always possible to draw multiple conclusions from the same data both in science and philosophy, and as such plurality does not invalidate the veracity and relevance of divergent readings. In fact, one may even argue that the apparent diversity of traditional cosmologies is rooted in an underlying unity in that such postulates as the universe as a sign of God (*ayat Allah* in Arabic and *vestigia Dei* in Latin), teleology, intrinsic intelligibility of the world, order and harmony, and so on are all shared by various schools of thought. At this point, the concept of Islamic science has a lot to offer to the current religion-science debate especially if this term is understood in a broader sense to include the reassertion of the religious view of the universe as an alternative vision to the profane and secular worldview of modern scientism.

Considering the eroding impact of scientism on traditional beliefs and practices and the disastrous consequences of scientific and technological development without boundaries, the Islamic world can make a strong case for a new vision of science that will both cater to the practical needs of modern society and preserve the spiritual and ethical significance of the world of nature – a case for which people of other religious traditions have to collaborate to foster a common ground for a science that is in peace and harmony with both heaven and earth at the same time.

Islamic World and Science Today

There are two important aspects to how the question of science is addressed in the Islamic world today. On the one hand, the Islamic intellectual and scientific tradition, going back to the rise of Islam as a world civilization in the 9th and 10th centuries, remains a major source of knowledge and inspiration for the contemporary Muslim world in its quest for self-identity and self-esteem. The glory of Islamic civilization stretching from Andalusia and the Balkans to Persia and India and the historic contributions of such Muslim scientists as Ibn al-Haytham, Khwarazmi, Ibn Sina, Nasir al-Din al-Tusi and others to the development of science are remembered throughout the Islamic world as more than a mere grandeur of the past.

Rather, this tradition of remarkable scientific achievement and philosophical articulation is a witness to the study of the world of nature within a religious and sacred framework that delivered to both the spiritual and practical needs of human society. In this sense, the historical experience of Islamic science is an invaluable asset for the development of an Islamic philosophy of science today. The big challenge facing the Islamic world is to show the relevance of this tradition today. This brings us to the second aspect of the science debate in the Islamic world and it is how to deal with modern science without succumbing to the temptations of secular scientism.

There is a world of difference between Ibn Sina's Neoplatonic cosmology and modern science not only in terms of cumulative knowledge and heuristic advancement but also in the philosophical outlook of the two systems of the universe. For a devout follower of modern science like John Searle, "there is really nothing in the universe but physical particles and fields of force acting on physical particles", and this makes matters supposedly easier once we rest our case for a spiritual vision of the universe. The question for the Islamic world, however, is this: after four centuries of not practicing science in full scale and for the last century trying to transfer of science and technology from the West, will the Islamic world ever be in a position where it will put its own 'paradigm' in place and re-develop a scientific tradition that will be in harmony with its religious tenets and aspirations on the one hand, and cater to its practical needs, on the other?

The confusion that plagues the minds of countless scientists in the Muslim world and across the globe arises precisely from the lack of a balance between the discourse and practice of science in an Islamic context. For some, the question of religion or any other philosophical consideration is simply not there. The scientist goes about her own work and fulfills her function in her scientific community without bothering herself with any such philosophical issues. In most cases, however, the Muslim scientist is split between her profession as a scientist and her value system as a believer. The scientist works as part of a global scientific community and remains mostly indifferent to questions of ethics, cosmology, religion, etc.

The believer practices her religion but brings very little from her devotion to bear on his scientific work. We thus end up having split identities with very little ground to integrate the two in a meaningful and cogent manner. Now, part of this problem has to do with the resistance of the scientisticly minded Muslim professionals to accept any alternative to modern science except, perhaps, when it comes to the ethical and environmental misdeeds of modern science. This is a common phenomenon in spite of the fact that the groundwork for an Islamic concept of science and its conceptual scheme has already been done by a long list of Muslim scholars that include S. H. Nasr, Rene Guenon, O. Bakar, Alparslan Acikgenc, Muzaffar Iqbal, Mahdi Golshani, Ziauddin Sardar, Zaki Kirmani, and many others with important differences among them. The task at hand, however, is rendered more difficult by the simple nonexistence of a strong and parallel scientific tradition in the Muslim world.

The possibility of applying an Islamic framework of science to actual scientific work is alarmingly limited in the sense that the level of scientific infrastructure in Muslim countries from physics and engineering to medicine and astronomy is simply not comparable with that of the West that controls the world over the pace and direction of scientific research and technological innovation. Further-more, the global network of scientific programs and technological novelties, funded by governments and powerful transnational corporations, makes it extremely hard if not impossible for any scientist to go against the grain and open up new venues for the flourishing of an alternative vision of the universe beyond the parameters of modern science.

This we see clearly in how Muslim scientists deal with such controversial issues as evolution versus creationism, genetic engineering, human cloning, and nuclear technology. The fact that some people in the Islamic world take pride in the creation of atomic bomb, or the so-called 'Islamic bomb', by Muslim scientists as a token of the return of the glory of Islamic civilization is an indication of the graveness of the problem. Needless to say, all these problems speak to the urgency of the question of science in the Muslim world.

Until and unless the Islamic world recovers its intellectual and scientific tradition on the one hand, and comes to terms with the challenges of modern science, on the other, we will either join the camp of scientific universalism and reduce reality to what the natural sciences can reveal, or join the camp of radical anti-realism of the postmodernists, as it has often been the case among the Muslim critics of secular science, and deny any validity to science or, for that matter, any other human endeavor. The Islamic intellectual and scientific tradition can provide a comprehensive framework which will address the challenge of studying the universe in a non-reductionist way and preserve the sacred meaning of nature – a framework shared by other religious traditions from Judaism and Christianity to traditional Hinduism and Buddhism.

The Quran deserves to be evaluated from different points of view. One topic for examination is the artistic and verbal beauty of the Quran and its style which is neither poetry nor prose. It does not have the characteristics of poetry, which may be thought as giving free flight to the imagination and indulging in poetic exaggeration, and equally it does not exemplify conventional prose, for it is imbued with a distinctive rhythm and melody that are the means for it to exert a powerful and unique spiritual attraction on all who make its acquaintance.

Then the intellectual and scientific content of the Quran also calls for examination. It is true that it is not the aim of the Noble Quran to uncover and expound scientific phenomena, to set forth all the natural motions and events that occur within the system of being in accordance with a specific set of laws, or to explain the properties and mode of operation of nature. We should not expect the Quran to discuss, in an organized manner, the various branches of science and to analyze the topics connected with each of those branches, or to solve the various problems that are encountered in different fields of research.

The ability to experiment and to conduct scientific research has been made inherent in the human being's nature, and he can obtain the knowledge and the arts he needs in his life by means of thought and reflection. He makes valuable advances through his unceasing efforts to gain control over the forces of nature. Concerns such as these are alien to a book of moral edification. The aim pursued by the Quran is the training of the human being as a being conscious of his duties; it reinforces and accelerates his spiritual ascension, together with all of his qualities, toward a state of true loftiness and the dignity of which the human being is worthy. The emergence of such a being requires a comprehensive reform of the human being, involving various changes such as the negation of false values and meaningless criteria deriving from the Age of Ignorance and the creation and fostering of a creative energetic spirit within him.

The Quran can thus be said to melt the spirits of human beings and pour them into a new mould, where they acquire a different, richer and more valuable form. Although this may be said to be the principal aim of the Quran, it summons the human being insistently, at the very same time, to reflect and to ponder, and to acquire a realistic view of the world; it guides him on to the path of thought, of teaching and learning. In the very first verses of the Quran to be revealed, we encounter praise and ennobling of the pen, of the acquisition of knowledge and of the study of nature as one of the principal sources of cognition; a profound awareness of nature may lead to the boundaries of the supranatural realm.

Through the inspiration given by the Quran and as a result of the scientific movement launched by Islam, a vital and active people blossomed into maturity, uniquely gifted with knowledge and virtue. The viewpoint of Islam on science represented a major development that prepared the way for subsequent developments. Iqbal, the well-known Indo-Muslim thinker, says: "The birth of Islam, as I hope to be able presently to prove to your satisfaction, is the birth of inductive intellect...The constant appeal to reason and experience in the Quran, and the emphasis that it lays on Nature and History as sources of human knowledge, are all different aspects of the same idea of finality.

"Inner experience is only one source of human knowledge. According to the Quran, there are two other sources of knowledge - Nature and History; and it is in tapping these sources of knowledge that the spirit of Islam is seen at its best." All forms of scientific endeavor are necessarily based on respect for the intellect and for the development of the human being and on freedom of thought from all kinds of fetters. The principal advances and developments in the natural sciences are all due to these premises. The contemporary human being is heir to the knowledge and the researches of millions of thinkers and scholars who in their investigations discovered the foundations of the various sciences, and who gained access to some of the mysteries of being by means of their intellectual originality and creativity and their untiring efforts.

In the age when the Quran was revealed - an age known as the Age of Ignorance - creative and innovative thought, marked by the comprehensive spirit of science, was non-existent, and no one was able to discern the mysteries of the vast, unknown universe. When expounding the mysteries of creation, the Quran is clear and explicit whenever clarity and explicitness are desirable. In cases where the perception of complex truths was difficult for the people of that age, the Quran contents itself with making allusions, so that in the course of time as the intellects and knowledge of human beings developed and the mysteries of nature came more clearly to the fore, these matters would become more easily comprehensible.

In expounding the contents of the Quran, Muslim scholars have continually put forward different views, as a result both of their own researches, investigations and reflections, and of the vast spiritual richness of the Quran. Given this spiritual richness, it is inconceivable that such a great and infinite source of truth could have been produced by the talent and intellectual genius of the human being. If something takes place by way of natural causation, it should be possible for people living either at the time of its first occurrence or in a later age to produce something similar. But if a phenomenon takes place outside the natural course of things, so that natural laws and criteria are suspended, people will be unable at all times to attempt its replication.

In the case of the Quran, we see that all conventional criteria and principles were violated; the entirety of the book represents a transcendence of all norms. We have said that the Quran refers allusively to scientific truths, almost as secondary matters serving as a preliminary to the attainment of a greater and more glorious goal. We cannot, therefore, regard it as a technical work of specialization that discusses matters only from the viewpoint of science. The Quran refers to certain aspects of the life of the human being, the earth, the heavens and the plants, but it would be entirely wrong to imagine that it does so with the intention of elucidating the natural sciences or resolving dubious points connected with them. The purpose of the Quran is rather to expound truths that are relevant to the spiritual life of the human being and the exaltation of his being and conducive to his attaining a life of true happiness.

Furthermore, when expounding scientific truths which might be couched in a different terminology in every age, the Quran does not make use of technical terms. For although scientific truths and the laws governing all phenomena enjoy stability and immutability, and although they have always existed and always will exist, it is possible that scientific terminology might change from one age to the next and appear in a totally different form from before. Discussions in the Quran concerning the world of creation relate to a series of truths and principles that are not situated in the sensory realm. The human being can grasp these matters only by recourse to particular scientific instruments.

Dr. Bucaille, the French scientist, writes as follows: "A crucial fact is that the Quran, while inviting us to cultivate science, itself contains many observations on natural phenomena and includes explanatory details which are seen to be in total agreement with modern scientific data. There is no equal to this in the Judeo-Christian Revelation. "These scientific considerations, which are very specific to the Quran, greatly surprised me at first. Up until then, I had not thought it possible for one to find so many statements in a text compiled more than thirteen centuries ago referring to extremely diverse subjects and all of them totally in keeping with modern scientific knowledge...A thorough linguistic knowledge is not in itself sufficient to understand these verses from the Quran. What is needed along with this is a highly diversified knowledge of science.

A study such as the present one embraces many disciplines and is in that sense encyclopedic. As the questions raised are discussed, the variety of scientific knowledge essential to the understanding of certain verses of the Quran will become clear. "The Quran does not aim at explaining certain laws governing the Universe, however; it has an absolutely basic religious objective. The descriptions of Divine Omnipotence are what principally incite the human being to reflect on the works of Creation. They are accompanied by references to facts accessible to human observation or to laws defined by God who presides over the organization of the universe both in the sciences of nature.

"One part of these assertions is easily understood, but the meaning of the other can only be grasped if one has the essential scientific knowledge it requires..."

"The hypothesis advanced by those who see Muham-mad as the author of the Quran is quite untenable. How could a man, from being illiterate, become the most important author, in terms of literary merit, in the whole of Arabic literature? How could he then pronounce truths of a scientific nature that no other human being could possibly have developed at the time, and all this without once making the slightest error in his pronouncements on the subject?"

"The ideas in this study are developed from a purely scientific point of view. They lead to the conclusion that it is inconceivable for a human being living in the seventh century AD to have made statements in the Quran on a great variety of subjects that do not belong to his period and for them to be in keeping with what was to be known only centuries later. For me, there can be no human explanation to the Quran."

Let us briefly examine a few examples of this kind of topic. One, the best-known theory concerning the emergence of the solar system is the hypothesis of Laplace, some of whose views were later refuted by certain scientists as a result of further research. Although there are other views concerning the factors that caused the emergence of the solar system, all scientific circles in the world today are agreed that the planets were originally composed of a mass of sodium gas: first the heavens and the earth were joined together as a single entity and then they separated from each other.

Centuries ago, the Quran alluded to this scientific theory. It says, when describing the creation of the heavens: "Then God turned to the creation of the heavens (the planets), when they were but a smoky substance." (41:11) "Do the unbe-lievers not see that the heavens and the earth were joined together before We separated them, and that We brought all living things into existence from water? Why do they still not believe in God?" (21:30) The well-known scientist Gamof says: "As we know, the sun came into being out of cumulative gases, and the sun then emitted a series of gases from itself that came into being after the separation from it of the planets. How did this burning mass of planetary matter come into being and what forces were involved in its origination? Who assembled the materials needed for their construction?

"These are questions which confront us with respect to the moon as well as every other planet in the solar system; they form the basis of all cosmological theories and are riddles that have preoccupied astronomers for centuries."

James, an English scientist, writes: "Millions of centuries ago, a planet was passing in the vicinity of the sun and created an awesome tidal effect, so that matter separated from the sun in the shape of a long cigarette. Then this matter was divided: the weightier portion of the cigarette became the great planets, and the lighter portions brought the lesser planets into being."

The words used by the Quran in the verse quoted above, attributing the origin of the heavens to smoke (=gas), indicates the profundity with which this Divine book treats matters. All scientists are of the opinion that sodium is a gas mixed with ferrous materials, and the word smoke/gas may be taken to include both gas and iron. The word 'smoke' is, then, the most scientific expression that might be employed in the context. Thus the Quran unveils one of the great mysteries of nature: the separation of the planets from a huge object and then their separation from each other. Since at the time of the revelation of the Quran, the general level of knowledge and science was extremely low, does this not constitute a proof of the heavenly nature of the Quran?

Does not the exposition of these matters by the Quran, in a manner conforming to quite recent discoveries made by astronomers, prove that the voice speaking in the Quran belongs to one who is acquainted with all the mysteries and truths of existence? Dr. Bucaille makes the following open admission: "At the earliest time it can provide us with, modern science has every reason to maintain that the Universe was formed of a gaseous mass principally composed of hydrogen and a certain amount of helium that was slowly rotating. This nebula subsequently split up into multiple fragments with very large dimensions and masses, so large indeed, that specialists in astrophysics are able to estimate their mass from 1 to 100 billion times the present mass of the Sun (the latter represents a mass that is over 300,000 times that of the Earth).

These figures give an idea of the large size of the fragments of primary gaseous mass that were to give birth to the galaxies. "It must be noted, however, that the formation of the heavenly bodies and the Earth, as explained in verses 9 to 12, surah 41....required two phases. If we take the Sun and its sub-product, the Earth as an example (the only one accessible to us), science informs us that their formation occurred by a process of condensation of the primary nebula and then their separation. This is exactly what the Quran expresses very clearly when it refers to the processes that produced a fusion and subsequent separation starting from a celestial 'smoke'. Hence there is complete correspondence between the facts of the Quran and the facts of science.

"Such statements in the Quran concerning the Creation, which appeared nearly fourteen centuries ago, obviously do not lend themselves to a human explanation." Two, one of the most subtle problems in science concerns the expansion of the universe, its tendency constantly to extend its boundaries. This was something completely unknown to the human being until the last century. This mystery is, however, mentioned by the Quran in the following terms, which again bear witness to its remarkable profundity when discussing such matters: "We created the heavens with Our strength and power, and constantly expand them." (51:47)

This verse speaks in categorical terms of the expansion of the universe, its constellations and galaxies, although not more than a century has passed since the discovery of the expansion of the universe. The well-known scholar Baresht writes as follows: "Astronomers gradually became aware that certain regular motions were underway in the most distant galaxies that were barely visible to their telescopes. Those distant galaxies appear to be moving away both from the solar system and from each other.

"The regular flight of these galaxies, the closest of which is five hundred light-years away from us, is completely different from the placid motion of attraction exerted by bodies close to us. Those distant motions may have an effect on the curvature of the universe. The universe is not, then, in a state of immobility and balance; it is more like a soap bubble or a bellows in its constant expansion."

Another scholar, John Pfeffer, writes as follows: "The universe is expanding. Wherever we look, we see the galaxies becoming more distant from each other; the distance between them is constantly growing. The most distant galaxies are becoming ever more removed from us, at the greatest conceivable speed. For example, while you have been reading this sentence, some of the galaxies will have become 250,000 miles farther removed from the earth. "The parts of the universe are becoming farther removed from each other. It is as if a bullet had exploded in the air, the galaxies corresponding to the particles of the bullet as they hasten farther and farther apart. The theory of the big bang is based on precisely such a comparison.

"According to this theory, there was a time when all the matter in the universe was gathered together into a single dense mass. It was a substance suspended in space, with a volume hundreds of times greater than the sun, and resembled a bomb ready to explode. Then, about ten billion years ago, the explosion took place with a blinding flash, and the huge ball of matter became scattered in space. Its components are still being scattered forth in every direction, in a process of unceasing expansion - gases, rays, galaxies."

The Glorious Quran draws people's attention to the splendor inherent in the ordering of the universe and the complexity of its creation, and it reminds them that the signs of the Creator's workmanship are so numerous in the universe that if the human being reflects aright he will inevitably come to believe in the eternal power of God, the source of all being. Then he will bow humbly before His magnificence. We read in Surah al-Imran: "Certainly in the creation of the heavens and earth and in the alternation of night and day, there are clear signs for the intelligent, those who at all times make remembrance of God and constantly reflect on the creation of the heavens and the earth and say: 'Oh Creator! You have not created this expanse of splendor and magnificence in vain; you are pure and transcendent, so preserve us through your favour from the torment of the fire.' "(3:190-91)

6

In the history of medicine, Islamic medicine or Arabic medicine refers to medicine developed in the medieval Islamic civilization and written in Arabic, the lingua franca of the Islamic civilization. Despite these names, a significant number of scientists during this period were not Arab. Some consider the label Arab-Islamic as historically inaccurate, arguing that this label does not appreciate the rich diversity of Eastern scholars who have contributed to Islamic science in this era. Latin translations of Arabic medical works had a significant influence on the development of modern medicine. Islamic medicine was a genre of medical writing that was influenced by several different medical systems, including traditional Arabian medicine of Muhammad's time, ancient Hellenistic medicine

3

Science and Medicine

The treasure-houses of Islamic science are just beginning to be opened. In Constantinople alone there are more than eighty mosque libraries containing tens of thousands of manuscripts. In Cairo, Damascus, Mosul, and Baghdad, as well as in Persia and India, there are other collections, few have been listed, much less described or edited. Even the catalogue of the Escorial Library in Spain, which contains a large part of the wisdom of western Islam, is not yet complete. During the last few years the mass of material recovered has gone far to subvert our former conceptions and has thrown a flood of new light on the early history of scientific thought in the Islamic world. Thus at present even an outline of the medical and scientific achievement of Islam can, at best, be but tentative.

In the history of medicine, Islamic medicine or Arabic medicine refers to medicine developed in the medieval Islamic civilization and written in Arabic, the *lingua franca* of the Islamic civilization. Despite these names, a significant number of scientists during this period were not Arab. Some consider the label "Arab-Islamic" as historically inaccurate, arguing that this label does not appreciate the rich diversity of Eastern scholars who have contributed to Islamic science in this era. Latin translations of Arabic medical works had a significant influence on the development of modern medicine. Islamic medicine was a genre of medical writing that was influenced by several different medical systems, including the traditional Arabian medicine of Muhammad's time, ancient Hellenistic medicine such as Unani, ancient Indian medicine such as Ayurveda, and the ancient Iranian Medicine of the Academy of Gundishapur. The works of ancient Greek and Roman physicians Hippocrates, Dioscorides, Soranus, Celsus and Galen had a lasting impact on Islamic medicine.

In Islamic tradition, the first Muslim physician is believed to have been Muhammad himself, as a significant number of hadiths concerning medicine are attributed to him. Several Sahaba are said to have been successfully treated of certain diseases by following the medical advice of Muhammad. The three methods of healing known to have been mentioned by him were honey, fire cupping, and cauterization, though he was generally opposed to the use of cauterization unless it "suits the ailment." According to Ibn Hajar al-Asqalani, Muhammad disliked this method due to it causing "pain and menace to a patient" since there was no anesthesia in his time. Muhammad also appears to have been the first to suggest that there is always a cause and a cure for every disease, according to several hadiths in the Sahih al-Bukhari, Sunan Abi Dawood and Al-Muwatta attributed to Muhammad, such as:

"There is no disease that Allah has created, except that He also has created its treatment."

"Make use of medical treatment, for Allah has not made a disease without appointing a remedy for it, with the exception of one disease, namely old age."

"Allah has sent down both the disease and the cure, and He has appointed a cure for every disease, so treat you medically."

"The one who sent down the disease sent down the remedy."

"For every disease, Allah has given a cure."

The belief of the cure for every disease encouraged early Muslims to engage in biomedical research and seek out a cure for every disease known to them. Many early authors of Islamic medicine were usually clerics rather than physicians, and were known to have advocated the traditional medical practices of prophet Muhammad's time, such as those mentioned in the Quran and Hadith. For instance, therapy did not require a patient to undergo any surgical procedures at the time. From the 9th century, Hunayn ibn Ishaq translated a number of Galen's works into the Arabic language, followed by translations of the *Sushruta Samhita, Charaka Samhita,* and Middle Persian works from Gundishapur. Muslim physicians soon began making many of their own significant advances and contributions to medicine, including the fields of allergology, anatomy, bacteriology, botany, dentistry, embryology, environmentalism, etiology, immunology, microbiology, obstetrics, ophthalmology, pathology, pediatrics, perinatology, physiology, psychiatry, psychology, pulsology and sphygmology, surgery, therapy, urology, zoology, and the pharmaceutical sciences such as pharmacy and pharmacology, among others.

Medicine was a central part of medieval Islamic culture. Responding to circumstances of time and place, Islamic physicians and scholars developed a large and complex medical literature exploring and synthesizing the theory and practice of medicine. Islamic medicine was initially built on tradition, chiefly the theoretical and practical knowledge developed in Arabia, Persia, Greece, Rome, and India. Galen and Hippocrates were pre-eminent authorities, as well as the Indian physicians Sushruta and Charaka, and the Hellenistic scholars in Alexandria. Islamic scholars translated their voluminous writings from Greek and Sanskrit into Arabic and then produced new medical knowledge based on those texts.

In order to make the Greek and Indian traditions more accessible, understandable, and teachable, Islamic scholars ordered and made more systematic the vast and sometimes inconsistent Greco-Roman and Indian medical knowledge by writing encyclopedias and summaries. It was through Arabic translations that the West learned of Hellenic medicine, including the works of Galen and Hippocrates. Of equal if not of greater influence in Western Europe were systematic and comprehensive works such as Avicenna's *The Canon of Medicine*, which were translated into Latin and then disseminated in manuscript and printed form throughout Europe. During the fifteenth and sixteenth centuries alone, *The Canon of Medicine* was published more than thirty-five times.

Muslim physicians set up the earliest dedicated hospitals in the modern sense, known as Bimaristans, which were establishments where the ill were welcomed and cared for by qualified staff, and which were clearly distinguished from the ancient healing temples, sleep temples, hospices, asylums, lazarets and leper-houses which were more concerned with isolating the sick and the mad from society "rather than to offer them any way to a true cure." These contrasted with hospitals in Christian Europe which were more concerned with prayer. The Bimaristan hospitals later functioned as the first public hospitals, psychiatric hospitals and diploma-granting medical universities.

In the medieval Islamic world, hospitals were built in all major cities; in Cairo for example, the Qalawun Hospital could care for 8,000 patients, and a staff that included physicians, pharmacists, and nurses. One could also access a dispensary, and research facility that led to advances, which included the discovery of the contagious nature of diseases, and research into optics and the mechanisms of the eye. Muslim doctors were removing cataracts with hollow needles over 1000 years before Western physicians dared attempt such a task. Hospitals were built not only for the physically sick, but for the mentally sick also. One of the first ever psychiatric hospitals that cared for the mentally ill was built in Cairo. Hospitals later spread to Europe during the Crusades, inspired by the hospitals in the Middle East. The first hospital in Paris, Les Quinze-vingts, was founded by Louis IX after his return from the Crusade in between 1254-1260.

Hospitals in the Islamic world featured competency tests for doctors, drug purity regulations, nurses and interns, and advanced surgical procedures. Hospitals were also created with separate wards for specific illnesses, so that people with contagious diseases could be kept away from other patients.

One of the features in medieval Muslim hospitals that distinguished them from their contemporaries and predecessors was their significantly higher standards of medical ethics. Hospitals in the Islamic world treated patients of all religions, ethnicities, and backgrounds, while the hospitals themselves often employed staff from Christian, Jewish and other minority backgrounds. Muslim doctors and physicians were expected to have obligations towards their patients, regardless of their wealth or backgrounds. The ethical standards of Muslim physicians was first laid down in the 9th century by Ishaq bin Ali Rahawi, who wrote the *Adab al-Tabib* (*Conduct of a Physician*), the first treatise dedicated to medical ethics. He regarded physicians as "guardians of souls and bodies", and wrote twenty chapters on various topics related to medical ethics.

Another unique feature of medieval Muslim hospitals was the role of female staff, who was rarely employed in ancient and medieval healing temples elsewhere in the world. Medieval Muslim hospitals commonly employed female nurses, including nurses from as far as Sudan, a sign of great breakthrough. Muslim hospitals were also the first to employ female physicians, the most famous being two female physicians from the Banu Zuhr family who served the Almohad ruler Abu Yusuf Ya'qub al-Mansur in the 12th century. Later in the 15th century, female surgeons were illustrated for the first time in Þerafeddin Sabuncuoðlu's *Cerrahiyyetu'l-Haniyye* (*Imperial Surgery*).

The first encyclopedia of medicine in Arabic was Ali ibn Sahl Rabban al-Tabari's *Firdous al-Hikmah* (*"Paradise of Wisdom"*), written in seven parts, and c. 860. It was the first to deal with pediatrics and child development, as well as psychology and psychotherapy. In the fields of medicine and psychotherapy, the work was primarily influenced by Islamic thought and ancient Indian physicians such as Sushruta and

Charaka. Unlike earlier physicians, however, al-Tabari emphasized strong ties between psychology and medicine, and the need of psychotherapy and counseling in the therapeutic treatment of patients.

Muhammad ibn Zakarîya Râzi (Rhazes) wrote the *Comprehensive Book of Medicine* in the 9th century. The *Large Comprehensive* was the most sought after of all his compositions, in which Rhazes recorded clinical cases of his own experience and provided very useful recordings of various diseases. The *Comprehensive Book of Medicine,* with its introduction of measles and smallpox, was very influential in Europe.

Ali ibn Abbas al-Majusi (Haly Abbas)'s *Kitab Kamil as-sina'a at-tibbiyya* ("*Complete Book of the Medical Art*"), c. 980, became better known as the *Kitab al-Maliki* ("*Royal Book*", Latin: *Liber regalis*) in honour of its royal patron 'Adud al-Dawla. In twenty sections, ten of theory and ten of practice, it was more systematic and concise than Razi's *Hawi,* but more practical than Avicenna's *Canon,* by which it was superseded. With many interpolations and substitutions, it served as the basis for the *Pantegni* (c. 1087) of Constantinus Africanus, the founding text of the Schola Medica Salernitana in Salerno.

Abu al-Qasim al-Zahrawi (Abulcasis), regarded as the father of modern surgery, contributed greatly to the discipline of medical surgery with his *Kitab al-Tasrif* ("*Book of Concessions*"), a 30-volume medical encyclopedia published in 1000, which was later translated to Latin and used in European medical schools for centuries. He invented numerous surgical instruments and described them in his *al-Tasrif.* Avicenna (Ibn Sina), a Hanbali and Mu'tazili philosopher and doctor in the early 11th century, was another influential figure. He is regarded as the father of modern medicine, and one of the greatest thinkers and medical scholars in history. His medical encyclopedia, *The Canon of Medicine* (c. 1020), remained a standard textbook in Europe for centuries, up until the renewal of the Muslim tradition of scientific medicine. He also wrote *The Book of Healing* (actually a more general encyclopedia of science and philosophy), which became another popular textbook in Europe.

Among other things, Avicenna's contributions to medicine include the introduction of systematic experimentation and quantification into the study of physiology, the discovery of the contagious nature of infectious diseases, the introduction of quarantine to limit the spread of contagious diseases, the introduction of experimental medicine, evidence-based medicine, clinical trials, randomized controlled trials, efficacy tests, clinical pharmacology, risk factor analysis, and the idea of a syndrome in the diagnosis of specific diseases, the first descriptions on bacteria and viral organisms, the distinction of mediastinitis from pleurisy, the contagious nature of phthisis and tuberculosis, the distribution of diseases by water and soil, and the first careful descriptions of skin troubles, sexually transmitted diseases, perversions, and nervous ailments, as well the use of ice to treat fevers, and the separation of medicine from pharmacology, which was important to the development of the pharmaceutical sciences.

Abû Rayhân al-Bîrûnî's *Kitab-al-Saidana* was an extensive medical encyclopedia which synthesized Islamic medicine with Indian medicine. His medical investigations included one of the earliest descriptions on Siamese twins. Ibn Al-Thahabi (d. 1033) was famous for writing the first known alphabetical encyclopedia of medicine. Ibn al-Nafis (1213-1288) wrote *Al-Shamil fi al-Tibb* (*The Comprehensive Book on Medicine*), a voluminous medical encyclopedia that was originally planned to comprise 300 volumes, but he was only able to complete 80 volumes as a result of his death in 1288. However, even in its incomplete state, the book is one of the largest known medical encyclopedias in history, though only a small portion of *The Comprehensive Book on Medicine* has survived.

During his lifetime, *The Comprehensive Book on Medicine* had eventually replaced Ibn Sina's *The Canon of Medicine* as a medical authority in the medieval Islamic world. Arabic biographers from the 13th onwards considered Ibn al-Nafis the greatest physician in history, some referring to him as "the second Ibn

Sina", and others considering him even greater than Ibn Sina. The last major medical encyclopedia from the Islamic world was Þerafeddin Sabuncuoðlu's surgical atlas, *Cerrahiyyetu'l-Haniyye* (*Imperial Surgery*). Though his work was mostly based on Abu al-Qasim al-Zahrawi's *Al-Tasrif,* he also introduced many innovations of his own.

George Sarton, the father of the history of science, wrote in the *Introduction to the History of Science*:

"Through their medical investigations they not merely widened the horizons of medicine, but enlarged humanistic concepts generally. Thus it can hardly have been accidental that those researches should have led them that were inevitably beyond the reach of Greek masters. If it is regarded as symbolic that the most spectacular achievement of the mid-twentieth century is atomic fission and the nuclear bomb, likewise it would not seem fortuitous that the early Muslim's medical endeavor should have led to a discovery that was quite as revolutionary though possibly more beneficent."

"A philosophy of self-centeredness, under whatever disguise, would be both incomprehensible and reprehensible to the Muslim mind. That mind was incapable of viewing man, whether in health or sickness as isolated from God, from fellow men, and from the world around him. It was probably inevitable that the Muslims should have discovered that disease need not be born within the patient himself but may reach from outside, in other words, that they should have been the first to establish clearly the existence of contagion."

"One of the most famous exponents of Muslim universalism and an eminent figure in Islamic learning was Ibn Sina, known in the West as Avicenna (981-1037). For a thousand years he has retained his original renown as one of the greatest thinkers and medical scholars in history. His most important medical works are the Qanun (Canon) and a treatise on Cardiac drugs. The 'Qanun fi-l-Tibb' is an immense encyclopedia of medicine. It contains some of the most illuminating thoughts pertaining to distinction of mediastinitis from pleurisy; contagious nature of phthisis; distribution of diseases by water and soil; careful description of skin troubles; of sexual diseases and perversions; of nervous ailments." "We have reason to believe that when, during the crusades, Europe at last began to establish hospitals; they were inspired by the Arabs of near East.... The first hospital in Paris, Les Quinze-vingt, was founded by Louis IX after his return from the crusade 1254-1260."

Like in other fields of Islamic science, Muslim physicians and doctors developed the first scientific methods for the field of medicine. This included the introduction of mathematization, quantification, experimentation, experimental medicine, evidence-based medicine, clinical trials, dissection, animal testing, human experimentation and postmortem autopsy by Muslim physicians, whilst hospitals in the Islamic world featured the first drug tests, drug purity regulations, and competency tests for doctors.

In the 9th century, al-Kindi (Alkindus), in *De Gradibus*, demonstrated the application of mathematics and quantification to medicine, particularly in the field of pharmacology. This includes the development of a mathematical scale to quantify the strength of drugs, and a system that would allow a doctor to determine in advance the most critical days of a patient's illness, based on the phases of the Moon.

In the 10th century, Razi (Rhazes) introduced controlled experiment and clinical observation into the field of medicine, and rejected several Galenic medical theories unverified by experimentation. The earliest known medical experiment was carried out by Razi in order to find the most hygienic place to build a hospital. He hung pieces of meat in places throughout 10th century Baghdad and observed where the meat decomposed least quickly, and that was where he built the hospital. In his *Comprehensive Book of Medicine*, Razi recorded clinical cases of his own experience and provided very useful recordings of various diseases. In his *Doubts about Galen*, Razi was also the first to prove both Galen's theory of humorism and Aristotle's theory of classical elements false using experimentation. He also introduced urinalysis and stool tests.

Avicenna (Ibn Sina) is considered the father of modern medicine, for his introduction of systematic experimentation and quantification into the study of physiology, the introduction of experimental medicine, clinical trials, risk factor analysis, and the idea of a syndrome in the diagnosis of specific diseases, in his medical encyclopedia, *The Canon of Medicine* (c. 1025), which was also the first book dealing with evidence-based medicine, randomized controlled trials, and efficacy tests.

According to Toby Huff and A. C. Crombie, the *Canon* contained "a set of rules that laid down the conditions for the experimental use and testing of drugs" which were "a precise guide for practical experimentation" in the process of "discovering and proving the effectiveness of medical substances." Avicenna's emphasis on tested medicines laid the foundations for an experimental approach to pharmacology. The *Canon* laid out the following rules and principles for testing the effectiveness of new drugs and medications, which still form the basis of clinical pharmacology and modern clinical trials:

1. "The drug must be free from any extraneous accidental quality."
2. "It must be used on a simple, not a composite, disease."
3. "The drug must be tested with two contrary types of diseases, because sometimes a drug cures one disease by its essential qualities and another by its accidental ones."
4. "The quality of the drug must correspond to the strength of the disease. For example, there are some drugs whose heat is less than the coldness of certain diseases, so that they would have no effect on them."
5. "The time of action must be observed, so that essence and

accident are not confused."

6. "The effect of the drug must be seen to occur constantly or in many cases, for if this did not happen, it was an accidental effect."
7. "The experimentation must be done with the human body, for testing a drug on a lion or a horse might not prove anything about its effect on man."

One of the earliest physicians known to have performed human dissection and postmortem autopsy in his medical experiments was Ibn Zuhr (Avenzoar), who introduced the experimental method into surgery, for which he is considered the father of experimental surgery. There were a number of other early practitioners of human dissection and autopsy at the time, including Ibn Tufail, Saladin's physicians al-Shayzari and Ibn Jumay, Abd-el-latif, and Ibn al-Nafis.

The experimental method was introduced into botany, materia medica and the agricultural sciences in the 13th century by the Andalusian-Arab botanist Abu al-Abbas al-Nabati, the teacher of Ibn al-Baitar. Al-Nabati introduced empirical techniques in the testing, description and identification of numerous materia medica, and he separated unverified reports from those supported by actual tests and observations.

The first documented description of a peer review process is found in the *Ethics of the Physician* written by Ishaq bin Ali al-Rahwi (854–931) of al-Raha, Syria, who describes the first medical peer review process. His work, as well as later Arabic medical manuals, state that a visiting physician must always make duplicate notes of a patient's condition on every visit. When the patient was cured or had died, the notes of the physician were examined by a local medical council of other physicians, who would review the practising physician's notes to decide whether his/her performance have met the required standards of medical care. If their reviews were negative, the practicing physician could face a lawsuit from a maltreated patient.

In anatomy and physiology, the first physician to refute Galen's theory of humorism was Muhammad ibn Zakarîya Râzi (Rhazes) in his *Doubts about Galen* in the 10th century. He criticized Galen's theory that the body possessed four separate "humors" (liquid substances), whose balances are the key to health and a natural body-temperature. Razi was the first to prove this theory wrong using an experiment. He carried out an experiment which would upset this system by inserting a liquid with a different temperature into the body resulting in an increase or decrease of bodily heat, which resembled the temperature of that particular fluid.

Razi noted particularly that a warm drink would heat up the body to a degree much higher than its own natural temperature, thus the drink would trigger a response from the body, rather than transferring only its own warmth or coldness to it. This line of criticism was the first comprehensive experimental refutation of Galen's theory of humours and Aristotle's theory of the four classical elements on which it was grounded. Razi's own chemical experiments suggested other qualities of matter, such as "oiliness" and "sulfurousness", or inflammability and salinity, which were not readily explained by the traditional fire, water, and earth and air division of elements.

The contributions of Avicenna to physiology include the introduction of systematic experimentation and quantification into the study of physiology in *The Canon of Medicine* (c. 1020). The contributions of Ibn al-Haytham (Alhacen) to anatomy and physiology include his correct explanation of the process of sight and visual perception for the first time in his *Book of Optics*, published in 1021. Other innovations introduced by Muslim physicians to the field of physiology by this time include the use of animal testing and human dissection.

Ibn Zuhr (Avenzoar) (1091-1161) was one of the earliest physicians known to have carried out human dissection and postmortem autopsy. He proved that the skin disease scabies was caused by a parasite, a discovery which upset the theory of humourism supported by Hippocrates and Galen. The removal of the parasite from the patient's body did not involve purging, bleeding, or any other traditional treatments associated with the four humours. In the 12th century, Saladin's physicians al-Shayzari and Ibn Jumay were also among the earliest to undertake human dissection, and they made explicit appeals for other physicians to do so as well. During a famine in Egypt in 1200, Abd-el-latif observed and examined a large number of skeletons, and he discovered that Galen was incorrect regarding the formation of the bones of the lower jaw and sacrum.

Ibn al-Nafis, the father of circulatory physiology, was another early proponent of human dissection. In 1242, he was the first to describe the pulmonary circulation, coronary circulation, and capillary circulation, which form the basis of the circulatory system, for which he is considered the one of the greatest physiologists in history. The first European descriptions of the pulmonary circulation came several centuries later, by Michael Servetus in 1553 and William Harvey in 1628. Ibn al-Nafis also described the earliest concept of metabolism, and developed new Nafisian systems of anatomy, physiology and psychology to replace the Avicennian and Galenic doctrines, while discrediting many of their erroneous theories on the four humours, pulsation, bones, muscles, intestines, sensory organs, bilious canals, esophagus, stomach, and the anatomy of almost every other part of the human body.

The Arab physician Ibn al-Lubudi (1210-1267), also from Damascus, wrote the *Collection of discussions relative to fifty psychological and medical questions*, in which he rejects the theory of four humours supported by Galen and Hippocrates, discovers that the body and its preservation depend exclusively upon blood, rejects Galen's idea that women can produce sperm, and discovers that the movement of arteries are not dependent upon the movement of the heart, that the heart is the first organ to form in a fetus' body (rather than the brain as claimed by Hippocrates), and that the bones forming the skull can grow into tumors. He also advises that in cases of extreme fever, a patient should not be released from hospital.

In the 15th century, the *Tashrih al-badan* (*Anatomy of the body*) written by Mansur ibn Ilyas contained comprehensive diagrams of the body's structural, nervous and circulatory systems.

Muslim physicians were pioneers in pulsology and sphygmology. In ancient times, Galen as well as Chinese physicians erroneously believed that there was a unique type of pulse for every organ of the body and for every disease. Galen also erroneously believed that "every part of an artery pulsates simultaneously" and that the motion of the pulse was due to natural motions (the arteries expanding and contracting naturally) as opposed to forced motions (the heart causing the arteries to either expand or contract). The first correct explanations of pulsation were given by Muslim physicians.

Avicenna was a pioneer of sphygmology after he refined Galen's theory of the pulse and discovered the following in *The Canon of Medicine*:

"Every beat of the pulse comprises two movements and two pauses. Thus, expansion: pause: contraction: pause. The pulse is a movement in the heart and arteries ... which takes the form of alternate expansion and contraction."

Avicenna also pioneered the modern approach of examining the pulse through the examination of the wrist, which is still practiced in modern times. His reasons for choosing the wrist as the ideal location is due to it being easily available and the patient not needing to be distressed at the exposure of his/her body. The Latin translation of his *Canon* also laid the foundations for the later invention of the sphygmograph.

Ibn al-Nafis, in his *Commentary on Anatomy in Avicenna's*

Canon, completely rejected the Galenic theory of pulsation after his discovery of the pulmonary circulation. He developed his own Nafisian theory of pulsation after discovering that pulsation is a result of both natural and forced motions, and that the "forced motion must be the contraction of the arteries caused by the expansion of the heart, and the natural motion must be the expansion of the arteries." He notes that the "arteries and the heart do not expand and contract at the same time, but rather the one contracts while the other expands" and vice versa. He also recognized that the purpose of the pulse is to help disperse the blood from the heart to the rest of the body. Ibn al-Nafis briefly summarizes his new theory of pulsation:

"The primary purpose of the expansion and contraction of the heart is to absorb the cool air and expel the wastes of the spirit and the warm air; however, the ventricle of the heart is wide. Moreover, when it expands it is not possible for it to absorb air until it is full, for that would then ruin the temperament of the spirit, its substance and texture, as well as the temperament of the heart. Thus, the heart is necessarily forced to complete its fill by absorbing the spirit."

In etiology and epidemiology, Muslim physicians were responsible for the discovery of infectious disease and the immune system, advances in pathology, and early hypotheses related to bacteriology and microbiology. Their discovery of contagious disease in particular is considered revolutionary and is one of the most important discoveries in medicine. The earliest ideas on contagion can be traced back to several hadiths attributed to Muhammad in the 7th century, who is said to have understood the contagious nature of leprosy, mange, and sexually transmitted disease. These early ideas on contagion arose from the generally sympathetic attitude of Muslim physicians towards lepers (who were often seen in a negative light in other ancient and medieval societies) which can be traced back through hadiths attributed to Muhammad and to the following advice given in the Quran:

"There is no fault in the blind, and there is no fault in the lame, and there is no fault in the sick."

This eventually led to the theory of contagious disease, which was fully understood by Avicenna in the 11th century. By then, the pathology of contagion had been fully understood, and as a result, hospitals were created with separate wards for specific illnesses, so that people with contagious diseases could be kept away from other patients who do not have any contagious diseases. In *The Canon of Medicine* (1020), Avicenna discovered the contagious nature of infectious diseases such as phthisis and tuberculosis, the distribution of diseases by water and soil, and fully understood the contagious nature of sexually transmitted diseases. In epidemiology, he introduced the method of quarantine as a means of limiting the spread of contagious diseases, and introduced the method of risk factor analysis and the idea of a syndrome in the diagnosis of specific diseases.

In order to find the most hygienic place to build a hospital, Muhammad ibn Zakariya ar-Razi (Rhazes) carried out an experiment where he hung pieces of meat in places throughout 10th century Baghdad and observed where the meat decomposed least quickly. Razi also wrote the *Comprehensive Book of Medicine* in the 9th century. The *Large Comprehensive* was the most sought after of all his compositions, in which Razi recorded clinical cases of his own experience and provided very useful recordings of various diseases, as well as the discovery of measles and smallpox.

The *Large Comprehensive* also criticized the views of Galen, after Razi had observed many clinical cases which did not follow Galen's descriptions of fevers. For example, he stated that Galen's descriptions of urinary ailments were inaccurate as he had only seen three cases, while Razi had studied hundreds of such cases in hospitals of Baghdad and Rayy. Chickenpox was also first identified by Razi, who clearly distinguished it from smallpox and measles. The *Comprehensive Book of Medicine*, especially with its introduction of measles, smallpox and chickenpox, was very influential in Europe.

Ibn Zuhr (Avenzoar) was the first physician to provide a real scientific etiology for the inflammatory diseases of the ear, and the first to clearly discuss the causes of stridor. He also gave the first accurate descriptions on neurological diseases, including meningitis, intracranial thrombophlebitis, and mediastinal germ cell tumors. Averroes suggested the existence of Parkinson's disease and attributed photoreceptor properties to the retina. Maimonides wrote about neuropsychiatric disorders and described rabies and belladonna intoxication.

The study of allergology and immunology originate from the Islamic world. Muhammad ibn Zakarîya Râzi (Rhazes) was responsible for discovering "allergic asthma", and was the first physician known to have written articles on allergy and the immune system. In the *Sense of Smelling*, he explains the occurrence of rhinitis after smelling a rose during the Spring. In the *Article on the Reason Why Abou Zayd Balkhi Suffers from Rhinitis When Smelling Roses in Spring*, he dicusses seasonal rhinitis, which is the same as allergic asthma or hay fever. Al-Razi was the first to realize that fever is a natural defense mechanism, the body's way of fighting disease.

The distinction between smallpox and measles also dates back to al-Razi. The medical procedure of inoculation was practiced in the medieval Islamic world in order to treat smallpox. This was later followed by the first smallpox vaccine in the form of cowpox, invented in Turkey in the early 18th century.

In hematology, Abu al-Qasim al-Zahrawi (Abulcasis) wrote the first description on haemophilia, a hereditary genetic disorder, in his *Al-Tasrif*, in which he wrote of an Andalusian family whose males died of bleeding after minor injuries.

Muslim physicians speculated on the existence of bacteria

and microorganisms, though these early theories were not proven or observed until the 17th century, when investigations into microbiology were only made possible with the invention of the microscope. These early ideas did, however, influence Girolamo Fracastoro.

Avicenna hypothesized that bodily secretion is contaminated by foul foreign earthly bodies before being infected.

When the Black Death bubonic plague reached al-Andalus in the 14th century, Ibn Khatima hypothesized that infectious diseases are caused by small "minute bodies" which enter the human body and cause disease. Another 14th century Andalusian physician, Ibn al-Khatib (1313-1374), wrote a treatise called *On the Plague*, in which he stated:

"The existence of contagion is established by experience, investigation, the evidence of the senses and trustworthy reports. These facts constitute a sound argument. The fact of infection becomes clear to the investigator who notices how he who establishes contact with the afflicted gets the disease, whereas he who is not in contact remains safe, and how transmission is affected through garments, vessels and earrings."

In parasitology, Ibn Zuhr, through his dissections, was able to prove that the skin disease scabies was caused by a parasite, a discovery which upset the theory of humorism supported by Hippocrates, Galen and Avicenna. The removal of the parasite from the patient's body did not involve purging, bleeding, or any other traditional treatments associated with the four humours.

Muslim dentists were pioneers in dentistry, particularly dental surgery and dental restoration. The earliest medical text to deal with dental surgery in detail was the *Al-Tasrif* by Abulcasis. He gave detailed methods for the successful replantation of dislodged teeth.

Another 10th century Arab dentist, Abu Gaafar Amed ibn

Ibrahim ibn abi Halid al-Gazzar, from North Africa, described methods of dental restoration in his *Kitab Zad al-Musafir wa qut al-Hadir* (*Provision for the traveler and nutrition for the sedentary*), which was later translated into Latin as *Viaticum* by Constantine the African in Salerno. He provided the earliest treatment for dental caries:

"With caries purging must take place first, and then the teeth can be filled with gallnut, dyer's, buckthorn, terbinth resine, cedar resine, myrrh, pellitory and honey, or fumigated with colocynthis root." Al-Gazzar also recommended arsenic compound in his prescription for holes in the teeth, as well as against dental caries, loosening, and relaxing of the nerves as a result of too many fluids.

Avicenna dedicated many chapters of *The Canon of Medicine* to dentistry, particularly dental restoration. Influenced by al-Gazzar, he provided his own treatment for dental caries, stating that carious teeth should be filled with cypress, grass, mastix, myrrh, or styrax, among others, with gallnut, yellow sulfur, pepper, camphor, and with drugs for pain relief, like arsenic or wolf's milk. He further stated that arsenic boiled in oil should be dripped into the carious defect.

Both Avicenna and al-Gazzar, however, believed that dental caries were caused by "tooth worms" like what the ancients believed. This was proven false in 1200 by another Muslim physician named Gaubari in his *Book of the Elite concerning the Unmasking of Mysteries and Tearing of Veils* which dedicated a chapter to dentistry. He was the first to reject the idea of caries being caused by tooth worms, and he stated that tooth worms in fact do not even exist. The theory of the tooth worm was thus no longer accepted in the Islamic medical community from the 13th century onwards.

Muslim physicians made many advances in obstetrics, especially perinatology. In ancient times, Greek and Hellenistic writers such as Hippocrates, Galen, Ptolemy and Paul of Aegina erroneously believed that uterine contractions were only an indication of the onset of childbirth and that the fetus would subsequently swim its way out of the womb and birth canal. In the 10th century, Ali ibn Abbas al-Majusi proved this theory false as he discovered that uterine contractions are in fact the cause of delivery of the fetus.

Abu al-Qasim al-Zahrawi offered advice to midwives on childbirth and complex obstetrics in his *Al-Tasrif* (1000) and made a number of advances in the field. He pioneered the method of episiotomy for the delivery of obstructed labour, and he introduced the required surgical instruments for this operation. Caesarean sections were described in detail by Ferdowsi in his *Shahnameh* (1010) and by al-Biruni in his *Al-Athar al-Baliyah*.

Embryology was discussed to some extent in early Islamic literature, including the Quran and the Hadith literature. Ibn al-Nafis criticized previous Aristotelian, Galenic and Avicennian explanations of embryology and proceeds to develop his own theories on embryology and generation. He believed that when a male and female semen mix, and when they create a mixed matter that has an appropriate temperament to receive an animal or human soul, God issues a soul to this matter, which then develops into an embryo that grows and generates organs. He further writes:

"Galen believes that each of the two semen has in it the active faculty to fashion and the passive faculty to be fashioned, however the active faculty is stronger in the male semen while the passive in the female semen. The investigators amongst the *falasifa* believe that the male semen only has the active faculty, while the female only has the passive faculty. ... As for our opinion and God knows, the best either of the two semen has in it an active faculty to fashion."

He then shows that once the male semen and female semen are brought together in the womb, the female semen quenches the hot fire of the male semen through its own cool and wet nature.

The Arab physician Ibn al-Quff (1233-1305), a student of Ibn al-Nafis, described embryology and perinatology more accurately in his *Al-Jami*:

"The formation of a foam stage in the first 6 to 7 days which in 13 to 16 days gradually transformed into a clot and in 28 to 30 days into a small chunk of meat. In 38 to 40 days, the head appears separate from the shoulders and limbs. The brain and heart followed by the liver are formed before other organs. The fetus takes its food from the mother in order to grow and to replenish what it discards or loses ... There are three membranes covering and protecting the fetus, of which the first connects arteries and veins with those in the mothers womb through the umbilical cord.

The veins pass food for the nourishment of the fetus, while the arteries transmit air. By the end of seven months, all organs are complete ... After delivery; the baby's umbilical cord is cut at a distance of four fingers breadth from the body, and is tied with fine, soft woolen twine. The area of the cut is covered with a filament moistened in olive oil over which a styptic to prevent bleeding is sprinkled ... After delivery, the baby is nursed by his mother whose milk is the best. Then the midwife puts the baby to sleep in a darkened quiet room... Nursing the baby is performed two to three times daily. Before nursing, the mother's breast should be squeezed out two or three times to get rid of the milk near the nipple."

Al-Kindi was a renowned 9th century Arab doctor who wrote many books on the subject of medicine. His most important work in the field was *De Gradibus*, in which he demonstrated the application of mathematics to medicine, particularly in the field of pharmacology. This includes the development of a mathematical scale to quantify the strength of drugs, and a system that would allow a doctor to determine in advance the most critical days of a patient's illness, based on the phases of the Moon.

In his *Comprehensive Book of Medicine*, Razi (Rhazes) recorded clinical cases of his own experience and provided very useful recordings of various diseases. The *Comprehensive Book of Medicine*, with its introduction of measles and smallpox, was very influential in Europe. Razi also carried out an experiment in order to find the most hygienic place to build a hospital. He hung pieces of meat in places throughout 10th century Baghdad and observed where the meat decomposed least quickly, and that was where he built his hospital.

In the 10th century, Abu al-Mansur al-Muwaffak mentions for the first time some chemical facts to distinguish certain medicines. Avicenna's contribution to pharmacology and the pharmaceutical sciences in *The Canon of Medicine* (1020s) include the introduction of systématic experimentation and quantification into pharmacology and the study of physiology, the introduction of clinical pharmacology, experimental medicine, evidence-based medicine, clinical trials, randomized controlled trials, efficacy tests, the experimental use and testing of drugs, a precise guide for practical experimentation in the process of discovering and proving the effectiveness of medical substances, and the first careful descriptions of skin troubles, sexually transmitted diseases, perversions, and nervous ailments, as well the use of ice to treat fevers, and the separation of medicine from pharmacology, which was important to the development of the pharmaceutical sciences.

The *Canon* laid out the following rules and principles for testing the effectiveness of new drugs and medications, which still form the basis of clinical pharmacology and modern clinical trials.

In the field of pharmacy, the first drugstores were opened by Muslim pharmacists in Baghdad in 754, while the first apothecary shops were also founded by Muslim practitioners. The advances made in the Middle East by Muslim chemists in botany and chemistry led Muslim physicians to substantially develop pharmacology. Muhammad ibn Zakarîya Râzi (Rhazes) (865-915), for instance, acted to promote the medical uses of chemical compounds.

Abu al-Qasim al-Zahrawi (Abulcasis) (936-1013) pioneered the preparation of medicines by sublimation and distillation. H is *Liber servitoris* is of particular interest, as it provides the reader with recipes and explains how to prepare the 'simples' from which were compounded the complex drugs then generally used. Shapur ibn Sahl (d 869), was, however, the first physician to initiate pharmacopoeia, describing a large variety of drugs and remedies for ailments. Al-Biṙuni (973-1050) wrote one of the most valuable Islamic works on pharmacology entitled *Kitab al-Saydalah* (*The Book of Drugs*), where he gave detailed knowledge of the properties of drugs and outlined the role of pharmacy and the functions and duties of the pharmacist. Ibn Sina (Avicenna), too, described no less than 700 preparations, their properties, mode of action and their indications.

He devoted in fact a whole volume to simple drugs in *The Canon of Medicine*. Of great impact were also the works by al-Maridini of Baghdad and Cairo, and Ibn al-Wafid (1008-1074), both of which were printed in Latin more than fifty times, appearing as *De Medicinis universalibus et particularibus* by 'Mesue' the younger, and the *Medicamentis simplicibus* by 'Abenguefit'. Peter of Abano (1250-1316) translated and added a supplement to the work of al-Maridini under the title *De Veneris*. Al-Muwaffaq's contributions in the field are also pioneering. Living in the 10th century, he wrote *The Foundations of the True Properties of Remedies*, amongst others describing arsenious oxide, and being acquainted with silicic acid. He made clear distinction between sodium carbonate and potassium carbonate, and drew attention to the poisonous nature of copper compounds, especially copper vitriol, and also lead compounds. For the story, he also mentions the distillation of sea-water for drinking.

In the medieval Islamic world, Arabic physicians discovered the diuretic, antiemetic, antiepileptic, antiinflammatory, analgesic (pain killing) and antipyretic properties of medical cannabis, specifically cannabis sativa, and used it extensively as medication from the 8th to 18th centuries.

Razi (10th century) used mercurial compounds as topical antiseptics. From the 10th century, Muslim physicians and surgeons were applying purified alcohol to wounds as an antiseptic agent. Surgeons in Islamic Spain utilized special methods for maintaining antisepsis prior to and during surgery. They also originated specific protocols for maintaining hygiene during the post-operative period. Their success rate was so high that dignitaries throughout Europe came to Córdoba, Spain, to be treated at what was comparably the "Mayo Clinic" of the Middle Ages.

Razi, Avicenna, al-Kindi, Ibn Rushd, Abu al-Qasim, Ibn Zuhr, Ibn al-Baitar, Ibn Al-Jazzar, Ibn Juljul, Ibn al-Quff, Ibn an-Nafs, al-Biruni, Ibn Sahl and hundreds of other Muslim physicians developed drug therapy and medicinal drugs for the treatment of specific symptoms and diseases. The word "drug" is derived from Arabic. Their use of practical experience and careful observation was extensive.

Chemotherapeutical drugs were first developed in the Muslim world. Muslim physicians used a variety of specific substances to destroy microbes. They applied sulfur topically specifically to kill the scabies mite. Abulcasis developed a variety of medications, which he described in the cosmetics chapter of *Al-Tasrif* (c. 1000). For epilepsy and seizures, he invented medications called *Ghawali* and *Lafayfe*. For the relief and treatment of common colds, he invented *Muthallaathat*, which was prepared from camphor, musk and honey, similar to Vicks Vapour Rub, a modern topical cream. Abulcasis also invented nasal sprays and hand cream, and developed effective mouth washes.

Numerous Muslim chemists produced medicinal-grade alcohol through distillation as early as the 10th century and manufactured on a large scale the first distillation devices for use in chemistry. They used alcohol as a solvent and antiseptic.

Abu al-Qasim al-Zahrawi (Abulcasis), regarded as the father of modern surgery, contributed greatly to the discipline of medical surgery with his *Kitab al-Tasrif* (*Book of Concessions* or *The Method of Medicine*), a 30-volume medical encyclopedia published in 1000, which was later translated to Latin and used in European medical schools for centuries. His influential *al-Tasrif* introduced his famous collection of over 200 surgical instruments. Many of these instruments were never used before by any previous surgeons. Hamidan, for example, listed at least twenty six innovative surgical instruments that were not known before Abulcasis.

The surgical instruments he invented include the first instruments unique to women, as well as the surgical uses of catgut and forceps, the ligature, surgical needle, scalpel, curette, retractor, surgical spoon, sound, surgical hook, surgical rod, specula, bone saw, and plaster. His work also included anatomical descriptions and sections on orthopaedic surgery and ophthalmology. The influence of the *Al-Tasrif* eventually led to the decline of the barber surgeons who were prevalent before his time, and they were instead replaced by physician-surgeons in the Islamic world.

Ibn al-Haytham (Alhacen) made important advances in eye surgery, as he studied and correctly explained the process of sight and visual perception for the first time in his *Book of Optics*, published in 1021. Avicenna was the first to describe the surgical procedure of intubations in order to facilitate breathing, and he also described the "soporific sponge", an anesthetic imbued with aromatics and narcotics, which was to be placed under a patient's nose during surgical operations. He also described the first known surgical treatment for cancer, stating that the excision should be radical and that all diseased tissue should be removed, including the use of amputation or the removal of veins running in the direction of the tumor. Ammar ibn Ali al-Mawsili is also notable for inventing the injection syringe and hypodermic needle for the extraction of cataracts in the first successful cataract surgery.

Ibn al-Nafis dedicated a volume of *The Comprehensive Book on Medicine* to surgery. He described three stages of a surgical operation. The first stage is the pre-operation period which he calls the "time of presentation" when the surgeon carries out a diagnosis on the affected area of the patient's body. The second stage is the actual operation which he calls the "time of operative treatment" when the surgeon repairs the affected organs of the patient. The third stage is the post-operation period which he calls the "time of preservation" when the patient needs to take care of himself and be taken care of by nurses and doctors until he recovers. *The Comprehensive Book on Medicine* was also the earliest book dealing with the decubitus of a patient.

General anesthesia and general anesthetics were pioneered by Muslim anesthesiologists, who were the first to utilize oral as well as inhalant anesthetics. In Islamic Spain, Abu al-Qasim and Ibn Zuhr, among other Muslim surgeons performed hundreds of surgeries under inhalant anesthesia with the use of narcotic-soaked sponges which were placed over the face. Muslim physicians also introduced the anesthetic value of opium derivatives during the middle Ages. Laudanum was also used as an anaesthetic. Ibn Sina (Avicenna) wrote about its medical uses in his works, which later influenced the works of Paracelsus. Sigrid Hunke wrote:

"The science of medicine has gained a great and extremely important discovery and that is the use of general anaesthetics for surgical operations, and how unique, efficient, and merciful for those who tried it the Muslim anaesthetic was. It was quite different from the drinks the Indians, Romans and Greeks were forcing their patients to have for relief of pain. There had been some allegations to credit this discovery to an Italian or to an Alexandrian, but the truth is and history proves that, the art of using the anaesthetic sponge is a pure Muslim technique, which was not known before. The sponge used to be dipped and left in a mixture prepared from cannabis, opium, hyoscyamus and a plant called Zoan."

Ibn Zuhr (Avenzoar) is considered the father of experimental surgery, for introducing the experimental method into surgery in his *Al-Taisir*. He was the first to employ animal testing in order to experiment with surgical procedures before applying them to human patients. He also performed the first dissections and postmortem autopsies on humans as well as animals.

The surgical procedure of tracheotomy was invented by Ibn Zuhr (Avenzoar) in the 12th century.

Abu al-Qasim al-Zahrawi (Abulcasis), in his *Al-Tasrif* (1000), invented the modern plaster and adhesive bandage, which are still used in hospitals throughout the world. The use of plasters for fractures became a standard practice for Arab physicians, though this practice was not widely adopted in Europe until the 19th century.

Abu al-Qasim's use of catgut for internal stitching is still practised in modern surgery. The catgut appears to be the only natural substance capable of dissolving and is acceptable by the body.

Abu al-Qasim also invented the forceps for extracting a dead fetus, as illustrated in the *Al-Tasrif*.

A special medical instrument called a cauter, used for the cauterization of arteries, was first described by Abu al-Qasim in his *Kitab al-Tasrif*.

In the *Al-Tasrif*, Abu al-Qasim also introduced the use of ligature for the arteries in lieu of cauterization.

Al-Zahrawi was the first surgeon to make use of cotton (which itself is derived from the Arabic word *qutn*) as a medical dressing for controlling hemorrhage.

The surgical needle was invented and described by Abu al-Qasim in his *Al-Tasrif*.

The Iraqi surgeon Ammar ibn Ali al-Mawsili invented the first hollow hypodermic needle and injection syringe in *circa* 1000 using a hollow glass tube and suction to extract and remove cataracts from a patient's eye during a cataract surgery.

Other surgical instruments invented by Abu al-Qasim and first described in his *Al-Tasrif* (1000) include the scalpel, curette, retractor, surgical spoon, sound, surgical hook, surgical rod, and specula, as well as the bone saw.

Steam distillation was invented by Avicenna in the early 11th century for the purpose of producing essential oils, giving rise to aromatherapy. As a result, he is regarded as a pioneer of aromatherapy.

In cancer therapy, Avicenna described the first known treatments for cancer in *The Canon of Medicine*; one was a surgical method involving amputation or removal of veins, and the other was a herbal compound drug named "Hindiba", which Ibn al-Baitar later identified as having "anticancer" properties and which could also treat other tumors and neoplastic disorders. After recognizing its usefulness in treating neoplastic disorders, Hindiba was patented in 1997 by Nil Sari, Hanzade Dogan, and John K. Snyder.

Avicenna's *Canon* also described the first known surgical treatment for cancer, stating that the excision should be radical and that all diseased tissue should be removed, including the use of amputation or the removal of veins running in the direction of the tumor.

Chemotherapy was pioneered by al-Razi (Rhazes) in the 10th century, when he introduced the use of chemical substances and drugs as forms of medication. These chemicals included vitriol, copper, mercuric and arsenic salts, sal ammoniac, gold scoria, chalk, clay, coral, pearl, tar, bitumen and alcohol.

Avicenna, who viewed colour to be of vital importance in diagnosis and treatment, made significant contributions to chromotherapy in *The Canon of Medicine*. He wrote that "Color is an observable symptom of disease" and also developed a chart that related colour to the temperature and physical condition of the body. He further discussed the properties of colours for healing and was "the first to establish that the wrong colour suggested for therapy would elicit no response in specific diseases." As an example, "he observed that a person with a nosebleed should not gaze at things of a brilliant red color and should not be exposed to red light because this would stimulate the sanguineous humor, whereas blue would soothe it and reduce blood flow."

Hirudotherapy, the use of medicinal leech for medical purposes, was introduced by Avicenna in *The Canon of Medicine* (1020s). He considered the application of leech to be more useful than cupping in "letting off the blood from deeper parts of the body." He also introduced the use of leech as treatment for skin disease. Leech therapy became a popular method in medieval Europe due to the influence of his *Canon*. A more modern use for medicinal leech was introduced by Abd-el-latif in the 12th century, who wrote that leech could be used for cleaning the tissues after surgical operations. He did, however, understand that there is a risk over using leech, and advised patients that leech need to be cleaned before being used and that the dirt or dust "clinging to a leech should be wiped off" before application. He further writes that after the leech has sucked out the blood, salt should be "sprinkled on the affected part of the human body."

Muslim physicians developed a method of therapy that began with diet and physiotherapy; if this didn't work for the patient, then prescriptions for drugs and medication were given; and if this didn't work, then they resorted to surgery. The physiotherapy prescribed by Muslim physicians usually included physical exercise and bathing. Muslim Arab physicians developed an elaborate system of dieting, in which there was an awareness of food deficiencies, and proper nutrition was an important item of treatment. Medical drugs were divided into two groups: simple and compound drugs. As they were aware of the interaction between drugs, they used simple drugs first; if these failed, then compound drugs were used which are made from two or more compounds; and if these conservative methods failed, then surgery was undertaken as a last resort.

In phytotherapy, Avicenna introduced the medicinal use of Taxus baccata L. in *The Canon of Medicine*. He named this herbal drug as "Zarnab" and used it as a cardiac remedy. This was the first known use of a calcium channel blocker drug, which were not used in the Western world until the 1960s.

Muslim physicians from the Islamic world made many advances in the field of urology. Muhammad ibn Zakarîya Râzi introduced the methods of urinalysis and stool testing, while other physicians dealt with the medical management and treatment of kidney stones, inflammations, infections, and sexual dysfunction. They pioneered advanced surgical approaches to the treatment of bladder stones as well as penile and scrotal problems, using techniques that are still used by modern physicians. They were also the first to produce tested drugs for the treatment of many urological disorders.

In lithotomy, Abulcasis performed the first successful extraction of bladder and kidney stones from the urinary bladder using a new instrument he invented—a lithotomy scalpel with two sharp cutting edges—and a new technique he invented—perineal cystolithotomy—which allowed him to crush a large stone inside the bladder before its removal, significantly decreasing the death rates previously caused by earlier attempts at this operation by the ancients.

In sexual health, Muslim physicians and pharmacists identified the issues of sexual dysfunction and erectile dysfunction. They developed several methods of therapy for this issue, including the single drug method where a drug is prescribed, and a "combination method of either a drug or food." These drugs were also occasionally used for recreational drug use to improve male sexuality in general by those who did not suffer from sexual dysfunctions. Most of these drugs were oral medication, though a few patients were also treated through topical and transurethral means. Sexual dysfunctions were being treated with tested drugs in the Islamic world since the 9th century until the 16th century by a number of Muslim physicians and pharmacists, including al-Razi, Thabit bin Qurra, Ibn Al-Jazzar, Avicenna (*The Canon of Medicine*), Averroes, Ibn al-Baitar, and Ibn al-Nafis (*The Comprehensive Book on Medicine*).

Other medical contributions first introduced by Muslim physicians include the discovery of the immune system, the introduction of microbiology, the use of animal testing, and the combination of medicine with other sciences (including agriculture, botany, chemistry, and pharmacology), as well as the first drugstores in Baghdad (754), the distinction between medicine and pharmacy in the 12th century, and the discovery of at least 2,000 medicinal substances. Other medical advances came in the fields of pharmacology and pharmacy, and in the following fields of the biomedical sciences:

Muslims developed a scientific approach to botany and agriculture based on three major elements; sophisticated systems of crop rotation, highly developed irrigation techniques, and the introduction of a large variety of crops which were studied and catalogued according to the season, type of land and amount of water they require. Numerous encyclopaedias on botany were produced, with highly accurate precision and details. Al-Dinawari (828-896) is considered the founder of Arabic botany for his *Book of Plants*, in which he described at least 637 plants and discussed plant evolution from its birth to its death, describing the phases of plant growth and the production of flowers and fruit.

In the early 13th century, the Andalusian-Arabian biologist Abu al-Abbas al-Nabati developed an early scientific method for botany, introducing empirical and experimental techniques in the testing, description and identification of numerous materia medica, and separating unverified reports from those supported by actual tests and observations. His student Ibn al-Baitar published the *Kitab al-Jami fi al-Adwiya al-Mufrada*, which is considered one of the greatest botanical compilations in history, and was a botanical authority for centuries. It contains details on at least 1,400 different plants, foods, and drugs, 300 of which were his own original discoveries. The *Kitab al-Jami fi al-Adwiya al-Mufrada* was also influential in Europe after it was translated into Latin in 1758.

The earliest known treatises dealing with environmentalism and environmental science, especially pollution, were Arabic treatises written by al-Kindi, Qusta ibn Luqa, al-Razi, Ibn Al-Jazzar, al-Tamimi, al-Masihi, Avicenna, Ali ibn Ridwan, Ibn Jumay, Isaac Israeli ben Solomon, Abd-el-latif, Ibn al-Quff, and Ibn al-Nafis. Their works covered a number of subjects related to pollution such as air pollution, water pollution, soil contamination, municipal solid waste mishandling, and environmental impact assessments of certain localities. Cordoba, al-Andalus also had the first waste containers and waste disposal facilities for litter collection.

Ali ibn Sahl Rabban al-Tabari was a pioneer of pediatrics and the field of child development, which he discussed in his *Firdous al-Hikmah.*

His student Muhammad ibn Zakarîya Râzi (Rhazes) is considered the father of pediatrics for writing *The Diseases of Children*, the first book to deal with pediatrics as an independent field of medicine.

In endocrinology, Avicenna (980-1037) provided a detailed account on diabetes mellitus in *The Canon of Medicine*, "describing the abnormal appetite and the collapse of sexual functions and he documented the sweet taste of diabetic urine." Like Aretaeus of Cappadocia before him, Avicenna recognized a primary and secondary diabetes. He also described diabetic gangrene, and treated diabetes using a mixture of lupine, trigonella (fenugreek), and zedoary seed, which produces a considerable reduction in the excretion of sugar, a treatment which is still prescribed in modern times. Avicenna also "described diabetes insipidus very precisely for the first time", though it was later Johann Peter Frank (1745-1821) who first differentiated between diabetes mellitus and diabetes insipidus.

In the 12th century, Zayn al-Din al-Jurjani provided the first description of Graves' disease after noting the association of goitre and exophthalmos in his *Thesaurus of the Shah of Khwarazm*, the major medical dictionary of its time. Al-Jurjani also established an association between goitre and palpitation.

Avicenna's *The Canon of Medicine* was the first book to offer instruction for the care of the aged, foreshadowing modern gerontology and geriatrics. In a chapter entitled "Regimen of Old Age", Avicenna wrote that "old folk need plenty of sleep. Time spent on the couch should be liberal—more than is legitimate for adults." He wrote that after waking up, the body should be anointed with oil "to stimulate the sensitive faculties". Regarding exercise, he recommended walking or horse-riding. He stated:

"The factors to consider in regard to exercise in old people are the various bodily states of different persons; the sequels likely to arise from their ailments; and their previous habits as regards exercise."

He said that if the body is healthy, it can perform at tempered exercises, but if one part of the body is infirm, "then that part should not be exercised until after the rest", and that exercises are not to be strictly graduated "as if the body were to be strengthened". The *Canon* recognized four periods of life: the period of growth, prime of life, period of elderly decline (from forty to sixty), and decrepit age. He states that during the last period, "there is hardness of their bones, roughness of the skin, and the long time since they produced semen, blood and vapoural breath". However, he agreed with Galen that the earth element is more prominent in the aged and decrepit than in other periods. Avicenna did not agree with the concept of infirmity, however, stating:

"There is no need to assert that there are three states of the human body—sickness, health and a state which is neither health nor disease. The first two cover everything."

Thesis III of the *Canon* discussed the diet suitable for old people. Avicenna wrote that they should be given food in small amounts at a time and that they can have two to three meals a day, divided up according to the digestive powers and general condition of the old person in question. He also recommended fruits, such as figs and prunes. He also stated:

"Some laudable nutrition may be allowed at bedtime, [but] robust old folk may have a more liberal supper, as long as they avoid any gross aliment... all hot, sharp or desiccative foods, such as dishes made with vinegar, salt, hot aromatics, seasonings and pickles. [Milk is good for the aged, being] nutritious and humectant in nature. [Yet] articles of food with a laxative action are most appropriate for the elderly."

The famous Arabic physician Ibn Al-Jazzar Al-Qayrawani (Algizar, circa 898-980), also wrote a special book on the medicine and health of the elderly, entitled *Kitab Tibb al-Machayikh* or *Teb al-Mashaikh wa hefz sehatahom*. He also wrote a book on sleep disorders and another one on forgetfulness and how to strengthen memory, entitled *Kitab al-Nissian wa Toroq Taqwiati Adhakira*, and a treatise on causes of mortality entitled *Rissala Fi Asbab al-Wafah*. Another Arabic physician in the 9th century, Ishaq ibn Hunayn (died 910), the son of Hunayn Ibn Ishaq, wrote a *Treatise on Drugs for Forgetfulness* (*Risalah al-Shafiyah fi adwiyat al-nisyan*).

Of all the branches of Islamic medicine, ophthalmology was one of the foremost. The specialized instruments used in their operations ran into scores. Innovations such as the "injection syringe", invented by the Iraqi physician Ammar ibn Ali of Mosul, which was used for the extraction by suction of soft cataracts, were quite common. In cataract surgery, Ammar ibn Ali attempted the earliest extraction of cataracts using suction. He introduced a hollow metallic syringe hypodermic needle through the sclerotic and successfully extracted the cataracts through suction.

Ibn al-Haytham (Alhacen) made important contributions

to ophthalmology and eye surgery, as he studied and correctly explained the process of sight and visual perception for the first time in his *Book of Optics*, published in 1021. He was also the first to hint at the retina being involved in the process of image formation.

Ibn al-Nafis, in *The Polished Book on Experimental Ophthalmology*, discovered that the muscle behind the eyeball does not support the ophthalmic nerve, that they do not get in contact with it, and that the optic nerves transect but do not get in touch with each other. He also discovered many new treatments for glaucoma and the weakness of vision in one eye when the other eye is affected by disease.

The first psychiatric hospitals and insane asylums were built in the Islamic world as early as the 8th century. The first psychiatric hospitals were built by Arab Muslims in Baghdad in 705, Fes in the early 8th century, and Cairo in 800. Other famous psychiatric hospitals were built in Damascus and Aleppo in 1270. Unlike medieval Christian physicians who relied on demonological explanations for mental illness, medieval Muslim physicians relied mostly on clinical psychiatry and clinical observations on mentally ill patients. They made significant advances to psychiatry and were the first to provide psychotherapy and moral treatment for mentally ill patients, in addition to other new forms of treatment such as baths, drug medication, music therapy and occupational therapy.

The concepts of mental health and "mental hygiene" were introduced by the Muslim physician Ahmed ibn Sahl al-Balkhi (850-934). In his *Masalih al-Abdan wa al-Anfus* (*Sustenance for Body and Soul*), he was the first to successfully discuss diseases related to both the body and the mind, and argued that "if the *nafs* [psyche] gets sick, the body may also find no joy in life and may eventually develop a physical illness." Al-Balkhi was also a pioneer of psychotherapy, psychophysiology and psychosomatic medicine.

He recognized that the body and the soul can be healthy or sick, or "balanced or imbalanced", and that mental illness can have both psychological and/or physiological causes. He wrote that imbalance of the body can result in fever, headaches and other physical illnesses, while imbalance of the soul can result in anger, anxiety, sadness and other mental symptoms. He recognized two types of depression: one caused by known reasons such as loss or failure, which can be treated psychologically; and the other caused by unknown reasons possibly caused by physiological reasons, which can be treated through physical medicine.

Najab ud-din Muhammad (10th century) described a number of mental diseases in detail. He made many careful observations of mentally ill patients and compiled them in a book which "made up the most complete classification of mental diseases theretofore known." The mental illnesses first described by Najab include agitated depression, neurosis, priapism and sexual impotence (*Nafkhae Malikholia*), psychosis (*Kutrib*), and mania (*Dual-Kulb*). Symptoms resembling schizophrenia were also reported in later Arabic medical literature.

Muhammad ibn Zakarîya Râzi (Rhazes) and al-Balkhi were the first known physicians to study psychotherapy. Razi in particular made significant advances in psychiatry in his landmark texts *El-Mansuri* and *Al-Hawi* in the 10th century, which presented definitions, symptoms and treatments for problems related to mental health and mental illness. He also ran the psychiatric ward of a Baghdad hospital. Such institutions could not exist in Europe at the time because of fear of demonic possessions.

In al-Andalus, Abu al-Qasim (Abulcasis), the father of modern surgery, developed material and technical designs which are still used in neurosurgery. Ibn Zuhr (Avenzoar) gave the first accurate descriptions on neurological disorders, including meningitis, intracranial thrombophlebitis, and mediastinal germ cell tumors, and made contributions to modern neuropharmacology. Averroes suggested the existence of Parkinson's disease and attributed photoreceptor properties to the retina. Maimonides wrote about neurop-sychiatric disorders and described rabies and belladonna intoxication.

Ibn al-Haytham is considered by some to be the founder of experimental psychology and psychophysics, for his pioneering work on the psychology of visual perception in the *Book of Optics*. In Book III of the *Book of Optics*, Ibn al-Haytham was the first scientist to argue that vision occurs in the brain, rather than the eyes. He pointed out that personal experience has an effect on what people see and how they see, and that vision and perception are subjective. Along with al-Kindi and Ibn al-Haytham, al-Biruni was also a pioneer of experimental psychology, as he was the first to empirically describe the concept of reaction time.

Avicenna was a pioneer of psychophysiology and psychosomatic medicine. He recognized 'physiological psychology' in the treatment of illnesses involving emotions, and developed a system for associating changes in the pulse rate with inner feelings, which is seen as an anticipation of the word association test attributed to Carl Jung. Avicenna was also a pioneer of neuropsychiatry. He first described numerous neuropsychiatric conditions, including hallucination, insomnia, mania, nightmare, melancholia, dementia, epilepsy, paralysis, stroke, vertigo and tremor.

In rheumatology, Muhammad ibn Zakarîya Râzi reported a psychotherapeutic case study from a contem-porary 10th century Muslim physician who treated a woman suffering from severe cramps in her joints which made her unable to rise. The physician cured who by lifting her skirt, putting her to shame. He wrote: "A flush of heat was produced within her which dissolved the rheumatic humour."

In the zoology field of biology, Muslim biologists developed theories on evolution and natural selection which were widely taught in medieval Islamic schools. John William Draper, a contemporary of Charles Darwin, considered the

"Mohammedan theory of evolution" to be developed "much farther than we are disposed to do, extending them even to inorganic or mineral things." According to al-Khazini, ideas on evolution were widespread among "common people" in the Islamic world by the 12th century.

The first Muslim biologist to develop a theory on evolution was al-Jahiz (781-869). He wrote on the effects of the environment on the likelihood of an animal to survive, and he first described the struggle for existence and an early form of natural selection. Al-Jahiz was also the first to discuss food chains, and was also an early adherent of environmental determinism, arguing that the environment can determine the physical characteristics of the inhabitants of a certain community and that the origin of different human skin colours is the result of the environment.

Ibn al-Haytham wrote a book in which he argued for evolutionism (although not natural selection), and numerous other Islamic scholars and scientists, such as Ibn Miskawayh, the Brethren of Purity, al-Khazini, Abû Rayhân al-Bîrûnî, Nasir al-Din Tusi, and Ibn Khaldun, discussed and developed these ideas. Translated into Latin, these works began to appear in the West after the Renaissance and appear to have had an impact on Western science.

Ibn Miskawayh's *al-Fawz al-Asghar* and the Brethren of Purity's *Encyclopedia of the Brethren of Purity* (*The Epistles of Ikhwan al-Safa*) expressed evolutionary ideas on how species evolved from matter, into vapor, and then water, then mine-rals, then plants, then animals, then apes, and then humans.

After the 15th century, there were very few medical contributions from Muslim scientists until the 20th and 21st centuries, when Pakistani, Turkish, Iranian, Saudi Arabian, Yemeni, Malaysian and American Muslim scientists made significant contributions to modern medicine and biomedical research.

In the 20th century, Salimuzzaman Siddiqui was a leading Pakistani scientist in natural products chemistry. He is the pioneer in extracting chemical compounds from the Neem and Rauwolfia, and is also known for isolating novel chemical compounds from various other floras in the Indian subcontinent. As the director of H.E.J. Research Institute of Chemistry, he carried out extensive research with a team of scientists on pharmacology of various plants to extract a number of chemical substances of medicinal importance.

Behçet's disease is named after Hulusi Behçet (1889-1948), the Turkish dermatologist and scientist who first recognized the syndrome in one of his patients in 1924 and reported his research on the disease in *Journal of Skin and Venereal Diseases* in 1936.

In 1991, Saudi medical researchers discovered "neuro-Behcet's disease", a neurological involvement in Behcet's disease, considered one of the most devastating manifestations of the disease. In 1989, Saudi neurologists also discovered "neurobrucellosis", a neurological involvement in brucellosis.

Iranian scientist Samuel Rahbar was a pioneer in hematology and the understanding of diabetes. In 1969, he discovered glycosylated hemoglobin (HbA1C), a form of hemoglobin used primarily to identify plasma glucose concentration over time. He was also the first to describe its increase in diabetes.

Iranian physician and engineer Toffy Musivand invented a variety of medical technology, including the artificial cardiac pump as treatment for heart failure, "remote power transfer for implantable medical devices, remote patient monitoring (telemedicine), biofluid dynamics to reduce/eliminate thrombosis in blood conducting devices, patient care simulation centre, detection devices and methods for detection, in situ sterilization, medical devices (failure analysis and regulatory process), and medical sensors."

Dr. Muhammad B. Yunus is a Muslim American physician who practices internal medicine and rheumatology. In 1981, he published the "first controlled study of the clinical characteristics" of the fibromyalgia syndrome, for which he is regarded as "the father of our modern view of fibromyalgia." His work was the "first controlled clinical study" of fibromyalgia "with validation of known symptoms and tender points" and he also proposed "the first data-based criteria." In 1984, he proposed the important concept that the fibromyalgia syndrome and other similar conditions are interconnected. He showed serotonergic and norepinephric drugs to be effective in 1986, published criteria for fibromyalgia in 1990, and developed neurohormonal mechanisms with central sensitization in the 1990s.

He also made important advances in the understanding of the chronic fatigue syndromes in general, the biopsychosocial model, medical sociology, neurology, psychosocial development, and neurochemical pathology. His "biopsychosocial perspective" of fibromyalgia and other chronic fatigue syndromes is the "only way to synthesize the disparate contributions of such variables as genes and adverse childhood experiences, life stress and distress, posttraumatic stress disorder, mood disorders, self-efficacy for pain control, catastrophizing, coping style, and social support into the evolving picture of central nervous system dysfunction vis-a-vis chronic pain and fatigue."

In 2007, Malaysian scientist Sheikh Muszaphar Shukor, who is both an astronaut and orthopedic surgeon, became the first to perform biomedical research in outer space. His medical experiments on board the International Space Station were related to the characteristics and growth of liver cancer and leukemia cells, and the crystallisation of various proteins and microbes in space. His experiments relating to liver cancer, leukemia cells and microbes will benefit general science and medical research, while his experiments relating to the crystallisation of proteins, lipases in this case, will directly benefit local Malaysian industries.

Early Period to A.D. 750

When, in the seventh century, the Arabs first entered into the heritage of an ancient civilization, they brought with them apart from their religious and social ideals, no spiritual contribution save their music and their language. The rich and flexible tongue of Arabia was destined to become the scientific idiom of the Near East just as Latin grew into a medium of scientific understanding 'in the West.

The Arabian pre-Islamic and early Islamic poetry shows that the Bedouins possessed certain knowledge of the animals, plants, and stones of their vast peninsula. Their poets had a predilection for describing the qualities of their riding-camels and horses, and from their accounts in later centuries was derived a definite class of literature. The Quran expresses no clear conception of the nature of disease and gives hygienic directions only for social purposes. More elaborate material is afforded by Quranic traditions and commentaries formed during the first centuries of the Islamic faith. The contents of these, however, are of but little scientific value, being mere lists of diseases and remedies mingled with magic practices, description of talismans against the evil eye and protective prayers.

By the time the Arabs had penetrated into the Byzantine and Persian Empires., Greek science had for centuries ceased to be a living face. It had passed into the hands of scholars which copied or commented on the works of Aristotle, Hippocrates Galen, Ptolemy, Archimedes, and the rest. The Greek medic; tradition had found its most effective expositors in Aetios c Amida (ft. c. 550) and Paul of Aegina (fl. c. 625) who dwelt in Alexandria, in Alexander of Tralles (525-605) domiciled Rome, and Theophilos Protospatharios of Constantinop (fl. c. 640). During the centuries preceding the Arab invasion, the capital of Egypt saw some feeble revival of its ancient academy of new basis for medical learning was created by abstraction oft main works of Galen.

The soil is not favourable for any scientific development. For such reasons to act as an effectively mediary between that we must look to the Syriac-speaking world. The Aramaic or Syriac idiom had, from the third century onwards gradually replaced Greek in the learned circles of western Asia. The bearers of this Syro-Hcllenistic civilization were mainly the Nestorians. This Christian sect was founded in A.D. 428 by Nestorius, patriarch of Constantinople VI its adherents were condemned as heretical by the Council of Ephesus in 431 and thereon migrated to Edessa. Expelled thence in 480, by the Byzantine Empire, they emigrated to Persia, then under Sasanian rule, went they were well received. Pushing yet farther east-ward, with missionary zeal, they penetrated the heart of Asia and reached even as far as western China.

The Nestorian scientific centre, which included a medical school, was transferred from Edessa to Nisibison Mesopotamia and again in the first half of the sixth century to Jundeshapur in south-west Persia. There, besides a large hospital, an academy had been founded in the fourth century by the Sasanian monarch. The great' King Chosroes Nushirwan (531-79) made the city the most important intellectual centre of the time. Here Greek scholars who had left Athens when Justinian closed the philosophical schools in 529 came to meet Syrian, Persian, and Indian sages. Thus arose a scientific syncretism which later became important for the development of Islamic thought. Chosroes sent his own physician to India in search of medical books.

These were then turned from Sanskrit into Pahlavi (Middle Persian), and many other scientific works were translated from Greek in to Persian or Syriac. A disciple of the medical school of Jundeshapur and a contemporary of the Prophet was the first scientifically trained medical man in Arabia, and are cited by the Quranic traditionists. Versions of many important works of Galen are ascribed to him. Though crude, they were sufficient to maintain Greek medical tradition in western Asia for more than two centuries. During this period scholars began to write medical treatises of their own, based on Greek medicine. The writing of Ahlvon Tias not survived, but it seems to have contained the first description of small-pox, a disease unknown to ancient Greek medicine".

References to works on the natural sciences, from the centuries immediately preceding the rise of Islam, are rarer than those of a medical character. At some early period, the Parva naturalia of Aristotle and certain pseudo-Aristotelian books- *On the cosmos and On the Soul*, appeared in Syriac, as did also the Physiologus, a Christian theological treatise on animals and their legendary powers and qualities. In the same language appeared versions of Greek treatises on cattle-breeding, agriculture, and veterinary medicine, as well as alchemical tracts. Some early Syriac fragments on metallurgic technical procedure still survive. It is probable that during the Sasanian rule the main centres of alchemical and astrological study were the great towns in the eastern and northern provinces of Persia, where Chinese and Indian influences were being welded to form a new civilization.

When the Arabs overran North Africa and western Asia they left the Byzantine and Persian administrative and scientific institutions almost untouched. The academy of Jundeshapur continued as the scientific centre of the new Islamic empire. From here, during the Umayyad period (661-749), learned men, especially physicians, came to Damascus, the capital. They were mostly Christians or Jews bearing Arabic names. It was a Persian Jew, Masarjawaih, who translated Ahron's Pandects into Arabic, and was responsibility of what the earliest scientific book in that language. History however is almost silent concerning scientific aims at the court of the Umayyad Caliphs.

Age of Translations from about 750 to about 900

The rise of the Abbasids about 750 inaugurated the epoch of greatest power, splendour, and prosperity of Islamic rule. At the very dawn stands the figure of a Muslim whose shadow lies athwart the science of the Middle Ages in the Orient as in the Occident. Jabir ibn Hayyan called as-Sufi (that is 'the Mystic'), the Geber of Medieval Latin literature, was the son of an Arabic druggist in Kufa who died a martyr of the Shl'ite propaganda. Jabir practised as a physician, but no record of his medical writings has come down to us, though the author of this essay has recently been able to recover a work ascribed to him on poisons. As we write there arrives evidence, however, that the works ascribed to him are of the tenth century, where we shall accordingly consider them.

Jabir is said to have been closely attached to the family of the Barmecides, the powerful viziers of Harun ar-Rashid. He was implicated in their downfall in A.D. 803 and died in exile at Kufa, his father's birthplace, where it is said that his laboratory was found in ruins two hundred years later. In the time of the second Abbasid Caliph al-Mansur (754-75) the task of translation of Greek wisdom was taken up again, notably at Jundeshapur. From there the ruler, when sick, sent for Jurjis (George) of the Christian family of the Bukht-YismV ('Jesus hath delivered'), chief physician at the renowned hospital.

Another member of the same family was later consulted by the Caliphs al-Had! (d. 786) and Harun ar-Rashid (d. 809). The Bukht-Yishu' family produced no less than seven generations of distinguished physicians, the last of whom lived into the second half of the eleventh century A.D. It was doubtless the skill of the first Bukht-Yishu that made the caliphs desire to propagate Greek medical knowledge among the physicians of their empire. The ninth century was the period of greatest activity in the work of translation. The old Syriac versions of Sergius were revised and new ones added.

The translators, mostly Nestorian Christians, had a command of the Greek, Syriac, and Arabic languages and often also of Persian. Most of them wrote first in Syriac. The venerable Yuhanna ibn Masawayh (d. 857), however, who was for half a century physician to Harun ar-Rashid's successors, produced a number of medical works in Arabic. In general the

Syriac versions were prepared for Christian disciples and friends, while those in Arabic were intended for Muslim patrons who were themselves sometimes men of learning. During the reign of the Caliph Al-Ma'mun (813-33) the new learning reached its first climax. The monarch created in Baghdad a regular school for translation. It was equipped with a library. One of the translators there was Hunayn ibn Ishaq (809-77), a particularly gifted philosopher and physician of wide erudition, the dominating figure of this century of translators. We know from his own recently published Missive that he translated practically the whole immense corpus of Galenic writings.

This amounted to a hundred Syriac, and thirty-nine Arabic versions of Galen's medical and philosophical books. His disciples, of whom his son Ishaq and his nephew Hubaysh were the most prominent, produced some thirteen Syriac and sixty Arabic translations. Thus was transmitted to the Islamic world the whole legacy of the most voluminous of the Greek scientific writers. Hunayn's predilection for the scholastic turn in Galen's theories is everywhere apparent. It was Hunayn who gave Galen his supreme position in the Middle Ages in the Orient, and indirectly also in the Occident. Concerning the works of Hippocrates we are less well informed. Hunayn himself translated his Aphorisms, and this version remained classical for the later Arabs who frequently commented on it.

Most of the other Hippocratic works were translated by Hunayn's disciples. These versions were often revised by the master, who himself rendered into Syriac and Arabic nearly all the commentaries that Galen had himself written upon Hippocrates. Hunayn translated moreover the great Synopsis of Oribasius, the Seven Books of Paul of Aegina both voluminous works and the important and exceedingly influential Materia Medica of Dioscurides which had been badly rendered by a former translator. This work was yet again translated into Arabic in Spain during the second half of the tenth century. Magnificent illustrated Arabic manuscripts of these Arabic translations of Dioscurides are contained in various libraries. Among the Arabic translations ascribed to Hunayn are works of other Greek physicians and veterinary writers, together with several Aristotelian physical works and the Greek Old Testament (the Septuagint).

Many of Hunayn's translations are still extant in manuscript, particularly in the libraries of Constantinople. They exhibit a free and sure mastery of the language, an easy adaptation to the Greek original, and a striking exactness of expression without verbosity. The superiority of Hunayn's workmanship was so generally recognized that many of the minor translators ascribed their productions to the great master. Hunayn's own compositions are nearly as numerous as his translations. They include many summaries of, and commentaries on, Galen's works, and skilful extracts and recapitulations in the form of text-books for students.

Among the Arabs and Persians the most renowned of his books were the Questions on Medicine, a manual in the form of query and answer, and Ten Treatises on the Eye, which is the earliest systematic text-book of ophthalmology known. Several important works of Galen, though lost in their Greek original, have been preserved for us in the Arabic translations made by Hunayn or his pupils. Hunayn ibn Ishaq had several contemporaries who are considered 'great' translators, besides some ninety pupils who undertook similar work of less importance.

In the former class were his nephew Hubaysh, his son Ishaq (d. 910), the great physician and mathematician, Thabit ibn Qurra (825-901) of Harran in Mesopotamia, and Qusta ibn Luqa. All these except Thabit were Christians, like the majority of the physicians of the ninth century. Thabit himself was a heathen 'Sabian' or star-worshipper. Hunayn and Hubaysh translated medical writings almost exclusively, their colleagues devoted themselves rather to astronomical, physical, mathematical, and philosophical Greek works.

All of them produced also works of their own composition, the titles of which run into many hundreds. In the first half of the ninth century scientific works in the Syriac language predominated, but as the century wore on Arabic works became more numerous. Accompanying this process was the disappearance of the old school of Jundeshapur, all its famous physicians and scientists having been gradually transferred to Baghdad and Samarra, the brilliant residences of the caliphs. About 856, al-Mutawakkil re-founded at Baghdad the library and translation school, the direction of which was entrusted to Hunayn. The caliphs and their grandees furnished the necessary means to allow the Christian scholars to travel in search of Greek manuscripts and to bring them to Baghdad for translation.

Thus Hunayn himself relates concerning a work of Galen now lost, and rare even at that date, 'I sought it earnestly and travelled in search there of in Mesopotamia, Syria, Palestine, and Egypt, until I reached Alexandria. He says that he always tried to work from at least three manuscripts of a Greek book so as to collate them and restore their text properly a very modern conception of the duty of an editor. As for medical learning in Baghdad, an interesting passage in Hunayn's recently published Missive on the Galenic Translations shows us the Greek traditions fully alive there in 856. Thus he gives a picture of how the Twenty Books of Galen were being studied. 'The reading of the students of the Medical School at Alexandria was confined to these books, keeping to the order which I have followed in my list.

They were accustomed to meet daily to read and interpret one of the standard works, as in our days our Christian friends meet daily at the educational institutions known as schole (uskul) to discuss a standard work from among the books of the Ancients. The remainder of Galen's books they used to read each for himself, after an introductory study of the afore-mentioned books, just as our friends today do with the explanations of the books of the Ancients.' At this period, as well as later, full liberty to teach was granted in the schools and mosques of Baghdad. Besides the translations of Greek works and their extracts, the translators made manuals of which one form that of the 'pandects' is typical of the period of Arabic learning.

These are recapitulations of the whole of medicine, discussing the affections of the body, systematically beginning at the head and working down to the feet. Most of these pandect's are lost. One however was republished at Cairo only a few months ago. It was ascribed to Thabit ibn Qurra, more celebrated as a translator and astronomer than as a physician. It is divided into thirty-one sections. The subjects 'treated are hygiene, 'hidden' and general diseases, e. g. those of the skin ; then comes a section occupying the bulk of the work on diseases of parts from the head, down through the breast, stomach, and intestines to the extremities; then follows a discussion on infectious diseases, among which are small-pox and measles; and here also poisons find a place; next is an account of climate, then of fractures and dislocations, then of food-stuffs and diet, and lastly of matters of sex.

The exposition of each disease, its causes, symptoms, and treatment, is given in clear and succinct language. Many Greek and Syriac authors are quoted. Another kind of medical literature, much in favour with the Arab scholars, was the cram book in the form of questions and answers. Such books have survived in hundreds of manuscripts and have done much to give to Arabic medicine its scholastic aspect. As regards the process of translation of the Greek works on the sciences other than medicine, our sources of information are somewhat meagre. Most of the Aristotelian scientific corpus was rendered into Syriac and Arabic by unknown translators.

The Physics, the Meteorology, the De Anima, De Sensu, De Coelo, De Generatione et Corruptione, the Historia Animalium, together with works on botany, mineralogy, and mechanics spuriously ascribed to the great philosopher, all became accessible in these languages. Some treatises of neo-Platonic origin such as the Secret of Creation and the famous De Causis, ascribed to Apollonius of Tyana (called Balinus by the Arabs), and other apocryphal works of Hellenistic scientists appeared in Arabic dress. Many Greek alchemical works, all or most under false ascriptions, were also translated.

During the ninth century A.D., however, no progress in chemistry is recorded, and two of the great scientists, Hunayn and al-Kindi (d. c. 873), were violent opponents of alchemical practices which they considered fraudulent. We turn now from the translations to the original works of the period. In physics al-Kind is the most frequently named scholar. No less than works are ascribed to this first Muhammadan 'Philosopher of the Arabs'. Of these at least fifteen are on meteorology, several are on specific weight, on tides, optics and notably on the reflection of light, and eight are on music. Unhappily the bulk of al-Kinds scientific output is lost. His Optics preserved influenced Roger Bacon.

The technical arts were rapidly developing in Mesopotamia and Egypt, where irrigation works and canals for water-supply and communications were created. Theoretical mechanics roused much interest and many books on elevation of water, water-wheels, on balances and on water-clocks were written. The earliest treatise on mechanics extant appeared about 860 as the Book of Artifices by the mathematicians Muhammad, Ahmad, and Hasan, sons of Musa ibn Shakir, who were themselves patrons of translators.

This book contains one hundred technical constructions of which some twenty are of practical value, among them being accounts of vessels for warm and cold water, and water wells with a fixed level. Most are descriptions of scientific toys such as drinking-vessels with musical automata and the like, based on the mechanical principles of Hero of Alexan-dria. In natural history a special type of literature arose during the eighth century. It took the form of accounts of animals, plants, and stones composed with a literary aim, but containing useful information. One of the most prominent authors of such works was the famous Arabic philologist al-Asma f I of Basra (A. D. 740- 828).

He composed books On the Horse, On the Camel, On Wild Animals, On Plants and Trees, On the Vine and the Palm-Tree, On the Making of Man, and several other writers produced comparable works. A book that has caused much controversy is the Nabataean Agriculture of Ibn Wahshiyya (c. A.D. 800). It contains some useful information on animals, plants, and their cultivation, mingled with legends and forged translations from Babylonian and other Semitic sources. The Syriac version of the work on husbandry (Geoponica) by the Byzantine scholar Cassianus Bassus (c. 550) was translated into Arabic by different scholars. After the Arabic edition of Aristotle's apocryphal Mineralogy many Islamic writers composed books on stones, particularly precious stones, which form a special genre, the 'lapidary', after- US Y wards both translated and imitated in the West.

Nearly all those we have mentioned, from c Jabir ' to al-kind, were authors of such pamphlets. AJ-Kind moreover several small works on iron and or weapons. The increasingly close connexion between the caliphs' empire and eastern and southern lands, e. g., Turkistan, India, and the east African coasts, increased the afflux of rare and precious stones and the knowledge of them. Thus some modern names of stones still bear traces of Arabic or Persian contacts, for example the bezoar. Pharmacological and toxicological treatises were composed by many of the Arabic- writing physicians from Jabir ibn Hayyan onwards. Paper was introduced from China into the Islamic world in the eighth century and in A.D. 794 the first Islamic paper-manufacture was established in Baghdad.

The Golden Age

At the end of the period of translation, the physicians and scientists of the Islamic world stood on a firm foundation of Greek science, increased by a large share of Persian and Indian thought and experience. Their work had been learned but not very original. From this time on they begin to rely upon their own resources and to develop from within. The sciences, particularly medicine, now pass rapidly from the hands of Christians and Sabians into the possession of Muslim scholars, mostly Persians. In medicine, in place of pandects compiled from antique sources, we find imposing encyclopaedic works in which the knowledge of former generations is carefully classified and set against that of the moderns.

In his youth Rhazes practised as an alchemist, but in his later years, when his reputation attracted pupils and patients from all parts of western Asia, he devoted himself exclusively to medicine. His erudition was all-embracing, and his scientific output remarkable, amounting to more than 200 works, half of which are medical. The writings of Rhazes on medicine included many short missives of an ephemeral character. Their very titles bring a human element into what must be, for most readers, a somewhat arid theme. On the fact that even skilful 'physicians cannot heal all diseases. Why frightened patients easily forsake even the skilled physician; why people prefer quacks and charlatans to skilled physicians; why ignorant physicians, laymen, and women have more success than learned medical men, are among his lighter topics.

Other of his missives treats of separate diseases, for example of stone in the bladder and in the kidneys, both very common conditions in the 'near East. We have also the most celebrated of all the works of Rhazes is that on Small-pox and Measles. It was early translated into Latin and later into various languages, including English, being printed some forty times between 1498 and 1866. It gives the first clear account of these two diseases that has come down to us. An extract will convey to the reader something of the observing spirit of the original. 'The outbreak of small-pox is preceded by continuous fever, aching in the back, itching in the nose and shivering during sleep.

The main symptoms of its presence are: backache with fever, stinging pain in the whole body, congestion of the face, sometimes shrinkage, violent redness of the cheeks and eyes, a sense of pressure in the body, creeping of the flesh, pain in the throat and breast accompanied by difficulty of respiration and coughing, dryness of the mouth, thick salivation, hoarseness of the voice, headache and pressure in the head, excitement, anxiety, nausea and unrest. Excitement, nausea and unrest are more pronounced in measles than in small-pox, whilst the aching in the back is more severe in small-pox than in measles.'

Rhazes gives sound and detailed advice as to the treatment of the pustules after the full development of small-pox. These pustules are of course the cause of the unsightly scars left by the disease, which is still common in the East. The greatest medical work of Rhazes, and perhaps the most extensive ever written by a medical man, is his al-Hawi, i. e. 'Comprehensive Book', which includes indeed Greek, Syriac, and early Arabic medical knowledge in their entirety. Throughout his life Rhazes must have collected extracts from all the books on medicine which he had read, together with his whole medical experience. These he combined in his last years into this enormous manual. The Arabic biographies agree in saying that he could not finish his work and that after his death his disciples gave it its actual form.

He rendered the flame al-Hawl by continent, and as the Liber Continent this greatest work of Rhazes was propagated in numerous manuscripts during the following centuries. It was repeatedly printed from 1486 onwards. By 1542 there had appeared five editions of this vast and costly work, besides many more of various parts of it. Its Influence on European Medicine was very considerable. Besides medicine, Rhazes left writings on theology, philosophy, mathematics, astronomy, and the 'natural sciences'. His great Book of the Art (of Alchemy) was recently discovered in the library of an Indian prince.

Although dependent partly on the same sources as 'Jabir', Rhazes excels him in his exact classification of substances, and in his clear description of chemical processes and apparatus, which is always devoid of mystical elements. While 'Jabir' and the other Arabian alchemists divide mineral substances into 'Bodies' (gold, silver, &c.), 'Souls' (sulphur, arsenic, &c.), and 'Spirits' (mercury and sal-ammoniac), Rhazes classifies al-chemical substances as vegetable, animal, or mineral, a conception which comes from him into modern speech.

The class of minerals he divides into spirits, bodies, stones, vitriols, boraxes, and salts. He distinguished volatile 'bodies' and non-volatile 'spirits', placing among the latter sulphur, mercury, arsenic, and salmiac. A prominent contem-porary of Rhazes was the writer known to the West as Isaac Judaeus (855-955). This Egyptian Jew became physician to the Fatimid rulers of Qairawan in Tunisia. His works were among the first to be translated into Latin, the task being accomplished by Constan tine the African about 1080. They exercised much influence on Western medieval medicine, and were still being read in the seventeenth century. Robert Burton (1577-1640) quotes them freely in his Anatomy of Melancholy.

On simple Drugs and Aliments, and above all, his treatise On Urine dominated medicine for many centuries. Very remarkable is his little tract, extant in a Hebrew translation only, Guide for Physicians. It shows a high ethical conception of the medical profession. Some of the aphorisms in this work are worthy of record: 'Should adversity befall a physician open not thy mouth to condemn, for each hath his hour.' 'Let the own skill exalt thee and seek not honour in another's shame.' 'Neglect not to visit and treat the poor, for there is no nobler work than this,' 'Comfort the sufferer by the promise of healing, even when thou art not confident, for thus thou mayest assist his natural powers.'

A practical piece of advice excellent when dealing with Oriental patients is: 'Ask thy reward while the sickness is waxing or at its height, for being cured he will surely forget what thou didst for him!' Isaac's most distinguished disciple was Ibn al-Jazzar (d. 1009), a Muslim, whose chief work Provision for the Traveller was early translated into Latin as the Viaticum, Greek (Ephodia) and Hebrew. It was very popular with medieval physicians, because it gave a good record of internal diseases, but it was ascribed by its translator Constantine to himself and not to the real author. The alchemical writings to which the name of 'Jabir' is attached have long been a puzzle to scholars. If this 'Jabir' be the eighth-century mystic of that name, it is difficult to under-stand how he could have obtained any knowledge of the still inaccessible Greek alchemical literature.

As already indicated, however, evidence is now available that the works bearing the name of 'Jabir' were produced early in the tenth century. It appears that they were the work of a secret society similar to the so-called 'Brethren of Purity'. In the medical work of 'Jabir' only Greek authors are quoted, but the diction is independent of theirs and shows a distinct scholastic trend. Syrian and Indian names of drugs are rarely used, but Persian terms abound. Thus we may consider this remarkable book to be a mixture of Greek scientific research and Persian practical knowledge of medicines and poisons. Anyhow it is doubtless the last link in a long chain of scientific development during pre-Islamic and Islamic times.

'Jabir' is world-famed as the father of Arabic alchemy. This word, al-klmiyd, is usually said to be derived from the Egyptian kam-it or kem-it, 'the black', or, as some have thought, from the Greek ckyma, 'molten metal'. The fundamental premises of this 'science' as established by Egyptian and Greek scholars were (a) that all metals are in reality the same, and that consequently a transmutation of one into another is possible; (b) that gold is the 'purest' of all metals, and silver next to it, and (c) that there is a substance capable of continuously transforming base into pure metals. These conceptions had the merit of provoking experiment, but were unfortunately accompanied by an inordinate tendency to theorize. Moreover, at Alexandria, the centre of Greek learning, and indeed throughout the Islamic realm, certain mystical tendencies derived from the Gnostics and the neo-Platonists had a very detrimental effect upon the experimental spirit.

Alchemy, which in the hands of 'Jabir' was a matter for experimental research, tended to become the subject of ineffable speculation and superstitious practice passing into fraudulent deception. About a hundred alchemical works ascribed to 'Jabir' are extant. Many are little but confused jumbles of puerile superstition. But there are others which prove that the author recognized more clearly, and stated more definitely, the importance of experiment than any other early chemist. Thus he was enabled to make noteworthy advances in both the theory and practice of the subject. His influence can be traced throughout the whole historic course of European alchemy and chemistry. On the practical side, 'Jabir' described improved methods for evaporation, filtration, sublimation, melting, distillation, and crystallization.

He described the preparation of many chemical substances, e.g. cinnabar (sulphide of mercury), arsenious oxide, and others. He knew how to obtain nearly pure vitriols, alums, alkalis, sal-ammoniac, and saltpetre, how to produce so-called 'liver' and 'milk' of sulphur by heating sulphur with alkali, and so on. He prepared fairly pure mercury oxide and sublimate, as well as acetates of lead and other metals, sometimes crystallized. He understood the preparation of crude sulphuric and nitric acids as well as a mixture of them, aqua regia, and the solubility of gold and silver in this acid. Several technical terms have passed from 'Jabir Arabic writings through Latin into the European languages.

Among these are realgar (red sulphide of arsenic), tutia (zinc oxide), alkali, antimony (Ar: ithmid), alembic for the upper, and aludel for the lower part 'of a distillation vessel. A new chemical substance unknown to the Greeks which appears in 'Jabir works is sal-ammoniac. The ammoniacon of the Greeks was rock-salt, and it seems that the transference of the old name to a new salt was affected by the Syrians. A full appreciation of 'JabirY merits in chemistry will only be possible when the bulk of his chemical writings have been published, particularly his great Book of the Seventy. This composition of seventy discourses was till recently ' known only in an inferior and incomplete Latin version.

The chemical writings to which ' Jabir name is attached were soon translated into Latin. The first such version, the

Book of the Composition of Alchemy, was made by the Englishman Robert of Chester, in A. D. 1144. The translation of the Book of the Seventy into Latin was one of the achievements of the famous Gerard of Cremona. A work entitled the Sun of Perfection is ascribed to 'Jabir' by the English translator Richard Russell (1678) who describes nim as 'Geber, the Most Famous Arabian Prince and Philosopher'. Much evidence linking 'Geber' of the Latin writers with the Arabic alchemists has recently appeared from the pen of Dr. E. J. Holmyard.

In the Eastern caliphate there arose a generation of prominent physicians of whom we will first mention the Persian Muslim known to the Latins as Haly Abbas (d. 994). He composed an excellent and compact encyclopaedia, The Whole Medical Art, known also to the Latins as Liber regius (al-Kitdb al-Maliki). It deals with both the theory and practice of medicine. It begins with a most interesting chapter containing an explicit critique of previous Greek and Arabic medical treatises. This book was twice translated into Latin at an early date, but it was superseded by the Canon of the great Avicenna.

Abu 'All al-Husaynibn Sina, known universally to the West as Avicenna (980-103 7), was one of the greatest scholars of the Islamic world, though less remarkable as a physician than as a philosopher and physicist. Nevertheless his influence on European medicine has been overwhelming. Ibn Sma concentrated the legacy of Greek medical knowledge with the addition of the Arabs' contribution in his gigantic Canon of Medicine (al-Qanun ff t-Tibb), which is the culmination and masterpiece. This medical encyclopaedia deals with general medicine, simple drugs, and diseases affecting all parts of the body from the head to the feet, special pathology and pharmacopoeia.

The system of classification adopted in the Canon is most complex, and is in part responsible for the mania for subdivision which affected Western scholasticism. The book was translated into Latin by Gerard of Cremona in the twelfth century and his version exists in innumerable manuscripts. The demand for it may be gleaned from the fact that in the last thirty years of the fifteenth century it was issued sixteen times fifteen editions being in Latin and one in Hebrew, and that it was reissued more than twenty times during the sixteenth century. These figures do not include editions of parts of the work.

Commentaries on it in Latin, Hebrew, and the verna-culars, both in manuscript and in print, are without number, and the book continued to be printed and read into the second half of the seventeenth century. Probably no medical work ever written has been so much studied, and it is still in current use in the Orient. Some fifteen other medical works of Avicenna are known, together with about a hundred writings by him on theology, metaphysics, astronomy, and philology. Nearly all are written in Arabic except some poems which are in Persian, a language which acquired new importance during the tenth century.

To this day pious veneration surrounds the tomb of the great physician and philosopher at Hamadan in western Persia. While the eastern Islamic world was gradually acquiring supremacy in medicine, western Islam developed also as a centre of this science. In Spain during the glorious reigns of the caliphs 'Abd al-Rahman III and al-Hakam II of Cordoba, Has day ben Shaprut (d.c. 990), a Jew, was at once minister, court physician, and patron of science. In his younger years he translated into Arabic, with the help of the monk Nicholas, the splendid manuscript of the Materia Medica of Dioscurides which had been sent as a diplomatic present from the Byzantine emperor Constantine VII. Later Ibn Juljul, court-physician and medical historian, corrected this version and wrote a commentary on it.

The Muslim known to the Latins as Abulcasis (d.c. A.D. 1013) was likewise court-physician in Cordoba. His name is associated with a great Medical Fade mecum (at-Tasrif) in thirty sections, the last of which deals with surgery, an art which had till then been neglected by Islamic authors. The surgical treatise of Abulcasis is based largely on the sixth book of Paul of Aegina, but with numerous additions. His work contained illustrations of instruments which influenced other Arabic authors and especially helped to lay the foundations of surgery in Europe It was early translated into Latin, Provencal, and Hebrew. The celebrated French surgeon Guy de Chauliac (1300-68) appended the Latin version to one of his works.

In Egypt, Syria, and Mesopotamia there was much medical activity in the eleventh century A. D. 'All ibn Ridwan of Cairo (d.c. 1067) known to the Latins as Haly Rodoam, produced a fine medical topography of Egypt and was an ardent follower of Galen and the Greek authors. He declared that one could become a good physician solely by the study of the ancient works, which opinion gave rise to a long and violent polemic with his contemporary Ibn Butlan of Baghdad (d.c. 1063). Ibn Ridwan's commentary on Galen's Ars parva, as well as Ibn Butlan's Synoptic Tables of Medicine, a scholastic masterpiece, were translated into Latin.

Before leaving this period of Islamic medicine we have to consider some productions which are peculiar to it. First come the treatises on simple drugs which form parts of the great encyclopaedias, but which were also composed as separate monographs by a series of other authors. Such treatises are still highly esteemed in the Orient. Abu Mansur Muwaffaq of Herat in Persia wrote about 975 in Persian, The Foundations of the True Properties of Remedies describing 585 drugs. It contains besides Greek and Syriac, Arabic, Persian, and Indian knowledge. It is, moreover, the first monument of modern Persian prose. There were many treatises of the same type in Arabic.

4

Scientific Progress and Technological Advances in Muslim Countries

Recent decades have brought extraordinary transformations in information technology and in biotechnology, the collective impact of which has been felt worldwide. These transformations often reinforce feelings of powerlessness among those who have not benefited. This session explored the challenges that these developments pose for governments, societies, and traditional moral authorities, as well as for ordinary citizens. The session's chair, Ronald Lehman, director of the Center for Global Security Research at the Lawrence Livermore National Laboratory in the United States, opened by identifying the role of science in facilitating inter civilizational engagement and its ability to build bridges that transcend differences and to offer shared opportunities to improve lives around the world. However, particular scientific discoveries and applications of technology can create tensions when they conflict with cultural practices and religious beliefs.

Mr. Lehman raised four questions to lead the discussion. First, noting that participation in the global high-tech sector is made possible by education that is not equally accessible to all, he asked how science and technology can reach out to the different strata within communities. Second, he inquired whether faith and science advance together in the Muslim world and beyond, or whether they are adversaries. Third, Mr. Lehman wondered whether the Muslim world was transitioning from consumer to producer of technology at home and abroad and the implications of such evolution for the Muslim–Western relationship. Fourth, he asked how scientific cooperation between Muslims and Westerners could contribute to international peace and security and could mitigate the danger of "dual use" technology, such as nuclear energy.

The first speaker, Imran Ali, prefaced his remarks by making three underlying statements about the issue of technology. He noted, first, that there is no contradiction between Islam as a religion and the scientific pursuit of knowledge. Like all religions, however, Islam places certain moral limits on the application of science, proscribing, for example, the use of ultrasound technology in the service of fetal sex selection. Second, during the past five centuries, the Muslim world has been beset by a downturn in scientific production, while the Renaissance and the Industrial Revolution led to dramatic advances in Western technology. Third, the technology gap was reinforced by the subjugation of most Muslim countries during the colonial era. As global technological transformations continue to accelerate, will the gap widen, or will there be a breakthrough in the Muslim production of high-quality, scientific advancement?

Mr. Ali noted that in quantitative terms there are many centers of technological research in the Muslim world, but the limited quality of their contributions hinders the Muslim world's competitiveness. While there are many top-notch individuals in the sciences, they rarely aggregate into first-rate schools or departments. With the notable exception of Turkey, and, to a lesser extent, Indonesia and Iran, the Muslim world lacks industrial clusters that produce and patent technology. Excluding only the resource-based sectors (oil and gas), there are few, if any, companies based in the Muslim world that could be included in the top 500 worldwide.

These deficiencies urgently need to be addressed. Mr. Ali felt that current prospects for a scientific and technological revolution in the Muslim world are dim. On the economic front, where there are advances, such as in the large and dynamic "grey-market" sector, they tend to undermine the structural profitability of *bona fide* activities. Additionally, the removal of subsidies in many countries, compounded by rising production costs, has further diminished competitiveness. Apart from oil-driven activities, Muslim economies score low in innovation-based production. The private sector is still factory based and has not moved to a more agile, digital platform. This technological frailty also has military consequences: most Muslim countries have no significant technologically advanced weaponry.

The economic, geopolitical, and strategic implications of globalization are, hence, linked. The second speaker, Mustafa Ceric, grand mufti of Bosnia-Herzegovina, began by examining the relationship between faith and science. He noted that science is a tool used for achieving human goals, but it is not a goal in and of itself. This relationship has always underscored the interaction between theologians and scientists. Intellectual tolerance has been a distinctive feature of Islam for centuries, including lengthy periods during which other civilizations were stuck in their dark ages. The dramatic decline of the high scientific profile of the Islamic world challenges a staging of a "comeback," while avoiding both assimilation through secularization and the isolation that would result from a rejection of globalization.

The next speaker, Rainer Wessel, president of Ganymed Pharmaceuticals, began by highlighting that technology poses great challenges to us all, regardless of location or faith. Mr. Wessel stressed that the current era is witnessing a momentous technological revolution fueled by three areas of innovation: information technology, biotechnology, and nanotechnology. The publication of the human genome in 2001 constituted a landmark event encapsulating this recent history.

While scientists themselves have placed ethical limits on their own research, the overarching challenge today is closing the gap between fast-developing technology and legislation that is not keeping pace. He suggested that there is a role for nongovernmental organizations, such as the recently launched International Council for the Life Sciences, to provide independent, field-based regulation.

Mr. Wessel explained that the United States has led the way in recent scientific progress – particularly in biotechnology—with Europe and Asia closely following. As technology has become the principal driving force behind these economies, potential abuses of its products also increase. Technology is inherently neither good nor bad: what matters is the use to which it is put. Pressing ethical questions regarding the application of technology have been posed across different cultures, polities, and religions, with the debate constantly shifting along with scientific innovation. Mr. Wessel concluded by stating that sciences seem to flourish better in open societies. With science now a major driving force behind successful economies, he pointed to the need for economic and political liberalization in Muslim countries to stir scientific development.

The panel's discussant, Mark Smolinski, director of the Global Health and Security Initiative and vice president for Biological Programs at the Nuclear Threat Initiative (NTI) based in Washington, D.C., discussed the work of his organization to improve global capacity for prevention of and preparedness to biological threats through enhanced disease surveillance, early detection, and response. A consequence of globalization is that diseases spread quickly and over great distances, as demonstrated by recent severe acute respiratory system (SARS) and Asian bird flu epidemics. The NTI is working to establish regional organizations to monitor and respond to infectious diseases and has launched one such pilot program in the Middle East involving Israel, the Palestinian Authority, Egypt, and Jordan—demonstrating that regional cooperation in the arena of science and technology is possible even in a volatile area.

Mr. Bulliet launched this portion of the discussion by questioning the relationship between Western-trained Muslim scientists and scientific development in their home countries. Just as the repatriation of U.S.-based Chinese and Indian scientists has contributed in no small measure to these countries' recent economic successes, could the same not be true for the Muslim world? Mr. Ali responded that, at this point, many Muslim scientists return to their countries of origin only to find that they cannot make a significant contribution in the absence of a professional environment conducive to sustained scientific creation.

With scarce research possibilities and a culture of bureaucratic and institutional impediments—and with no apparent leadership invested in resolving these problems—Muslim scientists often find it impossible to live and work in their home countries. The Islamic world must culturally reinvest in the sciences to stem this brain drain. Mr. Bulliet also pointed out that major scientific contributions during the Muslim golden age took advantage of that civilization's permeability and lack of national boundaries. Today, technological pursuit is centered nationally, whereas Muslim scientists might fare best by creating regional networks. Hussein Solomon, director of the Center for International Political Studies at the University of Pretoria, endorsed Mr. Wessel's statement about the link between technology and open societies and added that changes in educational systems—shifting away from rote learning to critical inquiry—are necessary to foster a revival of technological progress in the Muslim world.

This must also be supported by active recruitment of and competitive salaries for promising scientists. Abdelmajid Charfi, professor emeritus of humanities and Islamic studies at the University of Tunis, concurred, adding that dogmatic training and memory-based education, as opposed to open-minded engagement, are conducive neither to proper education nor scientific production. Mina Al-Oraibi, a journalist for *Asharq Al-Awsat*, noted that these challenges are compounded by an urgent sense among Arab youth of having to catch up with fast-paced global trans-formations. Mr. Fücks questioned the existence of such a discipline as "Islamic science." Religion could be a source for ethical guidance in science, he offered, but religion should not interfere with science.

This concern is not unique to Islam, but one that is relevant to Christianity as well, with regard to the teaching of evolution, for example. Several participants agreed that Muslims should avoid adding the qualifier "Islamic" to science or other fields, as this demonstrates cultural insecurity and does not offer a constructive solution to the problems faced by Muslim countries. Vitaly Naumkin, president of the International Center for Strategic Studies in Moscow, wondered whether it might be useful to develop a Muslim scientific strategy or a joint Muslim vision of science. He also raised the question of whether measures adopted in the West for security reasons, such as the increased difficulty encoun-tered by Muslims applying for visas to work or study in the United States, were preventing Muslims from gaining access to the information and education necessary for technological advancement.

Mr. Wessel acknowledged that restrictions on the flow of knowledge are indeed a problem, not only between the Islamic and Western worlds, but within the West as well. Although such restrictions do not impair science itself and are mostly limited to regulating sensitive matters, certain people are excluded from information that could serve them better. For example, it is important that scientists in the Muslim world know about virulent viruses in order to make antibodies to fight them. The threat that such knowledge could fall into the hands of terrorists seeking biological weapons is offset by the benefits this knowledge would bring in the battle against infectious diseases.

The discussion then turned toward sources of funding for research and development in the Muslim world with Mr. Wessel remarking that although there is significant funding available from Muslim individuals—particularly in the Gulf countries—

such support is not always effectively distributed across the Muslim world. Mr. Nizami raised the problem of the widespread assumption of the West's centrality in scientific matters, specifically the idea that progress demands the mirroring of Western history. Although the Enlightenment made future scientific advances possible, these, in turn, depended on Muslim philosophical and scientific contributions of an earlier era. Furthermore, Mr. Nizami added, much of Europe's success rested on the institutionalized monopoly of patent protections and secured markets. Given that today's Muslim societies have neither of these capabilities, can they do the same?

Mr. Ali suggested that while the European system cannot be replicated in the Muslim world, there are other models for industrialization that could be instructive. To create climates conducive to scientific development, governments across the Muslim world must establish and institutionalize private property rights, which would stimulate a virtuous cycle of investment and returns. Ultimately, Muslim countries must "set their own shops right," and this begins with elites who all too often enrich themselves with little regard to the welfare of their less fortunate countrymen. The session closed with Mr. Ceric noting that Islam and the West have the opportunity to build trust around the interplay between science, politics, and theology by cementing technological interdependence and enabling strong international regulatory systems.

The Turkish-Islamic Union is a union of love. It is a union of affection, a union of hearts. The basis of this union is love, altruism, helping others, compassion, tolerance and understanding. The aim of the union is also to achieve the highest levels in respect for human beings and in art, science and technology. Once the union is established, not just Turkish societies and Muslims, but the whole world, will attain enlightenment. What truly makes the believers' union so strong is their faith and loyalty. Only genuine faith can engender true friendship and alliance. Muslims love one another with a pure heart and for the good pleasure of Allah, without the slightest selfish interest. A union built on the strongest foundation known to humanity—the fear and love of Allah—will never shatter, unless Allah wills otherwise.

The Turkish-Islamic Union will bring peace to the world. The Turkish-Islamic Union will first and foremost resolve the disputes between Muslim countries and bring peace to the Islamic world; it will also oppose all those movements that incite war and conflict in the world as a whole, and will be a force capable of preventing all initiatives aimed at provoking war. With the founding of the Turkish-Islamic Union, America, Europe, China, Russia, Israel and in short the whole world will breathe easier. Terror will come to an end, distribution of raw materials will be guaranteed, the economic and social order will be protected and cultural conflicts will disappear entirely. America will no longer have to send troops to lands thousands of kilometers away, Israel will no longer live behind walls, the countries of the EU will encounter no economic barriers, Russia will have no more security concerns and China will have no trouble finding raw materials.

With the founding of the Turkish-Islamic Union, the West's defense spending will fall. With its $400 billion military budget, the United States of America heads the armament list. Russia follows the USA with $60 billion, and China follows Russia with $42 billion. The Turkish-Islamic Union will give rise to a climate of global peace and security by eradicating all conflict and tensions regarding the Islamic world, and will also lead to a reduction in military spending, not just in Muslim countries, but on the part of a great many countries of the world. Investment in arms technology and money spent on weapons development will thus be diverted to such spheres as education, medicine, science and culture.

Freedom of ideas and expression are inherent in the Turkish-Islamic Union. People holding all kinds of beliefs and views will be able to express their ideas free from pressure and obstruction. These people's rights will be protected by all means and everyone's ideas will be met with toleration. Under the leadership of the Turkish-Islamic Union, Muslim societies will be communities in which people respect one another's views, communities will be dominated by equality, justice and freedom, and oppression and injustice will be banished. The Islamic world will not bring peace and security to Muslims alone, but will play a leading role in global culture and civilization.

The Turkish-Islamic Union will revitalize trade and strengthen the economy. Union among Muslim countries in the economic, political and cultural arenas will permit the less developed to make rapid progress and those countries which already possess the requisite means and infrastructure to use these as efficiently as possible. Economic growth and investment in science and technology will rise. With economic development will come a natural rise in education levels, and society will make progress on a number of fronts. The Turkish-Islamic Union will cause regeneration throughout the Muslim world. Thanks to the Islamic common market to be set up, products from one country will be easily marketed in another, without becoming caught up in quotas or national frontiers. Trade zones will grow, all Muslim countries will enjoy an increase in market share, exports will rise, leading to an acceleration of industrialization in Muslim countries, and economic development will lead to technological advances.

A Turkic-Islamic world with a powerful economy will be a major cause of prosperity for the Western world and other societies. These societies will find a power with which they can co-operate and engage in mutual trade with no feelings of concern. In addition, the funds that Western institutions and organizations constantly pour in for the region to regenerate will no longer be required, and these funds will be used to strengthen the global economy instead. With the founding of the Turkish-Islamic Union, energy resources will be guaranteed. Under the Turkish-Islamic Union, peace and stability will prevail in regions with rich underground reserves, and the democratic system will function in a most well-ordered manner there. A model will thus emerge in which these resources are used in the most efficient manner, and neither Islamic countries nor other communities will be disadvantaged. This, in turn, will make stable and balanced political policies possible in those matters of particular importance in maintaining global economic stability, particularly oil production and prices.

The Turkish-Islamic Union will encourage art and build a magnificent civilization. Peace and security will take hold, economic problems will be resolved in the Turkic-Islamic world, and a massive cultural advancement will take place, for there will be growing budgets for education, science, and culture. As friendship and fraternal feelings will prosper, people will find more time to reflect and conduct research, and they will be more free-thinking and open-minded when they do so. Environments free of chaos, destitution, and troubles are places in which new ideas take shape, new products emerge, beneficial inventions are made, and continuing progress is achieved. The Turkish-Islamic Union will create such an environment throughout the Islamic world. Is there really a problem? To judge by 'the correspon-dence in the TLS in January and February of 2007, there is. In a review (January 19) of Richard Dawkins's The God Delusion, the Nobel Prizewinning physicist Steven Weinberg denied that there had been any developments in Islamic science after the death of the scholar and mystic al-Ghazali in 1111.

In response, James Ragep, a historian of science, adduced, in rather general terms, all sorts of advances in Islamic science that had occurred after al-Ghazali's death. Weinberg responded by denying or diminishing some of Ragep's examples, such as the discovery of the pulmonary circulation of the blood, or a pre-Copernican presentation of a heliocentric system by Muslims. Weinberg, having reiterated that Islamic science never achieved much of importance after the early twelfth century, ended by quoting a 2002 survey by Nature which "identified just three areas of science in which Islamic countries excel: desalination, falconry and camel reproduction".

Evidently there is more at stake here than getting the chronology of the advance of science right. Ever since the nineteenth century there have been European thinkers, such as Ernest Renan, who have argued that the scientific outlook and Islam are incompatible; that the explosion of scientific translation and discovery was largely the achievement of non-Arabs; and that an increasingly strict and ossified Islam curtailed further scientific and speculative thought. Historians have wondered why the scientific movement in Islamic lands from the eighth to the eleventh centuries did not lead on to a scientific and an industrial revolution. Some Muslims might choose to detect an anti-Islamic agenda among those historians.

After all, the scientific and industrial revolutions did not occur anywhere in the world except in Europe, and therefore one needs to explain the peculiarity of European history, rather than adduce some kind of Islamic brake or blinker. Muzaffar Iqbal, who is a well-known scientist and Islamic scholar based in Canada, has written a book about science and Islam that is weighted towards the Middle Ages and has nothing to say about camel breeding or falconry. He has an agreeably caustic and aggressive approach to outdated and erroneous ideas about the history of science. The book is a polemical essay, rather than a history, and welcome as such. One of the targets is the notion that Islamic science was little more than a reheated version of ancient Greek science: "many histories of science tend to regard the eight hundred years of scientific activity in the Muslim world as being no more than some kind of depot where Greek science was parked and from where it was retrieved by Europe in later centuries".

He points out that the Arab scientific movement in the eighth century pre-existed the translation movement of the ninth and tenth centuries. He draws attention to a curious genre of literature that developed later, called shukuk, which was devoted to casting doubt on the findings of the Greeks, and he has no difficulty in adducing instances of Muslim scientists improving on, empirically testing or refuting Greek ideas. But, while he has some good sources to support the early development of what can be seen as an Islamic science, Iqbal is unwise to rely so heavily on the alleged writings of Jabir ibn Hayyan (whose notional dates are c721–815).

People who are only aware of Jabir (or Geber as he was known in the medieval West) as the name of an early scientist, may not be aware of what richly bizarre treasures are to be found in his strangely diverse writings: sperm is a crucial ingredient in the elixir of life; bird sperm is needed for producing a man with wings; the effigy of a Chinaman in bed will keep one awake at night; a picture of a man killing snakes done in magical ink will actually kill snakes; there is a fish called "the doctor of the sea" that carries a stone in its head that has the power to cure all ills; putrefied hair generates serpents; demons can be usefully trapped in statues.

In the monumental Jabir ibn Hayyan: Contribution à l'histoire des idées scientifiques dans l'Islam, Paul Kraus (1904–44), a genius who committed suicide at an early age, surveyed the Jabirian corpus, which covered sexology, alchemy, the art of warfare, the manufacture of talismans, artisanal techniques, religious polemic, grammar, music, invisible inks, the artificial generation of human beings and much else. Kraus showed that the corpus was not the work of a single hand. Moreover, most of the treatises dated from the late ninth and early tenth centuries and contained radical Shia propaganda.

Iqbal is aware of Kraus's findings but oddly refuses to engage with them and continues to treat Jabir as a real person who lived when he is supposed to have done and who wrote several hundred miscellaneous treatises. In general, Iqbal elides the pervasiveness of occult thinking in Islamic science. Also when writing about cosmology, he refers en passant to a genre of literature known as the "Wonders of Creation" (in Arabic aja'ib al-makhluqat), but the treatises in this genre that I have consulted have more in common with Ripley's Believe It or Not! than anything seriously scientific.

But Iqbal is successful in arguing that the "Quran itself lays out a well-defined and comprehensive concept of the natural world, and this played a foundational role in the making of the scientific tradition in Islamic civilization". Faith impelled rather than impeded the Islamic scientist. The Koran commands man to study Allah's creation. The eleventh-century cosmologist al-Biruni wrote: "Sight was made the medium so that [man] traces among the living things the signs and wisdom, and turns from the created things to the Creator". At a more practical level, astronomy and mathematics were studied and further developed to assist in such matters as the orientation of mosques, the determination of prayer times and the division of inheritances according to Islamic law.

It is odd that the life and writings of al-Ghazali should ever have been selected as marking some kind of watershed in the history of Islamic science. However, the immensely influential Hungarian Orientalist, Ignaz Goldziher, in his essay "Stellung der alten islamischen Orthodoxie zu den antiken Wissenschaften", published in 1915, argued that there was from the first an inherent antagonism between the ancient sciences and orthodox Islam. Those who studied these sciences were regarded with suspicion by the conservative religious establishment and, according to Goldziher, al-Ghazali's Tahafut al-falasifa ("Incoherence of the Philosophers") was accepted by the Muslim community as a decisive refutation of the independent validity of science. After al-Ghazali, an intellectual darkness spread over the Islamic lands.

Although Iqbal misrepresents Goldziher in presenting him as hostile to Islam, he is right to argue that the Tahafut al-falasifa was not really the attack on science that Goldziher claimed it to be. Indeed, al-Ghazali was explicit in his approval of mathematics, the exact sciences and medicine. What he was concerned to refute philosophically was the notion of causality espoused by Ibn Sina and other philosophers. For al-Ghazali, God is the real cause of all that happens. The notion of causality espoused by the philosophers whom he was criticizing was something that he thought was conjured up by men on the basis of what they regularly perceived. Whatever one thinks of al-Ghazali's idea of causality (which allowed space for miracles to happen), it is hard to imagine the Muslim scientific community of the twelfth century downing tools once word of the contents of the Tahafut got about.

Furthermore, it is perfectly clear that important advances in science were made after the twelfth century. For example, Ibn al-Shatir (d 1375) improved on the Ptolemaic model of the solar system by removing its eccentrics and equants, and his model for the rotation of the Sun anticipated that of Copernicus. Again, Al-Kashi (d 1429), besides compiling an improved set of astronomical tables, also provided the first systematic exposition of decimal fractions, as well as a way of extracting the nth root of a number.

Quite a large part of the religious establishment was opposed to alchemy, but, given the fraudulent tripe written by most of the alchemists, that was no bad thing (and of course many scientists, doctors and philosophers joined in the attack on the practice). In most other respects there was no conflict between science and Islam in the pre-modern period, and Iqbal shows this. So problems remain. Why was there an apparent decline in scientific achievement sometime after the fifteenth century and why were there no scientific and industrial revolutions in the Islamic world? Iqbal, though he is clear and convincing about Islam being not to blame, has no answers and takes the reasonable view that the field is still too under-researched for even provisional answers to be attempted. Certainly, decades of further research are necessary.

No less certainly, most readers of the TLS are too impatient to wait for the outcome. I would suggest that the spread of the madrasa, or religious teaching college, throughout the Middle East in the central and late Middle Ages led to a certain narrowing of intellectual horizons. While scientists continued to do research and publish, they do not seem to have founded scientific societies of the sort that proliferated in Western

Europe in the seventeenth century. The Middle East is poor in the resources needed to get an industrial revolution going. It lacks iron, copper, wood and much else, including lots of rivers that could be harnessed for industrial purposes. There was also a kind of imperial complacency among the subjects of the Ottoman, Safavid and Mughal empires (a complacency that finds its parallel among the citizens of the Spanish and Portuguese empires in the same period).

There had been plenty to be complacent about and Iqbal points out "that at the beginning of the eighteenth century, the entire Middle East, a large part of Africa, the whole middle belt of Asia and the Malayan archipelago were under Muslim control . . .". Thereafter, things changed rapidly. Iqbal is at his most agreeably acerbic when dealing with the relationship between Islam and science in the past two centuries. He gives a fascinating account of how a kind of tafsir, or exegetical literature, developed that was devoted to demonstrating that the Koran had anticipated modern embryology and the theory of the expanding universe.

The Turkish scholar, Said Nursi (1877– 1960) maintained that the Koran alludes to railways and electricity. Iqbal describes the Islamic world's encounter with Western science from 1950 as being "like a rude awakening from a medieval siesta". Modern Muslim states produce "a caricature of Western science" and he remarks with only slight exaggeration that "Almost all Muslim states have ministries and ministers of science and technology, who ceaselessly issue statements on the need to acquire modern science, but none of these fifty-seven states produce any science worth its name and most able Muslim scientists live outside these states".

Given that Iqbal is capable of penetrating criticism of writings on science and the transmission of knowledge by such scholars as Goldziher, George Sarton and Dmitri Gutas, surprised at the bland endorsement he gives to the Philosophia Perennis, a body of doctrine espoused by the followers of René Guenon (d 1951) and Frithjof Schuon (d 1998), both of them converts to Islam. That body of doctrine is unmistakably Gnostic, elitist, occultist, misogynist, rightwing, opposed to the theory of evolution and ultimately anti-scientific.

On the other hand, Iqbal is sometimes rather hard on Western Orientalists. It is not true, for example, that most of the translations of the Koran into European languages derived ultimately from that by Robert of Ketton in the twelfth century. The great seventeenth-century translations by Lodovico Marracci and André du Ryer were largely guided by works by Muslim exegetes, and George Sale's eighteenth-century translation drew on Marracci and similarly gave prominence to Muslim commentaries. Orientalism owes more to Muslim scholarship than most Muslims realize.

The contributions of Islamic scientists and technologists in the varied fields of knowledge were fascinating and are discussed in the various histories of science. These contributions, using mainly the medium of Arabic, were made by a wide variety of individuals – Muslim and non-Muslim – living in a multi-national and multiracial society. The universal religion of Islam provided the matrix within which the multiracial and multicultural Islamic society could subscribe to a universal science. The ethnic and cultural diversity of the Islamic world was a source of strength and creativity to the movement of scientists, ideas and products.

The introduction of efficient and extensive means of transportation facilitated the expansion of trade and the movement of people and ideas. These advances in transport and trade gave force to the universal precepts of Islam by facilitating the transfer of knowledge within the Islamic world; and also to the widely different cultures of India, China and Europe. The locus of scientific creativity in the Muslim world was not fixed. Centres of considerable scientific activity flourished at different times and were generally closely associated with the seat of power. During the Umayyad and Abbasid periods, the capitals of the Islamic world attracted scholars and scientists. In modern parlance, there was a brain drain to Damascus and Baghdad. Once the centres of power moved to Cairo, Spain, Persia (Mongolian period) and Istanbul, the flow of scientists followed there.

During the first centuries of Islam, the rulers pursued policies which promoted rationality, communications, trade and economic prosperity. These policies increased the demand for science and technology. Almost every aspect of life – from agriculture to health and prayers – depended on some scientific or technical activity. The decline, which set in after a combination of internal and external circumstances and conditions, caused a decrease in the demand for science and technology.

Science Thrives only in Affluent Societies

The challenging question that is always asked is: what were the causes of the decline of scientific work in Islam, and why did the gap in modern science and technology become so great between the West and Islam from the end of the sixteenth century? This is a complex question which cannot be dealt with fully in this chapter, but we shall venture to discuss some aspects of the decline which, it is hoped, will stimulate further research into this question.

At the time when scientific communities in Europe were on the increase, all the regions of Islam were witnessing the decline of science and of scientific communities. This phenomenon is discussed by Ibn Khaldûn in more than one chapter in his Introduction (*al-Muqaddima*). He discusses the factors which are essential to the flourishing of the sciences and the other professions, and the factors which lead to their decline. One chapter carries the title: 'That the Professions are Perfected and Become Plenty when the Demand for them Increases.'

He says that if a profession is in great demand, people will try to learn it, whereas if there is no demand for a profession it will be neglected and will disappear. 'There is here another secret, and it is that the professions and their perfection are demanded by the state, which is the greatest marketplace for the professions', and the needs of the state are so great that the demands of private individuals are too small in comparison, which means that when the state declines all professions decline as well. Another chapter carries the title: 'That Regions which Approach a Ruinous State will Become Devoid of the Professions.'

When a region becomes weakened, loses its affluence, and its population decreases, the professions will diminish, because they can no longer be afforded, until they finally disappear. He devotes a special chapter to the sciences under the title: 'That the Sciences Increase with the Increase in Prosperity and with the Greatness of Civilization in a Region.' After a dis-cussion of his theory he says: 'Let us consider what we have known about conditions in Baghdad, Cordoba, al-Qairawan, al-Basra, and al-Kufa.

When these cities became populous and prosperous in the first centuries of Islam and civilization became established in them, the seas of science rose and overflowed and scientists marvelled in the terminology and the technicalities of learning and of the various sciences, and in devising various problems and theories until they excelled over the ancients and surpassed those who came after. But when the prosperity of these cities and their civilization decreased and when their population was dispersed, that carpet, with all that was on it, was completely folded and science and learning were lost in them and moved to other regions of Islam.'

In discussing the rational sciences, Ibn Khaldûn gives the same analysis, and he remarks that when the empire became established, and when Islamic civilization surpassed all others, Muslims studied eagerly the rational sciences of the ancients until they excelled over them. He remarks that during his time (the second half of the fourteenth century), the rational sciences in the Maghrib and in al-Andalus were diminishing because prosperity in these regions was at a low level, whereas in the Eastern regions of Islam, especially in Persia and beyond to

Transoxania, the rational sciences were flourishing because of the prosperity of these regions and the stability of their civilization. Ibn Khaldûn was aware also that during his time, the rational sciences in Rome and in Europe in general, were in great demand and that there existed in these countries active scientific communities.

The ideas of Ibn Khaldun are repeated by modern scholars. Thus Bernal in his book Science in History repeats in a similar argument that 'Science's flourishing periods are found to coincide with economic activity and technical advance. The track science had followed - from Egypt and Mesopotamia to Greece, from Islamic Spain to Renaissance Italy, thence to the Low Countries and France, and then to Scotland and England of the Industrial Revolution - is the same as that of commerce and industry. Between the bursts of activity there have been quiet times, sometimes periods of degeneration. These coincide with periods when the organization of society was stagnant or decadent.'

Stagnation of Medieval Science

The above discussion helps to explain why the Scientific Revolution did not take place in Islam. Until the end of the fifteenth century, scientific knowledge was dominated by few major systems which became dogmatic and static. The main ones were Aristotelian physics, Ptolemaic astronomy, Galenic medicine, and Jabirian alchemy. Science had reached a point where further progress became extremely difficult or even impossible.

This explains the scarcity of important scientific progress both in Islam and in medieval Europe between the thirteenth and the fifteenth centuries. To achieve major breakthroughs in science, it was necessary to overthrow the old dominant systems. In other words, a revolution in science was necessary. Such a revolution requires the existence of a large community of scientists who are working diligently within a flourishing economy and a stable atmosphere over a long period of time. Contrary to the world of Islam, this community existed in

Europe after the fifteenth century and it continued on the rise with the increase of European wealth and population, and the domination by Europe of other parts of the world.

From the nineteenth century, some writers have suggested that the decline of science in Islam was caused by the negative attitude of Muslim theologians. Thus Sachau says, 'The fourth century (Islamic calendar) is the turning point in the history of the spirit of Islam. But for al-Ash'ari and al-Ghazali, the Arabs might have been a nation of Galileos, Keplers, and Newtons Speaking about al-Ash'ari, E.G. Browne compared the destructiveness of his influence to that of Jenghiz Khan and Hûlâgû.

A similar point of view is adopted by George Sarton, who labels the views of al-Ash'ari and al-Ghazâlî as scholasticism, which 'were obstacles to the progress of science in the Middle Ages. Sarton says that until the sixteenth century, developments in science were taking place both in the East and the West, but after that time Western science began to grow at an accelerated pace, while Eastern civilization remained at a standstill, or even deteriorated. He concludes that the essential difference between East and West is that the latter overcame scholasticism, while the former did not.

It is true that the divergence between Islam and the West in science continued to increase after the sixteenth century, but the assumption that the opposition of theologians to science was the cause of this, cannot be supported. The real causes are both political and economic, as was demonstrated by Ibn Khaldun; the decrease of interest in the rational sciences and the continued interest in the study of the religious sciences are unrelated. The former was a symptom of the economic weakness of the Islamic states and of their decreasing political power. Had there been a need for science and technology, as was the case during the Golden Age of the Islamic Empire, the rational sciences would have continued to progress without interruption.

In Islam, there was no single religious authority that controlled the whole educational system, and this left the system free and not dominated by orthodoxy. The rise of scientists and the flourishing of the rational sciences in the Golden Age reflected the prosperity of the empire and its strength, and the large number of mathematicians, astronomers, physicians, engineers and other kinds of scientists was in response to the needs of society and of the empire in that period. It conformed to the law of supply and demand. It is not our purpose here to defend the theologians. It should be pointed out, however, that the debate which took place between them and the philosophers was not over the rational sciences.

From the beginning, the study of mathematics, astronomy, medicine, alchemy and the other sciences was greatly encouraged, and it was mostly undertaken by scholars who were non-philosophers and non-theologians themselves. The Golden Age of science took place at the same time as the debate between theologians and philosophers was taking place. The study of the rational sciences was not affected by such a debate, since the pursuit of these sciences was independent from both the theological and the philosophical studies. To illustrate our statement, let us take the reigns of al-Ma'mun and of al-Mutawakkil.

Al-Ma'mun (813-833) was a staunch supporter of the Mu'tazilites and the rational sciences flourished during his reign. Contrary to him, al-Mutawakkil (847-861) was, according to one orientalist, 'of the strictest orthodoxy and fanatical in his orthodoxy...'. During his time 'the forces of orthodoxy began to gather momentum', and the orthodox theologians , whose front was led shortly later by al-Ash'arî, put up an organized front against the Muctazilites But, with his 'orthodoxy and fanaticism',, al-Mutawakkil like al-Ma'mun 'was a patron of science and scholarship and reopened the Dar al-Hikma, granting it fresh endowments. The best work of translation was done during his reign... He was a generous patron of scientific research... The best work of Dar al-Hikma was done under him, for by that time experience told, and Hunayn was surrounded by well-trained pupils.'

The Madrasa System

In a similar line of thinking, the decline of the rational sciences in Islam is attributed by some writers to the fact that the madrasa system which flourished after the founding of the Nizâmiyya Madrasa in Baghdad by Nizâm al-Mulk. in 459/1067 favoured the study of theology and law. But the study of the rational sciences in Islam was always undertaken independently, and the theological studies were not usually undertaken under the same teachers or at the same institutions. Astronomy and mathematics were pursued mostly in the observatories, within a community of mathematicians and astronomers, where a specialized library was available and observational instruments were in constant use.

The medical sciences were studied, as they should be, in the medical school of a bîmâristân (hospital). The other sciences were studied under individual renowned scientists, most often patronized by the rulers, to whom students travelled from the far realms of Islam. The existence of these individual renowned teachers constituted what may be called a college of professors within a certain large city or a region. Let us not forget also the libraries and the academies, like Dâr al-Hikma in Baghdad, which were devoted to research and to the study of the rational sciences. Most of the madrasas, on the other hand, were established by persons in power or by pious and wealthy individuals who endowed a part of their wealth to a waqf which supported the school.

The purpose was always religious, and the studies were naturally mainly those of law and theology. It can be said therefore that the madrasa was mainly a college of theology and law, and it was, according to recent studies, the forerunner of the college system in Western universities. But the universities which appeared in the West and which comprised several colleges for theology, law, arts and sciences, and medicine, did not develop in Islam in the same period.

This is due to the fact that the madrasas which were supported by the waqf system, and with them the study of law and theology, continued to exist without interruption, whereas the centres for the study of the rational sciences, which were dependent on the strength and the prosperity of the state, deteriorated and ceased to exist with the decline of the Islamic states, and for this reason scientific knowledge did not keep in line with the quick advances of science in Europe after the Scientific Revolution.

In the period preceding this revolution it was possible to speak about the achievements of Muslim scientists and compare them to those of medieval Europe. Advances in both areas were parallel and there was not a significant difference between them. But after the new discoveries of Copernicus, Galileo and Newton and the fall of the old systems of knowledge, the university in the West became the centre of the new scientific activities. For the Scientific Revolution which took place in Europe to have happened in Islam at the same time, there would have to have been in existence at that time in history an efficient system of communications between members of the scientific communities in both cultural areas.

But such a system did not exist; there were no Islamic universities which comprised all branches of knowledge, and the Islamic scientific community was almost non-existent. It was only in modern times that universities on the model of the European ones started to appear in the Islamic countries. Some of the older universities, such as al-Azhar, which followed the madrasa system and were devoted to the study of Islamic law and theology, have only recently introduced science, engineering and medicine into their curricula.

Having thus established the link between the decline of Islamic science and the decline of the Islamic lands both in political power and material wealth, the question which remains to be answered is: what are the factors behind the decline of the Islamic lands? And although the discussion of this subject lies in the domain of political and economic history, and not in the scope of the history of science, yet we shall summarize what we think are the major factors in the decline.

Nature of the Land

Most of the core Islamic countries, or the lands of the Islamic Middle East, are composed of arid or semi-arid lands with some scattered inhabited lands and large uncultivated or desert areas. Taking the lands of the early Islamic empire, excluding Spain, the inhabited area did not exceed one quarter of the total, the rest being barren or desert lands. Even the inhabited areas are mostly dependent on irrigation for their cultivation, since the rainfall in most of the areas is not sufficient to support agriculture. This ecology of the Middle East meant that its most productive agriculture was confined mainly to the basins of the great rivers of the Nile, the Euphrates and the Tigris. But the harnessing or utilization of the waters of these rivers could not be attempted by individuals, and this job had been undertaken since the days of the ancient civilizations of Egypt and Babylonia by the strong central governments.

Also in the first centuries of the Islamic empire, during the Umayyads and the Abbasids, the caliphs and the governors of the provinces gave great attention to the construction and the maintenance of the irrigation systems. And it is well known that an agricultural revolution took place in the first centuries of the Islamic empire. When the central government was weakened or disappeared, the irrigation works were neglected, and when, in addition, these works were destroyed by the Mongol invasions, as had happened in Iraq in the thirteenth century, agricultural lands became arid or turned into marshes and the whole economy and civilization of the region were destroyed.

Some changes in climate and in the rate of rainfall contributed also to the conversion of agricultural lands into arid. At the beginning of the Islamic period and until the middle of the thirteenth century, the area east of Antioch in Syria was one of high rainfall, and it saw the founding of many cities and much farming was taking place. Yet within a few centuries, the territory became arid. The important consequence of this ecology is that the area is considered a poor one from an agricultural point of view. It cannot depend only on agriculture for its prosperity and for the development of its civilization.

The Nomads

Another result of the ecology of the Middle East is that the semi-arid nature of the region, and the decline and the destruction of its irrigation systems, resulted in a phenomenon which is also peculiar to it. There existed throughout the history of the civilizations of the area, nomadic tribes who utilized the peripheral lands as pastures for animal breeding. The nomadic tribes always affected the stability of the central government and the economy of the region. When the central government was strong and the economy was prosperous, the nomads were usually kept under control.

Whenever the central government was weakened, the nomadic tribes would prevail and influence or dominate the various individual governments in the region causing further disorder and anarchy. With the destruction of the irrigation works and the transformation of irrigated lands into pastures or marshes, the nomads increased the areas under their immediate control, and thus the decline of civilization was further accelerated. This process of the conversion of irrigated lands into arid or marsh lands and the encroachment of nomads into previously settled areas led also to the depopulation of Iraq and Syria from the thirteenth century until the modern era.

Natural Disasters

Another important phenomenon in the social and economic history of Egypt, Syria and Iraq in the middle Ages was the drastic depopulation caused by natural disasters. In 968, the low level of the Nile caused a terrible famine which resulted in the death of about 600,000 people. Similar famines followed. One terrible famine, which was caused also by a low level of the Nile, lasted seven years between 1066 and 1072. Peasants deserted their villages and agricultural production was diminished severely. These famines heralded the beginning of a series of natural disasters which resulted in the depopulation of Egypt. In 1201 and 1202 a terrible famine was followed by plague and large numbers of people died. In many villages only empty houses remained; and in some quarters in Cairo all the inhabitants died. This was one of the major demographic disasters which befell Egypt in the middle Ages.

However, the greatest catastrophe in the middle Ages was the plague of 1347, 1348 and 1349, which was known in Europe as the Black Death and which swept across the Islamic world and Europe. Thousands died every day, and the population of Egypt, Syria and Iraq was diminished by one third. The Black Death was followed by a series of plagues which continued into the nineteenth century. It was estimated that between 1363 and 1515 alone, sixteen epidemics occurred in Egypt and fifteen in Syria.

These recurring famines and plagues were instrumental in diminishing agricultural production. Death wiped out a large proportion of peasants and domestic animals. Industry collapsed with the deaths of great numbers of skilled workers. This also had adverse effects on the administration and the government. The Mamelukes no longer had sufficient resources to maintain their military organization. This led to instability, corruption and oppression which helped further to accelerate the economic decay.

Geographical Location

The geographical factor made Iraq, Syria and Egypt the targets of continuous external attacks, aggression or intervention from the First Crusade in AD 1006 until modern times. Geographical location gave a prime strategic asset to some countries such as Japan and the British Isles, since their insular location offered protection from overland invasion. The geography of Europe and its location in the west protected it also from similar invasions.

Europe's landscape was much more fractured, with mountain ranges and large forests separating the scattered population centres in the valleys, and its climate varied considerably. This had minimized the possibility that the continent could be overrun by an external force like the Mongol hordes. In contrast, Iraq, Syria and Egypt were central between East and West and their flat geography made them vulnerable to external invasions from both sides.

The Crusades

Between 1096 and their final defeat in 1291 no fewer than seven Crusades were mounted against the Arab lands; one Crusade was mounted against Constantinople. The first three (1096, 1147, 1189) focused on Syria, including Palestine. The Fourth Crusade (1204) pillaged Constantinople, while the Fifth, Sixth and Seventh Crusades (1218, 1244, 1250) were directed against Egypt. The last one (1270) was directed against Tunisia. Palestine, especially Jerusalem, was consi-dered holy for the three religions of Judaism, Christianity and Islam.

The declared object of the Crusades was to occupy the Holy Land, especially Jerusalem, and to replace the native Muslim population by a Latin one. During the conquest, the Muslim population of the captured Syrian towns was annihilated by mass slaughter, and was replaced by the members of the invading armies and those who accompanied them, such as adventurers, merchants and pilgrims. There were also other motives behind these wars. Around AD 1000, the population of Europe was growing, whereas that of the Islamic world was on the decline. The population of Europe was estimated at 38.5 million while that of the Islamic lands did not exceed 12.5. Some historians are of the opinion that 'the

Crusades were essentially an early experiment in expansionist imperialism, motivated by material considerations with religion as a psychological catalyst.'

The period of the Crusades was one of growth on all fronts in Western Europe. There was a growth in population and in production. The growth in profits led to the accumulation of capital and this stimulated all who engaged in trade, notably the members of the Italian commercial and banking houses. The Crusades offered huge opportunities for the expansion of the great maritime cities of northern Italy – Venice, Pisa and Genoa. The conquest, and the concessions given to these cities, allowed the establishment of Italian co-lonies in the towns of the Syrian coast.

These colonies flourished under the Crusaders' rule, and they survived under the Muslim re-conquest and developed a considerable trade both for export and import. They were instrumental in the transfer of the manufacturing technologies of some Near Eastern industries and the establishment of these industries in Italy. There came a time when the process was reversed and the Italian products of these industries started to be exported to the Near East. This was probably the chief permanent effect of the Crusades in the Near East.

The efforts to confront and oust the Crusaders, which lasted for two centuries, sapped the local economies and weakened the Arab urban centres. This enormous task required formidable military strength which could not be provided by Syria alone, with its limited human and economic resources. It was only through the unity of Syria and Egypt under the Ayyubids and the, Mamelukes, and through the military system that was adopted, that the Crusaders were finally defeated and expelled.

The Mongols

In the middle of the thirteenth century, and while the core Islamic lands were still busy with the expulsion of the Crusaders, another terrible invasion came from the East. Genghis Khan united the nomadic tribes of Mongolia and launched a devastating assault against the Eastern Islamic lands. By 1220-/1221 Samarkand, Bukhara and Khwârizm fell into their hands and were cruelly devastated. In 1221, they crossed the Oxus River and entered Persia. Genghis Khan died in 1227. In the middle of the century, a new plan to conquer all the lands of Islam as far as Egypt was entrusted to Hûlâgû, who marched with an army numbering 200,000 men according some Arabic sources.

In February 1258 Baghdad fell into their hands. The Abbasid caliph al-Musta'sim was killed and the caliphate was abolished. This marked the end of a remarkable era in Islamic civilization. The most disastrous effect of the Mongol invasion was depopulation. The capture of Baghdad and several towns was followed by horrible massacres. The number of inhabitants who were slaughtered in Baghdad after its conquest according to Arabic sources ranged between 800,000 and 2 million; non-Arabic sources give lower figures, but it probably exceeded 100,000.

There were massacres in every other city. It is beyond doubt that the conquest of Iraq by the Mongols was a demographic catastrophe. Many towns remained desolate, and there was carnage in the countryside too. According to Rashid al-Din, most of the towns on both sides of the Euphrates were devastated and destroyed. Under the Ilkhanids, there was a general and progressive decline of Iraq's population.

The decrease of the population of Iraq and the consequences of the Mongol conquest were so catastrophic that Hamd Allah al-Qazwini observed that 'there can be no doubt that even if for 1,000 years to come no evil befall the country, yet it will not be possible completely to repair the damage and bring back the land to the state in which it was formerly. Modern research has revealed that the population of the province of Diyala, including Baghdad, had declined from 870,000 in AD 800 to 60,000 after 1258.

Immediately after the fall of Baghdad, the Mongols continued their march and overtook Syria and according to their plan, they were heading towards Egypt which was threatened also with annihilation and destruction. The Mamelukes realized the immensity of this danger, and they stood up to the challenge. In the battle of 'Ayn Jâlut in Palestine, in 1259, the Mongols were defeated decisively, and their tide was checked. The Mamelukes gradually wrested all of Syria from Hulâgu and his successors. The last encounter in this era between the Mongols and the Mamelukes took place in 1304 when Ghazan, who was already converted to Islam, was defeated. The final expulsion of both the Crusaders and the Mongols from Syria was achieved at the same time.

Timur (Tamerlane, ruled 1370-1405) followed in the footsteps of Genghis Khan in ruthlessness, and in conducting worldwide conquests. Although he was a Muslim and claimed that his campaigns were made in the name of Islam, yet they inflicted all the horrors of barbarian devastation on the Islamic world. In 1400-1401 he invaded Iraq and Syria and sacked and pillaged Baghdad, Aleppo and Damascus. His spoils from Damascus included the learned men and the artisans whom he took back with him to his capital in Central Asia. This was a further blow to the civilization of the region.

Loss of International Trade

The economy of the core Islamic lands during the Golden Age of Islam was a commercial and a monetary one which could quite easily have continued to match that of Europe had it not been beset by various adverse factors. A main element in the prosperity of the Islamic economy was inter-national trade. The strategic location of the Islamic lands between East and West and their military strength enabled them to be the masters of international trade until the end of the fifteenth century. It is not a mere coincidence that the year 1492 witnessed the fall of Granada, and the expedition of Columbus in an effort to find a route to India which could bypass the Islamic lands where Ottoman power was on the rise.

Thus Columbus discovered the New World and Spain established its authority on the greater part of the newly discovered continent. In this same period, the Portuguese were seeking also uninterrupted political stability and economic, technological and scientific progress. Each of them established a worldwide commercial empire based on advanced gunnery and sailing techniques, in addition to utter ruthlessness in the pursuit of profits. The discovery of the New World and the new routes to the East brought untold riches to Europe, which prospered on the captured gold, silver, spices and other products.

The distribution of wealth between Europe and the Islamic lands had changed dramatically, and the centre of international trade had shifted from the Mediterranean and the Indian Ocean to the Baltic and the Atlantic. The rise of the commercial empires created a system of exploitation in which Europe became the supplier of high-value manufactured products and the colonized or dominated countries, including the Islamic lands, produced raw materials.

The Capitulations

The core Islamic lands did not encounter a frontal military assault from the West similar to that of the Crusades until the nineteenth century. But during the intervening period, they were penetrated and invaded economically in an indirect and a more insidious and damaging manner. Even when the Muslims were victorious following the expulsion of the Crusaders, the Italian maritime cities which established their presence during the Crusaders occupation of the Syrian coast continued their presence and activities in Egypt and Syria under the Mamelukes, with damaging economic effects for both Egypt and Syria. The Ottoman sultans adopted even more harmful policies.

Immediately after the capture of Constantinople in 1453, the Genoese in that city were given trading privileges. These privileges and immunities, which were given to foreign nonMuslim trading communities living in Muslim cities, came to be known as the Capitulations. The word means submission, surrender and subordination, which is contrary to sovereignty and independence. The Ottoman sultans thought that these concessions to foreigners would benefit the empire's economy. In 1535, the French secured commercial concessions in the empire, in addition to other important privileges. The English Levant Company acquired comparable privileges in 1580.

In Persia, Shah Abbas I, who was a powerful ruler, acted in a similar manner. He granted the English East India Company similar commercial concessions. These concessions granted by Muslim rulers gave Europeans the opportunity to gain control over a large share of the economic life of Islam. With the declining power of the Ottoman Empire, the Capitulations were confirmed and extended to give foreign powers non-commercial concessions as well, such as the right of foreigners to have their own consular courts, and the right to guard Christian holy places. In the Levant, France was granted the right to protect all native Latin Catholics. Russia and Britain claimed similar protective rights over other sectors of the native population.

The nineteenth century witnessed the rise of European imperialism led by Britain. Although British goods were invading the Ottoman Empire, yet Britain exerted powerful pressure on the Ottoman Empire and forced it to abolish the system of state monopolies. In 1838, an Anglo-Turkish treaty was signed giving Britain and the European powers the right to trade in the empire in return for a duty of 3 per cent only.

This treaty, known as the Commercial Code, deprived the Ottoman government of its revenue from state monopolies. It opened the door for the foreign economic domination of the empire. Cheaper European goods invaded the markets, and the local industries were virtually destroyed. The Ottoman economy declined into that of a satellite in its relationship with Europe, supplying it with raw materials which were Manufactured in Europe and then sold back in the empire.

Western Military Intervention to thwart Modernization

In the nineteenth century, some Muslim rulers realized the weakness of their economies and became aware of the urgent need to introduce reforms and to modernize. These attempts took place in the Ottoman Empire, in Egypt, and in Tunisia, and all of them were thwarted by direct or indirect intervention by European powers. The story of Mohammad Ali is an example of direct military intervention by Western powers to foil the attempt to modernize by a Muslim ruler. Mohammad Ali, who was described by Brockelmann as the most important man in the history of modern Islam, came to power in Egypt in 1805.

He realized from the start wherein lay the power of Western Europe. So he spent his lifetime in an attempt to modernize and to build the economy of Egypt. He realized that military strength does not lie in the number of men in the armed forces or the amount of amassed imported military equipment, but in the possession and control of the means of production and not being dependent on Europe. So he undertook a massive programme of modernization and industrialization. He started by abolishing the Mameluke military system and establishing a modern army of about 180,000, in which the sons of the Egyptian peasants were recruited.

He introduced a land reform in which he abolished the *iqtá* system and consolidated the agricultural lands as state property, and allotted them to the peasants. He encouraged agriculture and introduced the cultivation of cotton into Egypt as an export crop for securing the foreign exchange which was much needed for his reforms. He made foreign trade a state monopoly and refused to apply the Commercial Code which was imposed by Western powers on the Ottoman Empire, because he believed that it would destroy the economy of Egypt.

Mohammad Ali built many industrial factories to produce a wide range of products which were needed for the country as a whole and for the army and the navy. These included textiles, clothing, paper, dyes, sugar, chemicals, leather, glass, machine tools, pumps, guns and ammunition, and many other products. He even built naval vessels in Alexandria. The number of industrial workers reached about 400,000. He sent workers to Europe to be trained in European factories and hired foreign technicians for some industries. Missions of Egyptian students were sent annually to Europe to study and specialize. Many modern schools were built for the first time in Egypt, such as the schools for medicine, veterinary medicine, engineering, languages, secretarial services, infantry and artillery.

At one time, the number of students in these schools reached 10,000, all of whom were supplied with lodging, food and stipends. The aim was to create the cadres needed to run and supervise a modern government and a modern economy, and to provide the army with the needed trained manpower. Muhammad Ali created a united Arab state which included Egypt, Greater Syria, Hijaz and the Sudan all of which were neighbours. Syria in particular was of immense importance as was evident to him from the history of Egypt and Syria during the previous Islamic periods.

The major Western powers became increasingly concerned and alarmed by the threat that this rising Islamic power posed to their interests. Britain in particular regarded Muhammad Ali as a dangerous menace to its interests. Palmerston in an official correspondence to his ambassador in France wrote: 'I hate Muhammad Ali whom I consider him nothing better than a barbarian. I believe that he is a great tyrant and oppressor.' Britain was seriously alarmed by the spread of Muhammad Ali's power along the whole eastern coast of the Red Sea and along a part of the southern coast of Arabia in which they saw a threat to their route to India and the East.

All the major powers saw in his economic policies and his expanding power a threat to their interests and to their markets in the Islamic lands. Britain set about organizing the five major powers of Europe, Britain, France, Prussia, Austria and Russia, to join an alliance to oust Muhammad Ali from Syria and to curtail his power. Even though these powers had conflicting interests, yet in this case they agreed to unite against Muhammad Ali. In 1840, the fleets of the allies led by the British, assembled off the Syrian coast to attack Ibrahim (his son).

They instigated a local revolt exploiting the religious differences among the population, and then landed in Beirut. Ibrahim was obliged to retreat. Then Acre was besieged, bombarded and captured. This was followed by the siege of Alexandria. Muhammad Ali realized that he was beaten. His French allies deserted him, and he could not fight the European powers alone. Through the terms of the Treaty of London of 1841, Muhammad Ali was obliged to leave Syria and Hijaz, and to reduce his forces to 18,000 only from 180,000 (or 250,000 according to some reports.) He had to acknow-ledge the validity of the treaties concluded between the Ottoman Empire and the foreign powers, including the Commercial Code.

Rise and Decline of the Ottoman Empire

When the Ottomans were on the rise, they were always keen to encourage economic activities in the new areas which were added to their empire. In the new cities, all the trades and crafts were established as an important support for the military effort. During the sixteenth century, the Ottomans were the superior military power. Their artillery and armaments were unchallenged. The Ottoman and Islamic civilization in general developed unaided until it reached the point where it could not develop any longer without a great new advance or a revolution in science and technology. The Ottomans were a great power as long as their gunpowder technology was superior.

Gunpowder technology was developed by the Islamic civilization from the thirteenth century until the end of the sixteenth; nothing of significance in this technology was borrowed from the West. We can even safely say that, in general, Islamic technology in the sixteenth century represented the best that was known in that age. This is illustrated in the mechanical engineering books of Taqì al-Din, who flourished at the end of the sixteenth century in Istanbul, and who established also the advanced Istanbul observatory which was the last one in Islam. In that age an English traveller in Syria was studying why people in England were under the impression that the Turks were superior to people in the West.

How can we explain then the decline which followed, and why the West overtook and then surpassed the Ottomans after the sixteenth century? We have given above various factors which led to the decline of the Islamic lands including the Ottoman Empire, notably the capitulations. The Ottomans lost their advantage in military technology after the sixteenth century, and their economy and their science and technology did not advance beyond medieval standards. In Europe, things began to change dramatically. The sixteenth and seventeenth centuries saw the emergence of a European economy on a large scale. The geographical discoveries brought to Europe great riches from the New World and from the newly discovered trade routes with India and the Far East. Other internal factors were behind the economic progress of local trade and industry.

The fertility of the land in Europe and the growth of population were among the factors behind this economic growth. By about the middle of the nineteenth century, the population of the Ottoman Empire was barely 17 million. This included more than 5 million in the European part which was more of a liability, 6 million in Anatolia and Istanbul, 2-3 million in Egypt, about 1 million in each of Syria and Iraq, and 2-3 million in North Africa.

The population of Western Europe in this same period was about 190 million which is more than 11 times the population of the Ottoman Empire. And with Russia and Eastern Europe the total was 274 million or more than 16 times the size of the Ottoman Empire. Each of the following West European countries was larger than the Ottoman Empire in population: Great Britain (28.9 million), France (36.5), Spain and Portugal (19.7), Italy (23.9), Germany (31.7), and Austro-Hungary (31.3).

In face of this growing prosperity and power of Europe, the Ottoman Empire was to falter, and to turn inward. The Ottoman army, however well administered, became increasingly unable to maintain the lengthy frontiers without enormous cost in men and money; and the Ottoman Empire, unlike that of the Spanish, Dutch, and the British later, did not bring much in the way of economic benefit. By the second half of the sixteenth century, the empire was showing signs of strategic over-extension, with a large army stationed in central Europe, an expensive navy operation in the Mediter-ranean, troops engaged against Persia, in North Africa, the Aegean, Cyprus, and the Red Sea, and reinforcements needed to hold the Crimea against a rising Russian power.

An important element in the decline was the cultural barrier which existed between Christian Europe and the Ottomans and which isolated the empire from the revolutions which took place in science and technology. This resulted also in a hostile relationship with Europe, which was considered as a continuation of the Crusades and which sapped the energy of the empire. The gap between the levels of development continued to increase, and when the Ottomans realized in the nineteenth century the need to modernize, it was not as much the forces of reaction which delayed the reforms, but the obstacles which were created by the Western powers.

Future of Islamic Science

After the Second World War, most Islamic lands became independent once again, but the scars of long colonial rule remained. These are evident in the further fragmentation of Islamic and Arabic countries into smaller states, in the injustice and oppression inflicted against the Palestinians, in the destructive invasion of Iraq, in the renewed activities to strengthen the cultural barrier between the West and Islam and to distort the image of Islam, in the current sectarian and ethnic feuds and devastating civil wars within some countries in the economic and political dominance of foreign powers, and in the cultural domination exemplified in the use of foreign rather than national languages in higher education.

But despite all the adversities and obstacles facing the Islamic lands, the future holds hope and promise. These lands have been the cradle of some of the richest civilizations ever known. Science appeared in the Nile Valley, Syria and Mesopotamia. It continued uninterrupted over thousands of years, reaching its peak during the Islamic period. It flowed on incessantly, and the wide gap of today started only since the Industrial Revolution, less than 200 years ago. Thus there is a solid substratum to the civilization of the Muslim world, which has indigenous and inherent cultural traditions and customs, deeply rooted in the peoples of the area. In addition, there are the crafts and industrial skills inherited over thousands of years.

These inherited skills proved their importance in the wake of independence and after the Second World War, when some Islamic countries started to industrialize and thousands of workshops and industrial plants were established in all Muslim cities. Craftsmen in even the smallest machine shops were able to manufacture the most delicate modern machinery, in no way inferior to imported or imitated versions. In approaching modern science and technology, we must remind ourselves of those lessons of history that help us to look to the future. For history shows that there is nothing in the content of any part of science, or indeed of technologies high or low, that cannot be nurtured and developed by any people of any type of culture.

Almost no society or set of cultural conditions is hostile: on the contrary, almost all the great groups of mankind have throughout the ages made significant contributions to the common heritage of knowledge and techniques. Among the foremost of them are the peoples of Islam. Once we realize that the content of science and technology finds no cultural barriers, we arrive at another lesson of history. It has been established that in the past, as now, science and scientists flourish in large communities and linguistic groups rather than small, in affluent areas better than in poor. During historic times, science has indeed flourished only when an empire or a nation became mighty and rich, because it depends on the infrastructure provided by the existence of affluence. This is amply demonstrated throughout Islamic history.

The Islamic world is rich in human resources, and some areas are rich in petroleum and other natural resources. This is fortunate because the future of science in Islamic countries depends upon the successful utilization of a combination of these two ingredients. Development in all fields within a community depends significantly on the scientific size, which is itself proportional to the size of the population and the gross national product. Individually, most of the oil-rich countries are small in size. Each cannot by itself create an effective science and technology, or an independent industrial economy.

Similarly, those Muslim countries which are endowed with human resources lack the capital essential for the development of science and technology and, indeed, for their general development. Though most individual Islamic states now realize the importance of science and technology for their future development, and though some have achieved considerable success along this road, future progress in all Muslim countries, rich or poor, depend on the extent of economic co-operation and integration among them on a regional basis.

Speed of Technological Progress and Comparison to Western Scientific Progress

In recent years, globalisation, which has become one of the most widely discussed subjects in [illegible], has generally [illegible] writings which discuss the subject of globalisation [illegible] concentrate on the positive and negative effects of this unstoppable phenomenon [illegible] globalisation's importance from the point of view of technology and communications.

5

Speed of Technological Progress and Comparison to Western Scientific Progress

In recent years, globalization has become one of the most widely discussed subjects in the Islamic world, just as it has generally everywhere. Writings which discuss the subject of globalization concentrate on the positive and negative effects of this unstoppable phenomenon, and stress how Muslims should consider it. Globalization can be studied from many points of view, particularly scientific, technological, communications, religious, and cultural ones, because globalization encapsulates all of these. There are very different aspects to globalization, such as the mutual influences of different cultures and languages, the growing power of some as they eliminate others, the gradual disappearance of all countries' cultural identities, and its undesirable economic effects... But the subject we shall be stressing in this chapter is globali-zation's importance from the point of view of technology and communications.

With technological progress and the development of means of communication, the world has grown smaller, and the time factor in transport and communication has all but disappeared. Thanks to present-day satellite technology, Internet wireless communication, and television and radio, distances of thousands of miles between different countries are no longer of any importance. A single message can travel around the world in a matter of seconds. This is a most positive development from the point of view of Islamic countries. The spread of thoughts and ideas in particular has gained enormous speed. It has now become a great deal easier to explain Islamic morality, for Muslims to communicate with one another, to enable a current event to reach all Islamic societies, and for a reaction or request to be expressed by large social groups.

Muslim societies which used to live separated from one another, and out of contact, even in the same country, can now all act together, carry out studies with each other, and make their mark on important developments in the interests of Islam. For these reasons, this great speed conferred by superior technology is a great blessing for the faithful, and this blessing can be used in a much more powerful manner in order to spread Islamic morality. This speed that communications allows has made it easier to announce the beauty, peace,,tolerance, love and compassion of Islamic morality. A dialogue established in the framework of tolerance with different cultures and different religions will allow very many people to come to know Islam. Western societies today have prejudices against Islam, stemming entirely from ignorance or misinformation.

The way to do away with these prejudices is to explain Islamic morality to everybody, by all possible means, in a correct, wise, and clear style. Such communication will clearly be the means for a spiritual rapprochement, and the abolition of misunderstandings. It is also a fact that the new communications technologies, with the Internet at their head, are bringing Islamic societies from all over the world together. Developments such as this in recent years have played a major role in the Islamic awakening. Today, websites on the Internet bring involved people together from all corners of the world, and a great exchange of information is taking place. Another advantage conferred by a technology such as the Internet is the formation of an environment in which people who hold all kinds of different ideas and views can express themselves freely.

At last, many Muslim societies are able to overcome censorship and freely reveal the difficulties, pressure, and oppression they are suffering. Muslim minorities, living in countries that previously people never knew existed, and whose names they had never even heard, can now make their voices heard to the whole world in just a few minutes. Pictures and images of oppression of all kinds can now easily be set before the people of the world, from the death of a child in Palestine, to the bombing of a town in Chechnya. As we have emphasized above, this unstoppable process of globalization also raises a number of question marks. At the head of the list is the negative effect it will have on the youth of increasingly decadent Western society. Today, the subject people concentrate on most in the face of globalization is this degeneracy and decadence that may arise. However, it is possible to avoid this danger with proper education.

It is impossible for young people brought up with Islamic morality, who fear Allah, and possess conscience and pure faith, to undergo such degeneration, or to be affected by the negative aspects of Western culture. The Islamic morality and strong characters they possess will prevent such undesirable effects, and in fact, their superior virtues will actually enable them to act as examples to degenerate Western society. In fact, we can see reflections of this even now. A huge return to religion is being experienced in Western societies, which are today far from having any moral and spiritual values and have lost their own religious identities. Concepts such as the tolerance, compassion, self-sacrifice, love, affection, and uprightness that Islamic morality brings with it will beyond all doubt have a great influence on non-Muslim societies, and will be a means by which Islamic morality can spread over the entire world.

Globalization heralds an age when different cultures and beliefs in the world can meet, engage in dialogue, and evaluate each other, recognizing no obstacles or frontiers. Hesitation over this can only be the reflex of cultures and beliefs which have no confidence in themselves. Whereas Islam is the last true religion sent down to man by God, and calls everybody to the true path. For this reason, far from hesitating over globalization, Muslims must see it as an opportunity for the truths of Islam to be spread all over the world, and for people to be freed from the limits of narrow-mindedness, errors, and prejudices, and come to understand Islam. And to make use of this opportunity, Muslims must demonstrate a culture that will show the truths of Islam to the entire world, and make people hunger for it. The Muslim world, with its ideas, morality, knowledge, art, and aesthetics, must be an example to the world.

In order to carry out this great duty, Muslims must wage a cultural offensive all over the world. We must not forget that in order to succeed, the first thing that must be done is to live a genuinely Islamic life, turn towards God who has honoured us with Islam, and cling tightly to His book, as He has ordered us in the holy verse 'Hold fast to the book.' [Surah Maryam: 12]

The great British expert on Chinese science history Joseph Needham has written about how the "four great inventions of China," the compass, printing, papermaking and gunpowder, were exported to the rest of the world. Although Needham is good at writing about technology, he doesn't always provide sufficient evidence of transmission for these inventions. Only one of them, paper, can be said with absolute certainty to have reached the West as a fully developed product. According to Professor T.F. Carter, "Back of the invention of printing lies the use of paper, which is the most certain and the most complete of China's inventions."

As Lucien Febvre and Henri-Jean Martin write in The Coming of the Book, "It would have been impossible to invent printing had it not been for the impetus given by paper, which had arrived in Europe from China via the Arabs two centuries earlier and came into general use by the late 14th century." In the period from 1450 to 1550, Europe was becoming covered with paper mills. The traditional parchment was expensive and not well suited for mass production. During the Protestant Reformation in the sixteenth century, the reformers wanted the Bible to be available in the common language, not in Latin. Martin Luther thus helped shape the modern German language. As scholar Irving Fang states in the book A History of Mass Communication, "Vernacular printing also led French readers to think of themselves as being part of France, and English readers to regard themselves as part of England."

In some ways, we are witnessing a reversal of this trend towards nationalization now with global communications and the rise of English as an international lingua franca. Febvre and Martin believe, though, that about 77% of the books printed before 1500 were still in Latin, with religious books still predominant. This gradually gave way to secular books and other languages, but "it was not until the late 17th century that Latin was finally overthrown and replaced by the other national languages and by French as the natural language of philosophy, science and diplomacy. Every educated European then had to know French." They estimate that about 20 million books were printed in Europe before the year 1500 and that "between 150 - 200 million copies were published in the 16th century and this is a conservative estimate and probably well below the actual figure."

This is even more impressive if we remember that Europe of that day was far less populous than it is now and that only a minority could read. There was obviously a change then, and a swift one, compared to the slow, expensive and sometimes inaccurate process of copying each individual book by hand. Printing did have a major impact in East Asia, but it didn't trigger quite the same revolution as it did in the West. Buddhism came to Japan via China and Korea, and Buddhist monks also brought with them, in addition to tea and thus the basis for the elaborate Japanese tea ceremonies, other aspects of Chinese civilization, among them printing in the eight century. Yet until the late sixteenth century the Japanese printed only Buddhist scriptures. Europe also benefited from having a more diverse book trade than China and from having more competition in general.

As Irving Fang states, "Printing had not disturbed the monolithic Chinese empire. The introduction of printing in mid-fifteenth century Europe might also have made little headway if Europe were not ripe for change." According to him, the "establishment of European universities from the twelfth century onward marked the end of the 700-year-old Monastic Age. The more secular age that followed saw the emergence of a literate middle class and a rising demand for books of all kinds." Movable type printing had been invented in China by Bi Sheng around 1040, but it never gained widespread popularity. The nature of the Chinese language with its non-alphabetic script presumably didn't help.

To solve this dilemma, in the first half of the 1400s the Korean King Sejong the Great encouraged book production and ordered his scholars to create an alphabet for the common people as opposed to the complicated Chinese script with its thousands of characters. They produced hangul, "Korean letters," a phonetic system inspired by other alphabetic scripts, among them Sanskrit. Movable type printing with metal types and an alphabetic script was thus in use in Korea before Gutenberg began printing Bibles in Germany, but there are no indications of a connection between what happened in Korea and what happened in Europe. The geographical distance is too big and the time difference too small to make such a connection likely. The Chinese used baked clay for their characters, and only started employing metal types after their use in Europe. Gutenberg was a goldsmith and naturally created his letters out of metal.

According to Fang, "What Gutenberg produced that did not exist in Asia was a printing system. Most obvious among its elements were controlled, exact dimensions of alphabet type cast from metal punches made of hardened steel. These were not unlike the dies, stamps, and punches that were well known to European leather workers, metalsmiths, and pewter makers." Although possible, no link between the Eastern and the Western printing traditions has ever been conclusively proven. The different nature of the systems involved has caused many historians to believe that printing was developed in Europe independently of Asia. In contrast, we know with 100% certainty that Muslims were familiar with East Asian printing. The Mongols left a trail of devastation across much of Eurasia in the 1200s, but their vast empire did open up unprecedented opportunities for cultural exchange.

As scholar Thomas T. Allsen shows, however, being exposed to foreign ideas doesn't necessarily mean that you will adopt them. Local scholars often clung to the inherited tradition. He uses Russia at the time of Peter the Great as an example where some elements of that society were fanatically opposed to all innovation while others enthusiastically embraced all things foreign.

Allsen has described how the authorities in Iran under Mongolian rule in 1294 attempted to introduce Chinese-style printed banknotes, but failed, despite severe threats, due to massive popular resistance:

"Certainly the Muslim world exhibited an active and sustained opposition to movable type technologies emanating from Europe in the fifteenth century and later. This opposition, based on social, religious, and political considerations, lasted well into the eighteenth century. Only then were presses of European origin introduced into the Ottoman Empire and only in the next century did printing become widespread in the Arab world and Iran. This long-term reluctance, the disinterest in European typography and the failure to exploit the indigenous printing traditions of Egypt certainly argue for some kind of fundamental structural or ideological antipathy to this particular technology."

One of the most important inventions ever made has to be printing. Surely it is no coincidence that the Scientific Revolution decisively took off in Europe after the introduction of printing, just as it is not a coincidence that the one civilization that came closest to a similar breakthrough, China, was the one where printing had first been invented. It is likely that the rejection of printing alone set the Islamic world back centuries vis-à-vis non-Muslims. As David Crowley and Paul Heyer write in Communication in History: Technology, Culture, and Society, "Traditionally, the view has been that printing, along with numerous other developments, marked the transition between the end of the Middle Ages and the dawn of the modern era. However, the more we study this remarkable invention, the more we realize that it was not just one factor among many.

Although we hesitate to argue for historical 'primemovers,' certainly the printing press comes close to what is meant by this term. It was a technology that influenced other technologies - a prototype for mass production - and one that impacted directly on the world of ideas by making knowledge widely available, thereby creating a space in which new forms of expression could flourish. The repercussions of the printing press in early modern Europe did not come about in an inherently deterministic manner. Rather, they resulted from the existence of conditions whereby print could enhance a context receptive to its potential."

The spread of printing in East Asia was intimately connected to the Buddhist religion, just as it was used in Europe to print Bibles. Yet while Buddhists, Christians and Jews eagerly embraced this new technology, Muslims stubbornly rejected it. The contrast is striking if we compare this to how eagerly Muslims embraced another Chinese invention: gunpowder. Gunpowder wasn't the first chemical substance used in warfare.

According to legend, "Greek fire," a feared weapon in its time, was invented in the seventh century by Callinicus, a refugee from the Arab conquest of Syria. It was successfully used to defeat sieges by Arab Muslims of Constantinople in 674 and in 718, and helped the Byzantine Empire to survive for as long as it did. Its qualities appear to be somewhat similar to modern napalm. James R. Partington suggests in his book A History of Greek Fire and Gunpowder that it consisted of a mixture of "sulphur, pitch, dissolved nitre, and petroleum." The term "Greek fire" is a misnomer as the Byzantines called themselves Romans. The greatest revolution in the history of warfare, however, came with the introduction of gunpowder.

According to Dr James B. Calvert, professor of engineering, "The fundamental inventions of gunpowder and cannon had been made by 1300, but the sources are rare, difficult to interpret, hard to date, and often contradictory. The best guess is that gunpowder followed quickly after saltpetre was discovered (that is, a process for its purification was developed) by Chinese alchemists around AD 900 and introduced to Europe via trade routes and travellers around AD 1225, and that cannon were invented in southern Europe just before AD 1300."

One of the problems in determining this accurately is that Chinese writers can be just as ethnocentric as Western ones, sometimes more so. There is some debate whether gunpowder was invented independently in several regions, but most historians have settled for the explanation that it was first manufactured in China. Gunpowder (black powder) consists of charcoal, sulphur and potassium nitrate, or saltpeter, and was impossible to create until you could manufacture saltpeter with a high degree of purity. This was a specialty of Chinese alchemists quite early. The discovery reached the Middle East and Europe, probably via the Silk Road, and became known as "Chinese snow." Black powder remained the principle explosive until the nineteenth century, when the invention of unstable nitroglycerine made it possible for Swedish chemist Alfred Nobel to patent the more stable version of dynamite in 1867, and accumulate the great wealth which was later used to fund the various Nobel Prizes.

In the thirteenth century, the English Franciscan friar Roger Bacon, as well as the German Dominican friar Albertus Magnus, both theologians and scientists with an interest in alchemy, mentions a recipe for gunpowder. The Mongol conquests spread the knowledge of the fire-lance, a gunpowder-filled tube made of bamboo which could fire various projectiles, across Eurasia. The development of this weapon stagnated in China proper. According to James B. Calvert, "The place and time of the invention of the cannon is unknown, but its evolution from the fire lance among the Turks, Arabs and Europeans can hardly be doubted. The earliest use of cannon is not definitely known, but occurred sometime between 1300 and 1350. The use of cannon spread rapidly between 1350 and 1400."

Cannon were used during the Hundred Years' War between France and England, and Turkish Muslims successfully employed prolonged bombardment by massive Hungarian-made cannon during the conquest of Constan-tinople in 1453 to breach the walls of the city. Joel Mokyr, professor at the Department of Economics at Northwestern University and author of *The Gifts of Athena: Historical Origins of the Knowledge Economy* writes about innovation and economic history. According to him glass, although known in China, was not in wide use as tea was drunk in porcelain cups and the Chinese examined themselves in polished bronze mirrors. Islamic countries had a significant glass industry, yet they never came up with spectacles: "Tokugawa Japan had a flourishing industry making glass trinkets and ornaments, but no optical instruments emerged there either until the Meiji restoration [from 1867].

Not having access to the Hellenistic geometry that served not only Ptolemy and Alhazen, but also sixteenth century Italians such as Francesco Maurolico (1494-1575) who studied the characteristics of lenses, made the development of optics in the Orient difficult." The earliest known lenses were made of rock crystal, quartz, and other minerals, and have been used in Eastern and Western lands since ancient times. There is evidence that lenses were known in the Greco-Roman world.

They have been used as burning glasses and magnifying glasses for centuries, and so-called reading stones were in common use during the middle Ages, for instance the Visby lenses, lens-shaped rock crystals of high quality from in a Viking grave in Gotland, Sweden. The oldest one we know of is the Nimrud lens, found in modern Iraq.

Estimated to be almost three thousand years old, it indicates that the ancient Assyrians did have some basic understanding of optics. Iraq, seat of the Sumerian, Akkadian and Assyrian kingdoms, is home to one of the world's oldest astronomical traditions. Babylonian astronomy greatly influenced many subsequent cultures, Middle Eastern, Greek and Indian, and the sexagesimal (based on the number sixty) numeral system of the Sumerians is still with us today, in the form of sixty minutes to the hour and 360 degrees in a circle. The Iraqi-born scientist Ibn al-Haitham, known in the West as Alhacen or Alhazen, had a powerful influence on several Western scientists.

Alhazen was a pioneer in the scientific method by basing hypothesis upon systematic observation. He is most commonly remembered for his great contributions in the field of optics, where he pondered the nature of light, speculated on the colors of the sunset and described the qualities of magnifying lenses. His eleventh century Book of Optics was translated into Latin during the late twelfth century, and left a significant impact on Roger Bacon and others in the thirteenth century. Bacon was educated at Oxford and lectured on Aristotle at the University of Paris, the intellectual center among the small, but growing number of European universities. His teacher, the English bishop and scholar Robert Grosseteste, was a proponent of validating theory through experimentation.

Roger Bacon wrote about many subjects, including optics, and was among the first persons to argue that lenses could be used for the correction of eyesight. He asserted that "philosophy is the special province of the unbelievers," and urged scholars to learn Arabic. The Chinese experimented with lenses and mirrors, too, and produced a type of sunglasses, or eyeglasses with coloured lenses. However, these appear to have been mainly for decorative purposes and possessed no corrective properties. The science of optics stagnated in China after initial advances. The first fully developed spectacles were made in Europe, in Northern Italy from the late thirteenth century onwards. The American scientist and inventor Benjamin Franklin invented bifocals in the eighteenth century, during the early years of the United States.

In 1572 Freidrich Risner printed some of Alhazen's work on optics, as well as a work by the thirteenth century Polish friar Witelo which was similar to it, and thus made Alhazen widely known to new generations of scholars. Notable among them was the German astronomer Johannes Kepler. Danish astronomer Tycho Brahe, who died in 1601, was perhaps the most meticulous astronomer of the pre-telescopic era. During the final year of his life, Brahe passed on his observations of Mars to Kepler. These precise notes were important for Kepler's work on planetary motion, but another breakthrough that could verify his thesis was soon to come. As corrective lenses for near-sightedness became more sophisticated, the demand for high quality glass lenses grew.

In the Netherlands in the seventeenth century, Baruch Spinoza could make a decent living as a skilled lens grinder while working on his philosophical theories. This was during the Dutch Golden Age when the country was a refuge for many groups suffering from religious persecution, for instance Huguenots (Protestants) from France. Spinoza descended from Jews who had been expelled from Spain and Portugal following the Reconquista. The production of spectacles opened up new arenas for optics. A Dutch eyeglass maker, Hans Lippershey, is said to have created the first practical telescope and made it publicly available in 1608.

Within a few months of the news, Italian scientist Galileo Galilei had made his own telescope, and became the first person to turn the new invention towards the sky, discovering the four major moons of Jupiter in 1610. Kepler developed the Galilean telescope further by 1611 and described the theoretical basis for telescopic optics, in part inspired by Alhazen's work. The telescope had travelled from the Netherlands via Italy to Kepler in Prague within three years of its invention and had been improved along the way, a remarkable pace of innovation and diffusion of knowledge. Sir Isaac Newton's Principia Mathematica from 1687 and his laws of motion and gravity were derived from, among other things, Galileo's telescopic observations and Kepler's Laws of Planetary Motion.

Dutch eyeglass maker Zacharias Janssen and his father Hans are usually credited with inventing the first microscope in the late 1500s. The microscope was improved in the seventeenth century by their countryman Antonie van Leeuwenhoek, who was the first to spot bacteria and thus opened up an entirely new field of microbiology. This in turn led to great advances in the natural sciences. The German physician Robert Koch and the French chemist Louis Pasteur founded the science of bacteriology in the nineteenth century. The understanding that disease is caused by bacteria and microscopic germs produced the greatest strides in medicine in history.

According to the free online encyclopaedia Wikipedia, reading stone lenses were invented by polymath Armen Firman (Abbas Ibn Firnas) in Córdoba in Islamic-occupied Spain in the ninth century, and later spread throughout Europe. Wikipedia embodies both the good and some of the problematic aspects of the Internet. Let's assume for a moment that this information is correct. If so, how come lenses weren't developed further by Muslims? The telescope and the microscope were by-products of advances in the production of glass lenses. They made possible, for the first time ever, the study of what is not visible to the naked human eye and radically altered our understanding of the universe, both in the realms of the very small and the very big. All of this could have happened in the Islamic world.

So why didn't it, despite the fact that lenses were know there at least as early as in Europe, and despite the fact that the region produced a gifted optical scientist, Alhazen? Alhazen personally should be credited with being one of the greatest scientists of his age in any discipline, Eastern or Western, yet his inquisitive attitude and scientific mindset wasn't always appreciated by his contemporaries.

The opponents of those who are striving to build a genuine Islamic society argue with the most arrogant cynicism that Islamic civilization has vanished forever, that its era of creativity is past history and that it has nothing more to contribute to the world. They take supreme delight in relating how one Muslim country after another has succumbed to Western civilization. The various stages of acculturation are described in detail in order to prove that the disintegration of Islamic life and the complete triumph of Westernization are inevitable. It is furthermore asserted that nothing can stop this process. The assumption is that modern civilization is invincible. No propaganda technique in the hands of our enemies has proved so successful in demoralizing the rising generation of Muslim youth than the adoption of these clichés. Despite voluminous propaganda to the contrary, Western civilization is far from invincible.

Racial hatred, class conflicts, the epidemic of lawlessness, the perversion of scientific achievements for destructive purpose, the debility of the family, drug and alcohol addiction, universal indulgence in illicit sex and the waste of natural and human resources for luxurious living are some of its most vulnerable weaknesses. What has doomed all other civilization of the present? Our most precious asset over our adversaries is that genuine Islamic life is not contaminated with any of these corruptions. Western civilization only appears invincible because there is no rival. Once effective opposition appears on the scene, the corruption of modern culture will be exposed for all to see.

Most devastating to our cause are those of our writers

who escape from a practicable and realistic solution of present day problems by over glorifying the past, entirely overlooking the fact that the most extravagant praise of the achievements of Muslims a thousand years ago, provides no guarantee that the Islamic community will flourish in the future. These well meaning authors write reams in praise of our Holy Prophet and his companions, never tiring of rejoicing in the superiority of the "noble spiritual principles of Islam" coupled with a most vituperative condemnation of the "materialistic West" as if their effusive verbalism would automatically result in a beautiful Islamic utopia without any further effort needed on their part! As one Muslim writes about this problem: The Muslims of the world are passing through the most critical period in their history.

The western civilization called modernism has dominated over all other civilizations with the forceful hammerings of scientific advancement. Christianity fought against it desperately but it could not stand any longer for it had many vulnerable chinks in its armour. Other religions met the same fate as Christianity. There may still different customs prevailing in different countries but none can deny that they are highly influenced and imbued with modernism, so much so that they are totally changed and have lost their originality. Although the Muslims of all countries are trying hard to ward off the mighty blow dealt by modernism, they are losing ground against it. Even most of the Muslims themselves have welcomed it and are now gradually being absorbed into this universal civilization.

Superficially at least, the chances for the success of those determined to implement Islamic life on a significant scale would appear to be extremely remote. The recovery of political sovereignty from European rule has not at all weakened the influence of Western culture. On the contrary, under the slogan of "economic development", the westernization of Asia and Africa continues to progress at an ever-accelerating speed. The beginning of the 19th century witnessed the merging of Islamic society into the world-wide society of the present era. To become aware of these implications is in my view the greatest single problem of the Islamic society of our day. The influence of the West has been so great that even when the Islamic peoples regained their political independence they have found that a return to the traditional Islamic way of life was not possible. If the above quotation is so typical of the mentality of our modern-educated elite, must we Muslims yield to complete pessimism and bow to defeat?

If every other civilization has been vanquished by modernism, must we meekly resign ourselves to the same fate? Is there no hope for us? However bleak the prospect for an Islamic renaissance may appear at present, I still maintain that there yet remains considerable hope for us provided we take the appropriate action in time. This ray of optimism is based on the following assumptions:

1. The fundamental sources of Islam – the Quran and the Sunnah – are uncorrupted and intact. No other religion can claim this advantage.
2. As Islamic teachings are comprehensive, all-embracing in scope and entirely self-sufficient, Islam does not tolerate eclecticism or compromise with any culture in conflict with its principles. Islam alone provides adequate guidance for life in its totality. Not only does Islam tell us what to do but also specifically how to do it. The exant teachings of all other religions are limited, restricted and fragmentary.
3. The determination to preserve and propagate Islam in its original purity has been practically implemented in every period of Islamic history simultaneously in every Muslim country by a long series of Mujaddids. Although with the support and encouragement of Western scholars and politicians, the modernists attempt to force their distorted interpretation of Islam upon the entire community, happily they are encountering stiff resistance on every side from those who are not deceived by this hypocrisy and are determined to preserve an unadulterated Islam intact.

4. From Morocco to Indonesia the overwhelming majority want Islam and once inspiring leadership is prodded, they will be ready to follow most enthusiastically. This being the case, why has not Islamic leadership emerged in any Muslim country? We must realize that this is not on account of any intrinsic merit of Western culture, much less inherent inadequacy of Islam. The answer can be found by an insight into the nature of European imperialism.

In 1908, Lord Cromer wrote very revealingly in the last chapter of his book, Modern Egypt, that England was prepared to grant eventual political freedom to all of her colonial possessions as soon as a generation of intellectuals and politicians, imbued through English education with the ideals of English culture, were ready to take over, but under no circumstances would the British Government tolerate for a single moment an independent Islamic state. What was true in the case of Egypt is equally applicable to Pakistan and what was British policy was also French, Italian and Dutch policy and remains American and Russian policy to this day. Consequently, our political sovereignty is more nominal than real and the Western powers through economic means are determined to keep it that way. At this stage it is essential to examine the social structure of the Muslim countries in relation to the issues at stake.

On the top rung of our social and economic ladder we have our modern- educated elite who, although Arab, Indian Malay or African by blood, are carbon duplicates in their mentality of their ex-overlords, zealously determined to make their respective countries as closely as possible resemble the societies in Western lands. Although constituting only a small fraction of the total population, they hold all the power and unless their activities are stopped in time, the perverted moral and cultural values, hitherto limited to the aristocratic elite, will spread and contaminate all classes of the people. At the bottom of the ladder is the second group which is more than three quarters of the population in all Muslims countries—that is, the simple common folk. This second group includes all of these who by good fortune have remained removed from the impact of modern culture and not received a modern education.

Although these Muslims are mostly poor and illiterate people in humble occupations, the ulema and Imams of mosques who have received an exclusively madrassah type education (such as, al-Azhar or Deoband) also belong to this category. Although most of them are good Muslims at heart and some even in practice, because of their naïve ignorance, they are easily deceived and although they are numerous, because they are so weak disorganized, they are powerless. To make matters even worse, many, if not most, in this group observe Islam much more as habit and custom than personal conviction. Because there is no dynamism nor vitality left in the traditional culture they represent, the modern-educated youth cannot help but associate everything "Islamic" with what is old, primitive, backward, poor and dying while every thing "Western" appears to them as bright and beautiful.

And to the foreign tourist, this "traditional" culture is but the decaying remnants of the "exotic" Orient. Because no young person can bear to be stigmatized as backward or a reactionary fanatic and yearns to be praised as enlightened, modern and progressive, as soon as these youth can qualify at the government or Christian missionary higher institutions of learning as businessmen, technicians, doctors, teachers or social workers, to gain prestige and respect they are determined to put an end to all "traditionalism" and spread the "blessings" or modernism to the most remote corners of the land. With the full backing of the Government and the Western powers with their technical assistance programmers and foreign business investments, they are sure to succeed. The most the simple folk can do is offer passive resistance.

And even if they themselves do not succumb, their children after imbibing modern education inevitably must. If the question rested with these two groups alone our cause would indeed be hopeless but thanks to God there is slowly emerging a third group who, although smallest of all numerically, will decisively determine the future of the Muslim community. These are the men and women who, although having been thoroughly exposed to Western culture and received a modern education even to the extent of studying or working abroad in Europe or America, have by the grace and mercy of God maintained their faith and love for Islam, demonstrating in their daily lives, their zeal and readiness for self-sacrifice to implement their faith. Because this group possesses the necessary intellectual weapons to resist effectively modernist penetration into Islamic life, they alone are qualified for the leadership of the Muslim world.

The prevailing view of contemporary Muslim writers and scholars is that the Christian Church in Europe lost its power and influence between of its irrational dogmas of the Trinity, the Incarnation, Original Sin or the reactionary institution of the priesthood. Since Islam is a simple and straightforward doctrine having no inherent conflict with scientific progress and no priestly hierarchy set apart from the bulk of believers, it is immune to the catastrophe which befell Christendom. This line of reasoning, comforting as it may be, is dangerous wishful thinking. How ever contrary to Islam Christian dogma and institutions have always been, they themselves were not the cause of Christendom's downfall.

When the Catholic Church was confronted with the secular humanism of the Renaissance, the Protestant Reformation and tidal wave of atheist materialism which followed the French Revolution, all the Church did was resort to purely negative measures. Thus the Church welded all the power it could command to conduct a systematic persecution of non- conformists, organized heresy hunts, infamous inquisitions, invoked excommunication and the burning of heretical books.

Had the Catholic Church employed its best scholars to refute intellectually with logical and persuasive arguments the fallacy of the materialistic philosophers instead of merely hurling anathemas of heresy and placing their writings on the index of forbidden books, quite probably the Church would have succeeded in retaining its influence undiminished. Unfortunately, instead of appealing to the minds and hearts of its members and thus inspire love for Christianity in the minds of the Christians, these repressive actions incited nothing but hatred and rebellion. Even if, from the point of view of the Church, its heretics deserved what they received, repressive measures alone are not only cruel and inhuman but utterly ineffective, completely defeating their own purpose. Those who want to implement Islam by force and blood shed should take a lesson from the history of Christendom.

Although we Muslims, thank God, have never been guilty to such an intense degree of persecuting those who do not agree with us, still we must be honest with ourselves and confess that some of us have committed in a milder way, the same mistake. Merely cursing Western civilization as "materialistic", "ungodly" and "satanic" (as true as this is) cannot in the slightest counter its growing allurement for our modern educated youth. Hurling vituperative of heresy at the modernists is not going to stop them. The question at stake is not whether they deserve to be labelled as kafir. Quite probably they do but is this sufficient to accomplish anything constructive for our cause? The answer is an emphatic no!

The final judgment is God's—not ours—and we as believers can rest confident that if we exert ourselves to the utmost for Islam, God will punish as He sees fit. The crisis the Muslims are facing today is nothing new. Centuries ago we were faced with the same problem with the growing popularity of secular Greek humanism propagated by such Mu'tazilite philosophers as al-Kindi, al-Farabi, Ibn Sina and Ibn Rushd all of whom exactly like the modernists today, tried to concoct a new brand of Islam. But by the grace and mercy of God, al-Ghazzali in his Incoherence of the Philosophers ripped their fallacies and intellectual dishonesty that the Mu'tazilite movement was halted in its tracks. Ibn Taimiya dealt the rationalists the fatal blow. Henceforth Greek humanism lost all its influence and never again did the Mutazilite philosophy command any respect in the Muslim world. What the Muslim world today needs above all is a modern al-Ghazzali and a modern Ibn Taimiya.

The task of their successors would not be nearly so complicated it as may seem at first because the secular humanism of ancient Greece does not at all essentially differ from contemporary materialist philosophy. The latter is but a further development of the former. One of the most important tasks of our modern Ibn Taimiya is to refute the bogey of progress. Our obsession with "change" and "progress" and "moving with the times to meet the challenge of the age" is nothing but a modernist dogma derived from the Darwinian theory of evolution and incorporated into social philosophy as materialist concept of history by Karl Marx. As Muslims we should be concerned only with submission to the will of God through unquestioning obedience to Quran and Sunnah in its plain, literal meaning.

Once we attain cultural independence, we do not have anything to fear from a natural and spontaneous social evolution and development within the context of our indigenous Islamic values and ideals. So long as we remain slaves to modernism, however, change means nothing except progressive abandonment of Islamic values in exchange for the Western way of life and this is why under the present circumstances, every change is from the Islamic point of view to our detriment. There is nothing "new" or "progressive" about modernism.

Despite science, technology and economic development, ideologically Western civilization has not changed at all since the Age of Pericles nearly 2,500 years ago. Ibu Taimiya's modern successor must also expose the modernist dogma concerning the so-called necessity for complete freedom of inquiry on the part of students and teachers in higher institution of learning as just another bogey. This demand for complete freedom of "rational" and "scientific" inquiry is but another dogma of modernism derived from the philosophy of Socrates as recorded by his pupil, Plato and continuing to this day under the guise of "liberalism".

Divested of its sophistry, this so-called intellectual freedom is intended for the sole purpose of casting doubt and ridicule on the foundations of faith and mock God, His revelation and the hereafter which has found its legal expression in the Soviet Constitution of 1936 guaranteeing to all Russian citizens complete freedom of anti-religious propaganda. Freedom in its true sense must be freedom in every direction yet under the patronage of Western civilization; this so-called "reason" must always be pitted against revelation- never in its favour. Consequently, this so called "rational" and "scientific" inquiry is permitted to proceed in one direction only—the way of materialism.

These people never tire of condemning traditional Islamic education for its lack of critical, creative or independent thinking but we are at a complete loss to find any more originality or independence in respect to theirs! Another favourite technique of the modernists is to pit the "spirit" against the "letter" of Islam as if the two were irreconcilable! The letter of the Shariah, murders its spirit, so say the modernists. Consequently, the late Sayyid Ameer Ali in his well-known book The Spirit of Islam, suggests that the literal injunctions of Purdah are most "un-Islamic", but the Western concept of free mingling and absolute equality of the sexes is the true "spirit" and Islam; the letter of the Shariah permits polygamy, but only monogamy, and marriage a liberal Christians understand it, is in true conformity with the "spirit" of the Quran.

The plain injunctions of the Quran repeatedly urge Jihad against aggressive unbelievers as the most sacred duty of the Muslims, but Ameer Ali says that the "spirit" of Islam regards all warfare in the name of religion as a horrible sin, preferring peace at any price. The list could be added to indefinitely. The fallacy that the "letter killeth but the spirit giveth life" is a purely Christian idea taken from the Epistles of Saint Paul in the New Testament. Whatever Christian teachings may say, we as Muslims must summon the moral honesty to admit that this concept is totally foreign to Islamic values. Just as no creature can exist without its external shape, so in human society, the organization of institutions is essential because we cannot live as disembodied spirits. If the body of a human being were transformed into that of another creature, it could be human no longer.

Similarly, the letter of Islam lives in its spirit and its letter, the two indivisible and inseparable. Since the rise of modern technology, there has been endless and futile debate within the precincts of every religion as to its compatibility or incompatibility with modern scientific progress. If truth is one, then true faith could never conflict with true knowledge, that is, in its strict and impartial sense. The question arose only because modern science is not morally neutral but has evolved under the direct influence and patronage of materialist philosophy as its most important product and its most powerful weapon.

One of the most essential tasks of modern Muslim scholarship is to distinguish genuine, useful and constructive knowledge from pseudo-scientific, materialist theory and speculation. In my opinion the ideal Mujaddid or Mahdi will be a most modern leader of his age possessing unusually deep insight into all the current branches of knowledge and all the major problems of life. As regards statesmanship, political sagacity, and strategic skill in war, he will take the whole world by surprise and prove himself to be the most modern of the moderns. My view that the ideal Mujaddid will be a most modern leader does not mean that he will shave his beard, dress up in European clothes or live in the Western manner. I only mean to suggest that he will be fully conversant with the arts and sciences of his age, with its conditions and requirements and will use all scientific means and devices invented by it to the best advantage and all this is natural for unless a party captures all the available means of power and makes use of all existing arts and sciences, devices and techniques to propagate its influence, it cannot obtain its objectives and dominance in general.

This means that our only alternative is to come to grips with our enemy and fight and that we had better possess some effective weapons to fight with but here a word of warning. Coming to grips with modernism means fighting modernism—not compromising with it. And while waging our ideological and psychological warfare, we must never forget that once on the grounds of expediency we compromise and begin to resemble our adversaries, we shall have become as bad as they and have no reason to continue the struggle. The God fearing creed cannot survive under the Godless leadership. Therefore it is incumbent on the God fearing people to establish the God fearing leadership in the world.

The Muslims do not want leadership for selfish motives. Their contention with the materialists is not on the point of depriving them merely from the leadership. The Muslims want to regain the leadership on point of principle. The materialists are leading the world towards Godlessness and open rebellion against their Creator. It is extremely difficult in this environment of Godless culture and civilization that the God fearing theory, aims and principles of life may appeal to the minds and hearts of human beings because the entire trend of modern life is diagonally opposed to it. As opposed to this theory and practice, the Muslims are a group of God fearing people who place their belief in the obedience to Allah. This faith enjoins on the Muslims not only to keep themselves away from the materialist creed of the West but also to show to the world their own God fearing path. This duty cannot be performed by them successfully unless the Muslims take back the leadership of the world from the materialists.

There is hardly any subject as vexed and vital for the contemporary Islamic world as the question of modern science. Since its earliest encounter with modern Western science in the 18th and 19th centuries, the Islamic world has had to deal with science for practical and intellectual reasons. At the level of practical needs, modern science was seen as the sine qua non of the advancement and defense of Muslim countries in the field of military technology. The Ottoman political body, which, unlike the other parts of the Islamic world, was in direct contact with European powers, was convinced that its political and military decline was due to the lack of proper defense mechanisms against the European armies. To fill this gap, a number of massive reforms were introduced by Mahmud II with the hope of stopping the rapid decline of the Empire, and a new class of military officers and bureaucrats, who became the first point of contact between the traditional world of Islam and modern secular West, was created.

A similar project, in fact a more successful one, was introduced in Egypt by Muhammad Ali whose aspirations were later given a new voice by Taha Hussain and his generation. The leitmotif of this period was that of extreme practicality: the Muslim world needed power, especially military power, to stand back on its feet, and new techno-logies powered by modern science were the only way to have it. The modern conception of science as a medium of power was to have a profound impact on the relation between the Muslim world and modern science, which was then already equated with technology, progress, power, and prosperity – a mode of perception still prevalent among the masses in the Islamic world. The second level of encounter between traditional beliefs and modern science was of an intellectual nature with lasting consequences the most important of which was the re-shaping of the self-perception of the Islamic world.

Using Husserl's analysis of Selbstverstandnis, a key term in Husserl's anthropology of 'Western man', von Grunebaum takes the reception of modern science to be a turning point in the self-view of the traditional Islamic civilization and its approach to history. One of the recurring themes of this epochal even, viz., the incompatibility of traditional beliefs with the dicta of modern science, is forcefully stated in a speech by Ataturk, the founder of modern Turkey, who was as much aware of the practical urgencies of the post-independence war Turkey as he was passionately engaged in creating a new identity for Turkish people: 'We shall take science and knowledge from wherever they may be, and put them in the mind of every member of the nation. For science and for knowledge, there are no restrictions and no conditions. For a nation that insists on preserving a host of traditions and beliefs that rest on no logical proof, progress is very difficult, perhaps even impossible'.

On a relatively smaller scale, the revealing clash between the secular premises of modern science and the traditional Islamic worldview was brought home to many Muslim intellectuals with the publication of Renan's famous lecture L'Islamisme et la science given in Sorbonne in 1883, in which he strongly argued for the irrationality and inability of Muslim peoples to produce science. For us today, Renan's quasi-racist attack on the Islamic faith and crude promulgation of positivism as the new religion of the modern world makes little sense. Nevertheless, it was an eye opener for the Muslim intelligentsia of the time about the way the achievements of modern Western science were presented. Spearheaded by Jamal al-Din Afghani in Persia and Namik Kemal in the Ottoman empire, the Muslim men of letters took upon themselves the task of responding to what they considered to be the distortion of modern science at the hands of some anti-religious philosophers, and produced a sizable discourse on modern science with all the fervour and confusion of their tumultuous times.

Afghani, inter alia, came to epitomize the mindset of his time when he based his historical apology against Renan on the assumption that there could be no clash between religion and science, be it traditional or modern, and that modern Western science was nothing other than the original true Islamic science shipped back, via the Renaissance and Enlightenment, to the Islamic world. By the same token, there is nothing essentially wrong with modern science, and it is the materialistic representation of science that lies at the heart of the so-called religion-science controversy.

Namik Kemal joined Afghani with a rebuttal of his own in his Renan Mudạfanamesi (The Defense against Renan), focusing, unlike Afhgani, on the scientific achievements of the Arabs, namely the Muslim countries of the past. In contrast to these Muslim intellectuals who sought to place modern science within the context of Islamic worldview, a number of prominent Christian writers in the Arab world including Jurji Zaydan (d. 1914), Shibli al-Shumayyil (d. 1916), Farah Antun (d. 1922) and Ya'qub Sarruf (d. 1927), begun to advocate the secular outlook of modern science as a way of joining the European path of modernization, hence taking primarily a philosophical and secular stance on the ongoing debate between religion and science.

These two positions are still with us today as they continue to represent the ambitions as well as failures of the Islamic world in its elusive relation with modern science. Islamic countries spend billions of dollars every year for transfer of technology, science education and research programs. The goal set by the Ottomans in the 19th century has remained more or less the same: gaining power through technological advancement. Furthermore, the financial wedding between science and technology, begun with the industrial revolution, makes it ever harder to search for 'pure science', and the bottom line for the Muslim as well as the Western world becomes technology rather than science. The will of the Islamic countries to participate in the moderni-zation process through transfer of technology obscures the philosophical dimension of the problem, leading to the kind of simplistic and reductionist thinking upon which we will touch shortly.

As for the intellectual challenge posed by modern science, it can hardly be said to have dwindled or disappeared in spite of the diminishing sway of positivism and its allies among the learned. There is a peculiar situation in the wake of the rise of new philosophies of science with new developments in scientific research, extending from the ousting of positivism and physical materialism to quantum mechanics and anti-realism. The postmodernist wave has shaken our confidence in science with consequences far beyond the scientific field, and many young Muslim students and intellectuals see no problem with adopting the relativist and anti-realist stances of a Kuhn or Feyerabend.

The dike of modern science broken, it is assumed that religion and science can now begin talking to each other whereas the truth is that neither has a firm standing because both of them have been deprived of their truth-value by the anti-realist and relativist philosophies of our time. The popularity of the current discussions of philosophy of science in Muslim countries is indicative of the volatile nature of the subject as well as its long history among the Muslim intelligentsia.

It would not be a stretch to say that the contemporary Islamic world is gripped by the challenges of these two divergent yet related points of view, which shape its perception of science in a number of fundamental ways. On the one hand, the governments and ruling elite of Islamic countries consider it to be of the highest priority to keep up with the global race of technological innovation from communications and medical engineering to weapon industry and satellite technology. Arguments to the contrary are seen as a call for resisting the irreversible process of modernization, or for backwardness, to say the least.

On the other hand, it has become common wisdom that the consequences of the application of modern natural sciences to fields that have never been encroached upon before pose serious threats to the environment and human life. This is coupled with the threat of modern science becoming the pseudo-religion of the age, forcing religion to the margins of modern society, or at least making it a matter of personal choice and social ethics. This creates a bitter conflict of consciousness in the Muslim mind, a conflict between the sacred and the worldly power, between belief and scientific precision, and between seeing nature as the cosmic book of God and as a source of exploitation and domination.

When we look at the current discourse on science in the Islamic world, we see a number of competing trends and positions, each with its own claims and solutions. Without pretending to be exhaustive, they can be classified under three headings as ethical, epistemological and ontological/ metaphysical views of science. The ethical/puritanical view of science, which is the most common attitude in the Islamic world, considers modern science as essentially neutral and objective, dealing with the book of nature as it is, with no philosophical or ideological components attached to it. Such problems as the environmental crisis, positivism, materialism, etc., all of which are related to modern science in one way or another, can be solved by adding an ethical dimension to the practice and teaching of science.

The second position, which we may call the epistemological view, is concerned primarily with the epistemic status of modern physical sciences, their truth claims, and methods of achieving sound knowledge, and function for the society at large. Taking science as a social construction, the epistemic school puts special emphasis on the history and sociology of science. Finally, the ontological/metaphysical view of science marks an interesting shift from the philosophy to the metaphysics of science, and its most important claim lies in its insistence on the analysis of the metaphysical and ontological foundations of modern physical sciences. It is to this school, represented, inter alia, by such Muslim thinkers as Seyyid Hossein Nasr and Naquib al-Attas, that the concept of Islamic science goes back, a concept which has caused a great deal of discussion as well as confusion in Islamic intellectual circles.

Science as the Servant of God

The most common attitude towards science in the Islamic world is to see it as an objective study of the world of nature, namely as a way of deciphering the signs of God in the cosmic book of the universe. Natural sciences discover the Divine codes built into the cosmos by its Creator, and in doing so, help the believer marvel at the wonders of God's creation. Seen under this light, science functions within a religious, albeit overtly simplistic, framework.

The image of science as the decoder of the sacred language of the cosmos is certainly an old one, going back to the traditional Islamic sciences whose purpose was not just to find the direction of the qiblah or the times of the prayers but also to understand the reality of things as they are. Construed as such, science is surely a noble enterprise, and it was within this framework that the Muslim intellectuals, when they encountered the edifice of modern science in the 18th and 19th centuries, did not hesitate to translate the word 'ilm (and its plural 'ulum) for science in the sense of modern physical sciences.

This attitude can best be seen among the forerunners of Islamic modernism, especially among those who addressed the question of science as the most urgent problem of the Islamic world. Jamal al-Din Afghani in his celebrated attack on the 'materialists', i.e., Haqiqat-i mazhab-i naichiri wa bayan-i hal-i nachiriyan, translated into Arabic by Muham-mad Abduh as al-Radd 'ala'l-dahriyyin, was engaged in a self-proclaimed battle of saving science from the positivists, a battle for which he derived support from both the history of Islamic and modern sciences.

He had the following to say in his celebrated response to Renan:

'If it is true that the Muslim religion is an obstacle to the development of sciences, can one affirm that this obstacle will not disappear someday? How does the Muslim religion differ on this point from other religions? All religions are intolerant, each one in its way. The Christian religion, I mean the society that follows its inspirations and its teachings and is formed in its image, has emerged from the first period to which I have just alluded; thenceforth free and independent, it seems to advance rapidly on the road of progress and science, whereas Muslim society has not yet freed itself from the tutelage of religion. Realizing, however, that the Christian religion preceded the Muslim religion in the world by many centuries, I cannot keep from hoping that Muhammadan society will succeed someday in breaking its bonds and marching resolutely in the path of civilization after the manner of Western society...No I cannot admit that this hope be denied to Islam.'

Afghani's voice, which was carried on by such figures as Muhammad Abduh, Sayyid Ahmad Khan, Rashid Rida, Muhammad Iqbal, Mehmet Akif Ersoy, Namik Kemal, Said Nursi and Farid Wajdi, was the epitome of the sentiments of the time: modern science is nothing but Islamic science shipped back to the Islamic world via the ports of European Renaissance and Enlightenment. In other words, science is not a culture-specific enterprise, and as such it is not the exclusive property of any civilization. Afghani puts it in the following way:

'The strangest thing of all is that our ulama these days have divided science into two parts. One they call Muslim science, and one European science. Because of this they forbid others to teach some of the useful sciences. They have not understood that science is that noble thing that has no connection with any nation, and is not distinguished by anything but itself. Rather, everything that is known is known by science, and every nation that becomes renowned becomes renowned through science. Men must be related to science, not science to men.

The father and mother of science is proof, and proof is neither Aristotle nor Galileo. The truth is where there is proof, and those who forbid science and knowledge in the belief that they are safeguarding the Islamic religion are really the enemies of that religion. The Islamic religion is the closest of religions to science and knowledge, and there is no incompatibility between science and knowledge and the foundation of Islamic faith.' For this generation of Muslim thinkers, Western science was clearly and categorically distinguishable from Western values, the underlying assumption being that the secular worldview of modern West had no inroads into the structure and operation of the natural sciences.

The task is therefore not to unearth the philosophical underpinnings of modern science but to import it without the ethical component that comes from Western culture, which is alien to the Islamic ethos. The best example of this attitude was given by Mehmet Akif Ersoy, the famous intellectual of the Ottoman Empire and the poet of the national anthem of Turkey. Akif, who lived at a time when the Ottoman empire and parts of the Islamic world were being divided and fiercely attacked by European powers, made a clear-cut distinction between Western science and European life-style, calling for the full-fledged adoption of Western science while totally rejecting the manners and mores of European civilization.

The idea of locating modern science within the frame-work of Islamic ethics is an attitude that is still with us today. Most of the practitioners of science in the Islamic world, namely engineers, doctors, chemists, physicists believe in the inherent neutrality of physical sciences, and the questions of justification, domination, control, etc., simply do not arise for them. Since science is a value-free enterprise, the differences between various scientific traditions, if such a thing is allowed at all, come about at the level of justification, not experimentation and operation. Thus when a scientist, be he a Muslim, Hindu or simply non-believer, looks at the chemical components of the minerals, he sees the same thing, operates on the same set of elements under the same set of conditions, and arrives presumably at the same or commensurable conclusions. It is the practical application of these findings to various fields and technologies that makes the difference, if any, between Ptolemy, Ibn al-Haytham, or F. Bacon.

It is not difficult to see the imagery of the torch of science inherent in this view. Being the most prevalent attitude towards the history of science both in the Islamic and Western world, this view considers history of science progressing along a linear trajectory of discoveries and heuristic advancements. The torch of science transmitted from one nation to another, from one historical period to another, signifies the constant progress of scientific research, relegating such facts as religious convictions, philosophical assumptions and/or social infrastructure to a set of preparatory conditions necessary for the advancement of science. Thus the only difference between the science of the 13th century Islamic world and that of the 19th century Europe turns out to be quantitative, that is, in terms of the accumulation and further specialization of scientific knowledge about the physical world.

By the same token, the scientific revolution of the 17th and 18th centuries was a revolution not in the outlook of the modern man concerning nature and the meaning of scientific investigation but in the methodological tools and formulations of the natural sciences. This is how the majority of the 19th century intellectuals would have interpreted the history of science and the rise of modern natural sciences, and this is how the subject is still taught today in the schools in the Islamic world.

A logical result of this view of science is the incorporation of scientific findings as confirmations of the Islamic faith. In the pre-modern era when the religious worldview was strong, no scientist deemed it necessary to subject the Quranic verses to a 'scientific' reading, hoping, perhaps, to improve one's faith in religion or showing the religious basis of scientific investigation. As a trait of the modern period, however, many believers of different religions and denominations look for possible confirmations from the sciences for their religious belief, confirmations that would, it is hoped, both increase the truth-value of the sacred book and ward off the hegemonic onslaught of the positivists. A good example of this approach in the Islamic world is without doubt Said Nursi (1877-1960), the famous scholar, activist and founder of the Nurcu movement in Turkey.

Said Nursi's views on the relation between faith and science were formulated at a time when the rude positivism of the late 1900s was made the official ideology of the newly established Turkish republic. Unlike many of his contemporaries, Nursi had a considerable knowledge of the scientific findings of his time. His method in confronting Western science was a simple yet highly influential one: instead of taking a position against it, he incorporated its findings within the theistic perspective, thus pre-empting any serious confrontation between science and religion. Since Nursi, like many of his contemporaries, was acutely aware of the power of modern natural sciences, and, as we see in his great work Risale-i Nur, he certainly believed in the universal objectivity of their discoveries.

For him, reading the verses of the Quran through the eyes of modern physical sciences had not only an instrumental value for protecting the faith of the youth who were coming under the sway of the 19th century positivism and empiricism. It was also the beginning of a new method of substantiating the Islamic faith on the basis of the certainties of modern physical sciences, and reading the cosmic verses of the Quran within the matrix of scientific discoveries. As a religious scholar well grounded in traditional Islamic sciences, Nursi was aware of the apparent discrepancy between traditional cosmology articulated by Muslim philosophers and Sufis and the Newtonian world-picture which contained no religious terms. Instead of rejecting the mechanistic view of the universe presented by modern science, Nursi saw an interesting parallel between it and the kalam arguments from design (nizam).

In his view, the classical arguments from design, used profusely by Muslim and Christian thinkers alike, were meant to prove the eternal order and harmony built into the texture of the cosmos by the Divine creator, and as such they do not contradict Newtonian determinism. If the mechanistic view of the universe presents a world-picture in which nothing can remain scientifically unaccounted for, then this proves not the fortuitous generation of the cosmos but its creation by an intelligent agent, which is nothing other than the Divine artisan. Therefore the depiction of the universe as a machine or clock, the two favourite symbols of the deists of the 19th century, does not nullify the theistic claims of creation.

On the contrary, rationality as regularity, harmony and predictability, Nursi would wholeheartedly argue, lies at the heart of the religious view of the cosmos. Thus the mechanistic view of the universe, which was hailed by the secularists and positivists of the 19th century as the indisputable triumph of reason over against religion, poses no threat to the theistic conception of the universe. As Mardin points out, this attitude was so influential among Nursi's followers that vocabularies taken from 19th century thermodynamics and electricity became household terms of the Nurcu movement. Thus the physical world is described as 'a fabrika-i kainat (factory of the universe) (Lem'alar, 287); life is a machine of the future from the exalted benchwork of the universe (hayat kainatin tezgah-i azaminda ... bir istikbal makinesidir). Sabri, one of the first disciples of Bediuzzaman speaks of 'machines which produce the electricity of the Nur factory' when speaking of the work of disciples.'

Nursi's approach to modern science has been interpreted in a number of variant and, sometimes, conflicting ways. There are those who take his coping with science as a powerful way of deconstructing its metaphysical claims by using the language of Newtonian physics, chemistry and astronomy. The opposite side of the controversy is represented by those who tend to emphasize the influence of modern science and positivism on Nursi — an influence visible in the entire generation of 19th century Muslim scholars, intellectuals, and activists. Even though one can easily detect an apparent incongruity between what Nursi had intended by his so-called 'scientific commentary' (al-tafsir al-ilmi) and what his followers made out of it, the roots of his theistic scientism, one may claim, are ultimately traceable to his Risale-i Nur.

A few examples will suffice to illustrate this point. When discussing the miracles of the prophets mentioned in the Quran, Nursi identifies two main reasons for their dispensation by the Divine authority. The first reason pertains to the veracity of the prophets of God, viz., they have been sent with an undeniable truth (burhan) to summon people to God's eternal word. The second reason, and this is what concerns us here, is that the prophetic miracles contain in them the seed of the future developments of human civilization. The story of the Prophet Sùlayman (Solomon) mentioned in the Quran (Saba', 34/12), for instance, predicts the invention of modern aviation systems. As Nursi interprets it, the fact that God has given the wind under Sulayman's command to travel long distances in a short period of time points to the future possibility of travelling in the air in general, and to the invention of aircraft (teyyare) in particular.

Another example is the Prophet Moses' miracle to bring out water from the earth, as mentioned in the Quran, when he and his followers were searching for water in the middle of the desert. According to Nursi, this event predicts the development of modern drilling techniques to dig out such indispensable substances of modern industry as oil, mineral water and natural gas. Following the same line of thinking, so typical of his generation of Quranic commentators, Nursi explains the mention of iron and 'its being softened to David' (Saba', 34/10) as a sign of the future significance of iron and, perhaps, steel for modern industry.

Another striking example of how Nursi was deeply engaged in scientific exegesis is his interpretation of the verse of the light (Nur, 24/35), upon which such colossal figures of Islamic history as Ibn Sina and Ghazzali have written commentaries. Among many of the other profound and esoteric meanings of the light verse, which depicts God as the 'light of the heavens and the earth', is the allusion to the future invention of electricity whose continuous diffusion of light is compared to the Quranic expression 'light upon light' (nurun 'ala nur) mentioned in the verse. These examples, the number of which can easily be multiplied, and the way they are justified, were in tandem with a presiding idea, which Nursi adopted and elaborated with full force. This he called the 'miracle of the teaching of Divine names to Adam' (talim-i esma mucizesi).

The Quran tells us in Baqarah 2/31 that God, after creating Adam as his vicegerent on earth, to which the angels had objected for fear of corruption on earth, taught him 'all the names' (or according to another reading 'the names of all things', asma'a kullaha). Throughout the Islamic intellectual history, this verse has been interpreted in a myriad of different ways, ranging from the most literalist to the most esoteric readings. In a daring statement, Nursi takes this miracle of Adam, the father of humanity, as greater and more perfect than those of all the other prophets after him for it embodies and comprises the entire spectrum of 'all the progress and perfection human beings will ever achieve in the course of their history'.

Essentially, it is on the basis of this principle that Nursi justifies his scientific and 'progressive' exegesis of various verses of the Quran. True, interpretations of this kind can be found in traditional commentaries on the Quran or among the Sufis. What is peculiar about Nursi's new hermeneutics, if we may use such an appellation here, is the scientific and modern context in which it is articulated and carried out. In its vulgarized version, Said Nursi's encounter with modern science has led to a torrent of one-to-one correspondences between new scientific findings and Quranic verses, generating an unprecedented interest in natural sciences among his followers. Moreover, his position on science as the decoder of the sacred language of nature influenced a whole generation of Turkish students, professionals and lay people with repercussions outside the Turkish-speaking world.

Today, his followers are extremely successful in matters related to sciences and engineering, and continue Nursi's method of integrating the findings of modern physical sciences into the theistic perspective of Abrahamic religions. They are, however, also extremely poor and unprepared when it comes to the philosophical aspects of the subject. The pages of the journal Sizinti, published by Nursi's followers in Turkish, and its English version Fountain, are filled with essays trying to show the miracle of creation through comparisons between the cosmological verses of the Quran and new scientific discoveries. Expectedly, every new discovery, in this point of view, is yet another proof for the miracle and credibility of the Quran. In this sense, Nursi's progeny is the father of what we might call 'Bucaillism' in the Islamic world.

The idea of verifying the cosmological verses of the Quran via the scrutiny of the science of the day is a highly modern attitude by which it is hoped to confront and over-come the challenges of modern secular science. The fact that the same set of scientific data can equally be used within different contexts of justification and thus yield completely different and incommensurable results does not arise as a problem, neither the overtly secular nature of the world-view of modern science is considered to be a threat to the religious view of nature and the universe.

The deliberate ignorance of the problem is seen, we have to admit, as the solution, and the most poignant result of this is the rise of a class of Muslim scientists and engineers who pray five times a day but whose conception of science is largely determined by the postulates of modern scientific worldview. This, however, does not prevent the proponents of this view from seeing the problems inflicted upon the world of nature and human life by modern science. The environmental crisis, hazards of genetic engineering, air pollution, rapid destruction of countless species, nuclear and chemical weapon industry are all admitted as problems we have to deal with. Yet the proposed remedy is an expected one: inserting a dimension of social and environmental ethics will put under control, if not completely solve, the problems mentioned. In other words, science should be subjected to ethics at the level of policy decisions.

Accordingly, the aforementioned problems of modern science can be overcome by better management and advanced techniques of environmental engineering. Reminiscent of

Habermas' defence of the project of modernity which he considers incomplete as of yet, this view looks for the solution in the problem itself: further advancement in scientific research and technologies will create new methods of controlling the environmental crisis and all the problems associated with modern science. In short, we need more science to overcome its misdeeds. The great majority of people in the Islamic as well as Western world share the sentiments of the above view of science that we have just summarized. Many people from all walks of life believe in the necessity of upholding an ethical framework within which scientific investigation should be carried out and controlled.

This has certainly important policy implications for scientific research funded by federal governments and business corporations in many parts of the world. The point that is inevitably obscured, however, is much more crucial than having an influence on policy decisions. To limit ethics to policy implementations is to make it a matter of personal preference for the scientific community whose political and financial freedom against governments and giant corporations is highly questionable. The fact that the scientists who approve human cloning and genetic alteration believe in theistic evolution does not change the course of modern science. The conflict of consciousness to which we referred above resurfaces here in the form of people whose hearts and emotions are attached to the mandates of their respective religion but whose minds are empty of the religious view of the universe.

Epistemic View of Science

An important channel through which the contemporary Islamic world, especially in the last three decades of the 20th century, has come to terms with modern science is philosophy science as developed in the West. The impact of the deconstruction of the epistemological hegemony of 19th century positivism together with the critique of Newtonian physics and scientific objectivism and realism on the Islamic world has been stupendous and caused a torrential release of intellectual energy among students and intellectuals.

Needless to say, the influx of ideas associated with such names as Kuhn, Feyerabend and Popper and their current students continues almost unabated in spite of the fact that the post-antirealist thinking on science seems to have come to a serious stalemate. Being on the receiving end of this debate, many Muslim students and intellectuals are still experimenting with these ideas with little effort, as we shall see shortly, to extrapolate their full implications. Before doing that, however, a few words of clarification on the scope of contemporary philosophy of science are in order. The primary concern of the contemporary philosophy of science is to establish the validity, or lack thereof, of the truth claims of modern natural sciences.

The theory-observation dichotomy, fact-value distinc-tion, experimentation, objectivity, scientific community, history and sociology of science, and a host of other problems stand out, inter alia, as the most important issues of the field, which leaves no aspect of the scientific enterprise untouched. What concerns us here, however, is the emphasis of the philosophy of science on epistemology to the point of excluding any ontological or metaphysical arguments. The majority of contemporary philosophers of science, including such celebrated vanguards as Kuhn, Popper and Feyerabend, construe science primarily as an epistemic structure that claims to explain the order of physical reality within the exclusive framework of scientific methods. Scientific realism, anti-realism, instrumentalism, empiricism are all, needles to say, anchored in different notions of knowledge with profound implications for the natural as well as the human sciences.

Given its exclusive concern with epistemic claims involved, contemporary philosophy of science can be stated as the epistemology of science. In this regard, the epistemic view of science is surely a respected member of modern philosophy for which any concept other than the knowing subject and its paraphernalia is simply a non-starter for a proper understanding of the world. Thinking out the question of being in terms of how it is known, to use a Heideggerian language, is the leitmotif of modern philosophy, including its prima facie foes, rationalism and empiricism.

Whether we consider the knowing subject as a rationalist, empiricist, structuralist or deconstructionist, the anthropocentric ethos runs through the veins of how we perceive the world around us, how we interact with it, and how we position ourselves vis-à-vis the other human beings with whom we share the intentional as well as the physical space of our life-world. Here the eternal paradox of all subjectivist epistemologies is brought into clarity: to put the subject before the world, of which he is a part, is to claim the square inside the circle to be larger than the circle. Said differently, to ground the intelligibility of the world in the discursive constructions of the knowing subject is to see the world, or rather anything outside the subject, as essentially devoid of intrinsic meaning and intelligibility.

The Muslim critique of modern science based on the premises of modern epistemology has usually lost sight of this crucial fact as we see in the otherwise commendable literature produced by Ismail Faruqi and his protégé International Institute of Islamic Thought. There is no denying the fact that Kuhn's radical anti-realism or Popper's concept of verisimilitude cannot be interpreted as lending support to the epistemic hegemony of modern science. On the contrary, they are meant to destroy it once and for all. The anti-realist component of their positions, however, reinforces the anthropocentric imagery: it is the knowing subject who is willing to deny science its self-proclaimed objectivity and appeal to credibility.

It is this aspect of contemporary philosophy of science, I believe, that has been totally mistaken and ignored by its adherents in the Islamic world. Today we can hardly come across a book or article written in English, Arabic, Turkish or Bahasa Malaysia that does not have recourse to Foucault, Kuhn, Feyerabend or Lyotard to denounce the philosophical underpinnings of modern science. From the academic papers of Muslim graduate students to the writings of the so-called 'ijmalis' led by Ziauddin Sardar, the names of numerous philosophers of science sweep through the literature with indigenous additions from the Islamic point of view. To put it mildly, this has led to the overemphasis of epistemology and methodology among many Muslim thinkers and young scholars while questions of ontology and metaphysics have been either left out or taken for granted.

The concept of Islamic science, in this point of view, is centered on a loosely defined epistemology, or rather set of discrete ideas grouped under Islamic epistemology whose content is yet to be determined. In many ways, the idea of Islamizing natural and social sciences has been equated, by and large, with producing a different structure of knowledge and methodology within what we might call the epistemologist fallacy of modern philosophy. The crucial issue has thus remained untouched: to reduce the notion of Islamic science to considerations of epistemology and methodology, which are without doubt indispensable in their own right, is to seek out a space for the Islamic point of view within, and not outside, the framework of modern philosophy.

Ismail Faruqi's work known under the rubric of Islamization of knowledge is a good example of how the idea of method or methodology ('manhaj' and 'manhajiyyah', the Arabic equivalents of method and methodology being the most popular words of the proponents of this view) can obscure deeper philosophical issues involved in the current discussions of science. Even though Faruqi's project was proposed to Islamize the existing forms of knowledge imported from the West, his focus was exclusively on the humanities, leaving scientific knowledge virtually untouched. This was in tandem with his conviction that the body of knowledge generated by modern natural sciences is neutral and as such requires no special attention. Thus, Faruqi's work, and that of IIIT after his death, concentrated on the social sciences and education. This had two important consequences.

First, Faruqi's important work on Islamization provided his followers with a framework in which knowledge (al-'ilm) came to be equated with social disciplines, thus ending up in a kind of sociologism. The prototype of Faruqi's project is, we may say, the modern social scientist entrusted with the task of the traditional 'alim. Second, the exclusion of modern scientific knowledge from the scope of Islamization has led to the negligence, to say the least, of the secularizing effect of modern scientific worldview.

This leaves the Muslim social scientists, the ideal-type of the Islamization programme, with no clue as to how to deal with the question of modern scientific knowledge. Furthermore, to take the philosophical foundations of modern natural sciences for granted is tantamount to reinforcing the dichotomy between the natural and human sciences, a dichotomy whose consequences continue to pose serious challenges to the validity of the forms of knowledge outside the domain of modern physical sciences. A similar position, with some important variations, is to be found in the works of Ziauddin Sardar and a number of closely associated scholars known as the "ijmalis" and the "Aligarh School". Although the ijmalis do not accept the appellation of being a 'merely Kuhnian', one can hardly fail to see the subtext of their discourse based on Kuhn, Feyerabend and others in their critique of modern Western science.

Sardar's definition of science shares much of the instrumentalist and anti-realist spirit of the Kuhnian science. For him, science is 'a basic problem-solving tool of any civilization. Without it, a civilization cannot maintain its political and social structure or meet the basic needs of its people and culture.' The ijmali's socio-cultural point of view certainly points to an important component of scientific activity, *viz.*, and the social setting in which the sciences are cultivated and flourish. It is, however, to be noted that the relegation of physical sciences or any scholarly activity for that matter, to social utility is bound to have serious consequences insofar as the philosophical legitimacy of sciences is concerned. As we see in the case of Van Fraassen and Kuhn, the instrumentalist definition of science entails a strong leaning towards anti-realism, a position whose compatibility with the concept of Islamic science is yet to be accounted for.

Yet, there is another paradox involved here. The most common critique of modern science has been to present it as a culturally conditioned and historical endeavour with claims to universality and objectivity. Kuhn's philosophy of paradigm, which has become the most fashionable buzz word in the Islamic world, Feyerabend's defense of society against science, or Van Fraassen's scientific instrumentalism are all profusely used to show the utter historicity and relativity of modern science.

Since every scientific, and, by extension, human activity is embedded in a historical and cultural setting, we can no longer speak of sciences in isolation from their socio-historical conditions. This implies that no account of science, be it Western or Islamic, is possible without the history and, more importantly, sociology of science, whose task is to deconstruct the historical formation and genealogy of sciences. Furthermore, this approach has been applied to humanities as well, with almost total disregard to its implications for what is proposed in its place, i.e., Islamic science and methodology.

At this point, philosophy of science becomes identical with sociology of science, and any appeal to universal validity and objectivity by physical sciences is rejected on the basis of their utter historicity, contingency, ideology, cultural bias, and so on. Even though these terms are used as household terms by many Muslims writing and thinking on modern science, they rarely appear in their defense of Islamic science, which is proposed as an alternative to the Western conceptions of science. If science, as the advocates of this view seem to imply, is culture-specific with no right to universal applicability, then this has to be true for all scientific activity whether it takes place in the 11th century Samarqand or the 20th century Sweden.

This is in fact what is so clearly intended and stated by all the major expositors of the philosophy of science. If it is the modern secular science that is culturally and historically constructed, then Islamic science, as understood by this group of scholars, has to explain how and why it is entitled to universal validity and applicability. It will simply be short of logical consistency to say that Kuhn's language of paradigms is an adequate tool to explain the history of Western but not Islamic science. What I have called here the epistemic view of science, which has taken the form of an extremely common tendency rather than a single school of thought, has certainly raised the consciousness of the Islamic world about modern science, and contributed to the ongoing discussion of the possibility of having a scientific study of nature based on an Islamic ethos. We can, however, hardly fail to see the contradictions in this point of view especially when it is most vulnerable to the temptations of modern epistemology.

The emphasis put on epistemology to the point of excluding ontology and metaphysics has grave consequences for any notion of science, and it is for this reason that we do not see any serious study of philosophy, metaphysics or cosmology among the followers of this point of view. Furthermore there is a deliberate resistance to these disciplines in spite of the fact traditional Islamic philosophy and metaphysics had functioned as a gateway between scientific knowledge and religious faith. At any rate, it remains to be seen if the adherents of the epistemic view of science will be able to overcome the subjectivist fallacy of modern philosophy, i.e., building an epistemology without articulating an adequate metaphysics and ontology.

Metaphysics of Science

The last major position on science of which we can give here only a brief summary is marked off from the other two positions by its emphasis on metaphysics and the philosophical critique of modern science. Represented chiefly, inter alia, by such thinkers as Rene Guenon, Seyyed Hossein Nasr, Naquib al-

Attas, Osman Bakar, Mahdi Golshani and Alparslan Acikgenc, the metaphysical view of science consi-ders every scientific activity operating within a framework of metaphysics whose principles are derived from the immutable teachings of the Divine revelation. In contrast to philosophy and sociology of science, metaphysics of science provides sciences with a sacred concept of nature and cosmology within which to function.

At this point, the sacred view of nature taught by religions and ancient traditions takes on a prime importance in the formation and operation of physical sciences, and all of the traditional sciences, regardless of the historical and geographic setting they were cultivated in, were based on such principles which had enabled them to produce highly advanced sciences and techniques while maintaining the sacredness of nature and the cosmos. The traditional natural sciences, Nasr and others argue, derived not only their work-ethics and methodology but also metaphysical and ontological raison d'etre from the principles of Divine revelation because they were rooted in a conception of knowledge according to which the knowledge of the world acquired by man and the sacred knowledge revealed by God were seen as a single unity.

As a result, the epistemological crisis of the natural and human sciences that we try to overcome today did not arise for the traditional scientist who did not have to sacrifice his religious beliefs in order to carry out a scientific experiment, and vise versa. The traditional metaphysics envisages reality as a multi-layered structure with different levels and degrees of meaning. The polarity between the Principle and Its manifestation, which is translated into the language of theology as God and His creation, gives rise to a hierarchic view of the universe because manifestation already implies a domain of reality lower than its sustaining origin. Moreover, since reality is what it is due to the Divine nature, it cannot be seen as a play-thing or the product of a series of fortuitous events.

On the contrary, the cosmos, as the traditional scientists firmly believed, is teleological throughout, displaying a remarkable order and purpossiveness. Nature, depicted by modern science as a ceaseless flow of change and contingency, never fails to restore itself into an abode of permanence and continuity with the preservation of species and self-generation. Seen under this light, nature, which is the subject matter of physical sciences, cannot be reduced to any one of these levels.

With reductionism out, the traditional metaphysics of science uses a language built upon such key terms as hierarchy, telos, interconnectedness, isomorphism, unity and complexity. These qualities are built into the very structure and methodology of traditional sciences of nature, which can be taken to be one of the demarcation lines between the sacred and modern secular views of science. It is therefore impossible, the proponents of this view would insist, to create or resuscitate the traditional Islamic sciences of nature without first articulating its metaphysical framework. Any attempt to graft Islamic ethics and epistemology to the metaphysically blind outlook of modern science is bound to be a failure.

The philosophical underpinnings of Islamic science, as defined by Nasr, Attas, and others are derived from the metaphysical principles of Islam. Just as the Islamic revelation determines the social and artistic life of the Muslim civilization, it also gives direction to its understanding of the natural environment and its scientific study. The doctrine of tawhid, the most essential tenet of Islamic religion, affirms the unity of the Divine Principle, and it is projected into the domain of natural sciences as the essential unity and interrelatedness of the natural order.

A science can thus be defined as Islamic, Acikgenc states, to the extent to which it conforms to and reflects the cardinal principles of the Islamic worldview. In a similar way, Nasr insists that 'the aim of all the Islamic sciences – and more generally speaking, of all the medieval and ancient cosmological sciences – is to show the unity and inter-relatedness of all that exists, so that, in contemplating the unity of the cosmos, man may be led to the unity of the Divine Principle, of which the unity of Nature is the image.' Thus the Islamic sciences of nature function in a two-fold way. First, they look at nature as a single unity with all of its parts interconnected to each other. Second, they are meant to lead both the scientist and the layman to the contemplation of Nature as the sacred artifact of the Divine.

For Nasr, the sacred cosmology of the Sufis, which is grounded in metaphysics and inspiration rather than physical sciences per se, is related to the second function of the sciences of nature, and maintains its validity even today for it is based on the symbolic significance of the cosmos. This brings us to the other important feature of the Islamic sciences of nature, i.e., their intellectual function. Nasr uses the word 'intellect' in its traditional sense, viz., as related to contemplation. The modern connotation of the words intellect and intellectual as logical analysis or discursive thinking is the result of the emptying of their metaphysical and mystical content. Having rejected the usage of the word 'intellect' as abstract analysis or sentimentality, Nasr seeks to regain its medieval and traditional usage.

'"Intellect" and "intellectual" are so closely identified today with the analytical function of the mind that they hardly bear any longer any relation to the contemplative. The attitude these words imply toward Nature is the one that Goethe was to deplore as late as the early nineteenth century – that attitude that resolves, conquers, and dominates by force of concepts. It is, in short, essentially abstract, while contemplative knowledge is at bottom concrete. We shall thus have to say, by way of establishing the old distinction, that the gnostic's relation to Nature is 'intellective', which is neither abstract, nor analytical, nor merely sentimental.'

Defined as such, the Islamic sciences of nature do not lend themselves to being a means of gaining power and domination over nature. Their contemplative aspect, rooted in the Quranic teachings of nature as well as in traditional cosmologies, ties them to metaphysics on the one hand, and to art on the other. By the same token, the function of philosophy cannot be confined to being a mere interpreter of the data produced by natural sciences. In sharp contrast to the Kantian notion of philosophy, which has turned philosophy into a handmaid of Newtonian physics, Nasr assigns to philosophy an important role in establishing a harmonious relation between the givens of religion and the demands of scientific investigation.

In the post-Kantian period, philosophy was gradually reduced to a second-order analysis of the first-order facts of physical sciences, and this has assigned to philosophical pursuit a completely different task. In contrast to this new mission, Nasr insists on the traditional meaning and function of philosophy. On the one hand, philosophy is related to the life-world in which we live, including the physical environment, and as such it cannot remain indifferent to a veritable understanding of the universe and the cosmos. On the other hand, it is closely related to metaphysics and wisdom, and as such it cannot be reduced to a branch of physical sciences. In fact, this is how the relationship between philosophy and science was established in classical classifications of knowledge, both in the West and the Islamic world.

The scientist and the philosopher were united in one and the same person as we see in the case of an Aristotle or Ibn Sina, and this suggests that the scope of philosophical thinking could not be relegated to quantitative analysis of natural sciences. Thus, in Nasr's concept of science, philosophy, in addition to metaphysics and aesthetics, plays a crucial role that cannot be substituted for by any other science. Moreover, the sciences of nature always function within a definite framework of ontology and cosmology, which is articulated primarily and essentially by philosophy in the traditional sense of the term. This is why philosophy is an integral part of Nasr's metaphysical concept of science.

The metaphysical view of traditional civilizations concerning nature and its scientific study has been lost in modern science whose philosophical foundations go back to the historical rupture of the Western thought with its traditional teachings. The rise of modern science, Nasr and others would insist, was not simply due to some ground-breaking advancement in scientific methods of measurement and calculation. On the contrary, it was the result of a fundamental change in man's outlook concerning the universe. This outlook is predicated upon a number of premises, among which the following five are of particular significance. The first is the secular view of the universe, which allows no space for the Divine in the order of nature. The second is the mechanistic world-picture presented by modern science, which construes the cosmos as a self-subsistent machine and/or pre-ordained clock.

The third is the epistemological hegemony of rationalism and empiricism over the current conceptions of nature. The fourth is the Cartesian bifurcation, based on Descartes' categorical distinction between res cogitans and res extensa, which can also be read as the ontological alienation of the knowing subject from his/her object of knowledge. The fifth and the final premise of modern scientific worldview, which can be seen as the end-result of the preceding points, is the exploitation of the natural environment as a source of global power and domination. This is coupled with the hubris of modern science which does not accept any notion of truth and knowledge other than what is verifiable within the context of it's highly specialized, technical, and hence restricted means of verification.

The metaphysical view of science, which points to an interesting shift from the philosophy to the metaphysics of science, takes aim at the intellectual foundations of modern science and, unlike the other two views of science, proposes a well-defined philosophy of nature and cosmology based on the principles of traditional Islamic sciences. Its critique of modern science is not confined to ethical considerations or methodological amendments as it claims to restore the religious view of the universe. In this regard, the metaphysical view of science, as formulated by Nasr and others, is part of the larger project of deconstructing the modernist worldview, of which science is considered to be only an offshoot.

6

Islamic View of Social Sciences and their Applications

Western education is secular in outlook, skirts around moral issues central to Islam, and denies the idea that God is an active agent in human history. It is also highly Eurocentric, taking the key events in human history to be the Industrial Revolution in England and the French revolution, for example. It is built on a materialistic philosophy, stressing the primacy of physical objects over intangibles such as values, ideals and morals. Such a worldview is incompatible with Islam, which teaches us that the most significant event in human history was the twenty three year mission of our Prophet Muhammad (s.a.w.) during which he conveyed the message of Allah, the creator and sustainer of the Universes, to all human beings.

This Islamic worldview is fostered by traditional Islamic education systems, such as those of the madrassah's in Pakistan. These traditional educational systems are not adequate for modern needs, however. Their main failing is that they do not offer a coherent and integrated world view, which fits all historical, political, and technological developments into a unified perspective. However, this is just a reflection of the failure of the Ummah as a whole to cope adequately with the crisis created by losses on the battlefield, economic, and other fronts to an alien civilization with values radically different from our own. Our goal in this chapter is to spell out the outlines of an Islamic worldview which is capable of taking all modern developments and the recent history of the Ummah within its purview.

Spiritual and Psychological Aspects

The biggest challenge is a lack of confidence among Muslims, created by the shock of defeat and the continuing stagnation in the Islamic world. In fact Islam has a worldview which can comfortably encompass all developments, and the capacity to meet this shock as has been demonstrated in the past after the fall of Spain, and the sack of Baghdad. A precondition for undertaking and completing the intellectual exercises to be outlined is a strong faith, which can only be developed by spiritual training given to the companions of our Prophet (s.a.w.). One aspect of this training relevant for our present purposes is described in a Hadeeth as follows. Two men passed by the Prophet (s.a.w.) and his companions, and he asked them to compare the two. The first was a rich Kafir, and was held to be an honourable man esteemed in the community. The second was a poor Muslim, with no social standing.

The Prophet rejected this common view, indicating that the poor Muslim had much higher standing in the eyes of Allah than a whole world full of the first kind of persons. A precondition for intellectual revolution is a spiritual understanding that the most ignorant Muslim with faith has a treasure of knowledge more valuable than a world full of Einsteins, Galileos, Newtons, etc. Since these preconditions, relating to the heart and soul, cannot be adequately addressed on a piece of paper, we move on to the intellectual aspects of the worldview that we need to create, foster and teach as the backbone of an Islamic education.

Muslim Methodology Conflicts with Western

Two ideas must be central to any Muslim view of history. One is that God is in full control and all events which occur happen only with the will of Allah. No one other than Allah has the power to shape history. The second is that God responds to the moral behavior of mankind, and Muslims in particular, in shaping historical events. This denial of the effectiveness of material causes and invocation of God as an active agent in history is directly opposed to Western methodological assumptions, and will cause distress to many Muslims who see Islamic education as a suitable mix of Western and traditional Muslim education.

Nonetheless, it is not possible for us to compromise on this issue – we simply cannot accept a methodology which forbids us to invoke Allah as an explanatory factor, indeed the prime cause, of all historical events. Western Concept of Progress: One of the central unifying themes of Western education is the idea of progress: In all areas, mankind was backwards, and they have been progressing. It is often added that perfection has been achieved by the European civilization and all other races will eventually reach this stage through the process of development. Indeed the classification of Europe as developed and others as underdeveloped suggests that we will eventually become like them as we progress.

This picture, and all that it implies, are so pervasive that it will be hard to find Muslims who do not in some way or the other subscribe to at least some aspects of this. For example, if asked to describe golden periods in Islamic history, Muslims will mention the intellectual and scientific achievements at Baghdad and Granada. It is only on reflection that we realize that the golden age of Islam was the time of the prophet ("Khairul- Quroon Qarni"). This most perfect society was achieved only for a short period of time, and since then there has been only decline (punctuated by occasional periods of progress, for sure). Thus the Muslim worldview is dramatically different from the dominant Western one. However, in order to sustain this worldview we need our own analysis of history.

It is impossible to use conventional Western texts for this purpose. It is at this point that we have the key difficulty for an Islamic education, within or without a traditional madrassah. There do not exist texts written from an Islamic perspective which make sense of (that is, provide a coherent and meaningful perspective on) all historical, political, and technological developments of the past few centuries. In developing a strategy for Islamic education, this is the critical area for work: we need to develop texts which assimilate recent World history within an Islamic perspective. It is worth noting that this is a more ambitious project than the "Islamization of Knowledge," which seeks to modify Western knowledge to make it compatible with an Islamic perspective. Islam Centered History: Even though there do not currently exist texts that are fully suitable, there is a large amount of work which could serve as a satisfactory basis for what we seek to do in creating an Islamic worldview. The most important work which I am aware of is that of Syed Abul Hassan Ali Nadwi.

In particular, his early work on "The Rise and Fall of Islam and its impact on the World," is an excellent start for our project. This book traces the theme that Islam was responsible for a human-centered and civilized worldview, which brought benefits to all human beings. With the decline of Islam, materialistic values came to the fore, to the loss of all humans. The current prevalence of materialistic values, where it is considered acceptable to kill hundreds of thousands of human beings for financial considerations, and Machiavellian political considerations prevail over moral issues, is due to the decline of Islam. This is a broad theme, which has only been sketched briefly in the book. Developing it fully will require hundreds of scholars to trace the implications and work out the theme in many different particular historical contexts.

An early example of the kind of work that is needed is provided by a number of biographies of Salahuddin Ayyubi (by both Muslim and Christian authors) which show that the moral values and standards of conduct of the Muslims were substantially superior to those of the invading Christian Crusaders, regardless of their relative technological capabilities. The three volume work entitled "The Venture of Islam: Conscience and History in a World Civilization," by Charles

Hodgson provides an excellent sympathetic outsiders view which does much to debunk the traditional Eurocentrism and provide an analysis of history in terms much more sympathetic and favorable to an Islamic worldview.

We quote from the first few paragraphs: Muslims are assured in the Quran, 'You have become the best community ever raised up for mankind, enjoining the right and forbidding the wrong, and having faith in God.' Earnest men have taken this prophecy seriously to the point of trying to mould the history of the whole world in accordance with it. Soon after the founding of the faith, Muslims succeeded in building a new form of society, which in time carried with it its own distinctive institutions, its art and literature, its science and scholarship, its political and social forms, as well as its cult and creed, all bearing an unmistakable Islamic impress. In the course of centuries, this new society spread over widely diverse climes, throughout most of the Old World. It came closer than any had ever come to uniting all mankind under its ideals.

Those who have undertaken to rebuild life in Islamic terms have ventured on an enterprise with a high potential reward – that of winning through to the best that is open to mankind; but with correspondingly great risks of error and failure. Muslims have yet to implement the Quranic prophecy fully in all its implications. But they have perennially renewed their hopes and efforts to live the godly life not only as individuals but as a community. In every age, pious Muslims have reasserted their faith, in the light of new circumstances that have arisen out of failures, and also of successes of the past. The vision has never vanished, the venture has never been abandoned; these hopes and efforts are still vitally alive in the modern world. The history of Islam as a faith, of the culture of which it has formed the core, derives its unity and its unique significance from that vision and that venture.

The idea that the Muslim civilization is a venture to establish the Kingdom of God on Earth, to enjoin good and forbid evil, and that this is an ongoing enterprise with its successes and failures, can easily form the backbone of an alternative vision of history. Whereas the history of civilizations has been a story of the search for power and wealth, Muslims stand out as unique in their quest to establish justice in accordance with God's will on Earth. To establish this, it would be necessary to go into a deeper analysis of Muslim civilizations and their successes and failures. It would be crucial here to avoid the mistake of identifying civilizations with their rulers and studying lives of kings instead of that of ordinary citizens. Due to various quirks in European history, the idea of the nation-state as a central concept and driving force emerged with great power in the past century – this has led to a popular conception of history as being a history of rulers of states, or kings.

For Islam, we must realize that the Islamic history will focus on the religious lives of the people, and the best exponents of this life would be the Ulema and the Mashaikh, as well as the intellectual struggles associated with religion. Kings and their Islamic behavior or lack of it would only be a peripheral issue. Again, there exists substantial literature which can be pressed into service regarding this issue. The task required is to pull anecdotes of Muslim struggles for establishing justice on Earth into a coherent and integrated story, which portrays these struggles as a continuous struggle over the centuries.

An excellent example of the type of work needed is "Islamic Renaissance in South Asia 1707-1867: The Role of Shah Wali Allah and His Successors," by M. A. Ghazi. This book portrays the efforts of the Muslims as part of continuous and sustained struggle. As proper for an Islamic history, the religious leaders and Muslim intellectuals and the struggle for Islam is given primacy, and the kings and traditional historical topics are viewed as secondary adjuncts. Also important is that the defeats of Muslims are treated as local and temporary setbacks to our long term historical goals. Thus these setbacks necessitate reflection and reconsideration of our strategy, rather than being a source for despair and demoralization.

These themes need to be stressed in all Muslim approaches to history. Syed Abul Hasan Ali Nadwi has laid the foundations for this type of work in his "Tareekh-e Dawat Aur Azeemat," showing the struggles of various leading personalities in trying to bring about reform within the Islamic civilization. Muslim Struggles Against Oppression: In addition to the stories of our religious leaders, it is also necessary to show the popular struggles of Muslims for freedom all over the world in the past few centuries. In this dark period, there have been many unsung heroes in our struggle against many oppressive forces. It is sad that our own history textbooks, written in the post-Colonial period, do not present a picture of the worldwide struggle of Muslims against colonialism. Rather they paint the same picture favourable to colonialists of essentially benign and just British rule which replaced despotism and unenlightened rule.

In addition to stories of Muslim heroes (here again a start has been made by a number of biographies of Syed Ahmed Shaheed), we need to have a realistic history of colonialism. The flattering self- portrait of Western Civilization, with a depiction of colonization as a noble effort to spread the benefits of their advanced civilization to primitive peoples, needs to be questioned. There exist a number of realistic histories, which show the enormous amount of racism, cruelty, barbarity, opportunism and exploitation that went into colonialism.

For example, *Global Rift: The Third World Comes of Age* by L. S. Stavrianos gives a good account of the history of colonialism. A Peoples History of the USA by Howard Zinn gives an excellent account of US history, debunking the standard self-serving myths associated with this subject. Numerous other texts of this type are available. Vilification of the West is a rather common theme among certain classes of educated and uneducated Muslims. The psychology of this is to compensate for our own inferiority complex generated by centuries of losses by knocking down the West. This category of analysis (which has superficial resemblance to the texts under discussion here) is based on shallow caricatures of the West, promotes hatred, and generates obstacles to genuine understanding and further dialogue.

Our object would be to achieve a realistic picture of the West, painted with sympathy, accuracy, and understanding. Instead of a one-sided caricature, we would attempt to achieve a three dimensional view, portraying the history of the West as a struggle between forces for good and evil, much like those which occurred in our history. While debunking flattering portrayals of superior civilization of the West, we would avoid demonizing the West as the 'Great Satan,' seeking instead to achieve a realistic and humane understanding of their strengths and weaknesses. Non-Muslim Struggles Against Oppression: Another category of literature and history which needs to be assimilated into the Islamic worldview is the so-called postcolonial literature. This gives an account of the effects of colonialism on the people colonized from the perspective of the colonized.

The psychological consequences of the trauma resulting from colonization are similar across the world. Studying this literature would give deeper insight into our own history, and our reactions to colonization. An excellent example of this genre is Bury My Heart at Wounded Knee, written by an American Indian who gives an excellent account of the cruelty and oppression of the Americans against Red Indian tribes struggling to preserve their culture and way of life. Critical Evaluation of European Dominance: Some important themes need to be stressed as the background within which more detailed studies of the West by Muslim scholars need to be done. The first theme would be the savagery of the West – throughout their history; they have been more or less continuously at war with each other.

Indeed the idea of 'Europe' as a united entity emerges only in reaction to the threat of Islam during the crusades. If this could be contrasted to the (relative) peace which prevailed within the Islamic World, it would serve as an apparent cause of why Western sciences of war progressed much faster than ours. The second theme is the highly racist worldview, which despite efforts; they have never been able to overcome. This theme is rarely treated within European accounts of their own history, perhaps because they are justifiably ashamed of it. Nonetheless it is easily accessible, and plays a very important role in world history. European cultural centers never developed a cosmopolitan culture like those of the numerous centers of Islam.

As a result, they continue to have doubts about whether others of different shapes and colors are fully human. On different occasions, court decisions in England and USA declared Red Indians, Blacks and Australian Aborigines as being less than human. Indeed, it was permissible to hunt them like wild animals. This racism needs to be highlighted because it has had a monumental impact on history. British colonies with majority whites (like USA and Australia) developed along lines parallel to the mother country, while those with different races were brutally exploited and not allowed to develop.

Similarly, the stark developmental differences between the US colonies of Florida, Cuba, and Haiti are likely due to the racist factor. The third important theme is the decline of morality as a consequence of the rejection of Christianity in the West. Again there is a large amount of material available on this issue. On the whole, Western writers are inclined to view this process favourably and paint it in terms of liberation from restrictive ways of thinking based on (Christian) superstition. However, there are some who see that general immorality, breakup of families, teenage pregnancy, drugs and violence are all consequences of this process. The De-Moralization of Society, Humanity: a moral history of the Twentieth Century, and A Distant Mirror as well as many others. Most of the necessary material for an Islamic view is readily available; however it does need to be re-written from an Islamic perspective.

Conflict of Science and Religion in West

How should we fit in advances in science and technology into the general picture? This is a most important topic, on which it is necessary for us to depart substantially from Western views. Western views on the importance and relevance of science are deeply affected by the origins of science in conflict with Christianity, as illustrated by Galileo for example. Some contemporary elementary Western textbooks state that men invented religion to explain the occurrence of natural phenomena (like rainfall, thunder, etc.). With the development of science, factual knowledge replaced the religious superstitions.

This account ignores the fact that religion is concerned mainly with the moral domain – an area about which science is and must be silent. Due to the fact that science and religion are concerned with different domains (the positive and the normative, respectively) with little overlap, there is no natural conflict between them. Special circumstances in West, detailed by Catholic historian Hans Kung in "Does God Exist?" led to conflict, avoidance of which would have been beneficial to both parties according to Kung. Since science emerged as the victor of this conflict, the scientific outlook blended with its anti-religious bias permeates all Western education and thinking. This is of great importance and relevance to those of us seeking to benefit from Western developments within an Islamic framework. The full significance of this cannot be spelled out in detail here.

Loss of Faith in West

It is critical to realize that the loss of faith in the West was a consequence of the moral bankruptcy of the upper echelon of the Catholic Church. The crisis caused by openly flaunted moral corruption of a sequence of Popes (which involved living extremely luxuriously, legitimizing bastard progeny, selling pardons for sins to raise money for supporting lavish lifestyles, etc.) has been termed 'the most momentous event in the history of Europe.' This directly led to the rise of the Protestants, who attempted to preserve their faith while breaking from the corrupt Catholic Church. The other reaction, complete rejection of faith, eventually prevailed. This loss of faith, termed 'death of God' by Nietzsche, has been immensely consequential.

It has led to a glorification of science and scientific knowledge (as a replacement for religious knowledge). Since morality is outside the realm of science, morality was gradually expunged from scientific knowledge. The loss of faith led to the emergence of positivism, the philosophy that only what can be observed by the senses exists, as the dominant philosophy of the twentieth century. It also led to the emergence of a determinist point of view, which suggests that the world is organized like a machine and runs purely according to deterministic laws. Denying the tremendous capabilities for change in human beings leads to a mechanical social science which is not alive to the possibilities of change. From the Islamic point of view, (Lqd Khalaqnal Insana fi Ahsan-e Taqwim) human beings have tremendous potential.

The purpose of our existence is to achieve this potential to rise higher than the angels. This emphasis on humans and transformation of human beings (which was the great task accomplished by our Prophet s.a.w.) is central to the message of Islam. Causes of Muslim Decline (Western Explanations): For over a century, affluence and power have been concentrated in the West, while Muslim countries have been afflicted with poverty and powerlessness. Discovering the cause of this historical pattern is a problem of central importance, since remedies depend crucially on the diagnosis. Western thinkers have offered their own explanations for this pattern.

The once widely accepted racist explanation (that whites are intrinsically superior to non-whites) has been more or less discarded; nonetheless, it continues to play an important role in the undercurrents of modern thought, and continues to be advocated by a small but significant minority (for instance The

Bell Curve by Herrnstein and Murray). More sophisticated western explanations revolve around the 'three revolutions' in Europe: The revolt against God (already discussed), the revolt against Kings (epitomized by the French Revolution) which led to the emergence of democracy, and the Industrial revolution or the triumph of machines against nature.

Intelligentsia in Muslim countries who accept these western explanations would be forced to advocate democracy, development of science and technology, and the renunciation of religion as the only path to progress. In fact there is small but vocal minority which advocates the first two steps very strongly and the third step in a soft-spoken way to avoid difficulties with the Muslim populace which remains deeply committed to Islam throughout the Muslim World. Eastern Explanations: Every political leader (as well as every significant intellectual) in the East has had to take a stand on the causes of Muslim decline – the course of action and the goals to be advocated and struggled for depend directly on this diagnosis. Ataturk thought that the European culture was the source of European superiority. He therefore passed laws enforcing adoption of European dress and introduced theaters and dancing into Turkey.

Romanization of the Turkish script effectively cut off the Turkish people from their historical roots. Widespread translation of European novels and secular indoctrination in compulsory government schools has led to a deeply divided society. The conflicting values of Islam and the imposed European ones have led to social problems of tremendous magnitude in Turkey. In the case of British India, the British aristocracy felt that their superiority lay in the liberal and classical education they received. Sir Syed Ahmed Khan accepted this diagnosis and advocated a liberal British style education for Muslims as a cure for the ills of the Ummah. The scorn of the aristocracy for the working classes was reflected in the rejection of engineering and mechnical education in the original syllabus at Aligarh.

It is worth noting that around the same time the Turks were learning to dance and translating European novels, Japanese students were studying Engineering and Mathematics, and translating all technical, scientific and mathematical literature in English into Japanese. Since both started at ground zero, their current position is a good way to evaluate the relative effectiveness of their strategies. Islamic Explanations: An Islamic worldview must reject purely materialistic explanations of Western dominance. Even if science and technology are the apparent cause of Western superiority, we must ask why Allah T'aala chose to give the West this knowledge and did not choose this for the Ummat. The example of the Battle of Hunain shows that Allah T'aala punished Muslims by an initial defeat when they looked towards superior numbers as a guarantee of victory.

This is a clear lesson that attention to material causes without looking at the underlying cause - namely whether or not the help of Allah is with us - is a source of the displeasure of Allah T'aala. All explanations compatible with an Islamic worldview require us to look at the condition of Ummah and ask what are the most significant failings which have caused us to lose the help of Allah. In fact there are a large number of explanations which are compatible with an Islamic worldview and the issue is one which is deeply divisive among Muslims. Indeed, groups adhering to one Islamic explanation have sometimes considered other groups to be outside the pale of Islam.

The main categories of explanations are the following - each has many variants, which we need not detail here:

1. It is a religious imperative for Muslims to re-establish the Khilafah, failing which the help of Allah will not be with us.
2. It is a religious imperative for Muslims to establish the Kingdom of God on Earth (that is, create an Islamic state with the rule of Shariah).
3. It is a religious imperative for Muslims to invite all

mankind to Islam; failure of the Ummah in performing its collective responsibility has led to the current state of affairs.

4. The spread of Bid'ah and the abandonment of pure Islam has led to widespread shirk of the hidden as well as the apparent variety. This coupled with abandonment of Jihad is responsible for the sorry state of affairs of the Muslims.
5. Closing of the gates of Ijtihad by the Ulema, and their resistance and opposition to adoption of modern ideas led to stagnation and decline of the Ummah. In particular, we need to acquire science and technology of the West to progress.

For the purposes of developing an Islamic worldview, it is not necessary to take a stand on which of the above (or a number of other variant views not mentioned above) is the correct explanation for the Muslim decline. It is sufficient to realize that all Muslims agree that it is the failure of Muslims to adhere to Islam that is the root cause of Muslim decline. Also, all Muslims agree that Bid'a should be eliminated, Dawah is necessary, Jihad is farz, and establishment of Khilafat and enforcement of Shariat are essential goals. Disagreements exist as to the correct strategy and the sequencing in which we should approach these goals. Allah T'aala loves unity among the believers and disunity will cause us to lose the help of Allah.

The project of establishing the Islamic worldview as a viable competing alternative to the existing European materialistic and atheistic worldview is a large project which requires the co-operation of all Muslims. Our enemies and Shaitan have successfully exploited differences among Muslims to our disadvantage. We should concentrate on the areas of agreement (which are very large) and do not allow our hearts to be clouded against fellow Muslims for minor disagreements (which Shaitan magnifies and presents to us as very large). This will be essential for the purpose of developing a united alternative worldview to the prevailing dominant Western one.

Science and Technology

The biggest obstacle to developing a Muslim worldview is not the Western challenge, but the Muslims who have been affected by Western views. Muslims agree that renouncing religion is not needed, but most feel that we do need science and technology, as well as democracy to progress and reach Western levels of development. However, when we look at the training that our Prophet (s.a.w.) provided to the companions, we find that it was entirely spiritual and religious. This training enabled the companions to conquer two technologically advanced empires within thirty years.

Armed with materialist preconceptions, one might think that such conquests would require introduction of new weaponry, battle tactics, or at least an industrial and economic base, but we do not find any such material cause within the training of the companions. Examination of this and other episodes in Muslim history, as well as the corpus of religious knowledge, strongly suggest that if Muslims turn their attention to those A'amal which will attract the pleasure of Allah s.w.t., they will be rewarded by worldly benefits such as the science and technology or other causes of conquest. Since this line of reasoning goes strongly against the prevailing wisdom in the Muslim world, let us add an alternative way of reaching the same conclusion.

Consider the recent defeats in Afghanistan and Iraq. Some have considered it as a conclusive proof of the necessity of acquiring technology. Yet it seems abundantly clear that had the Muslims presented a united front, all of the technological dominance of USA would have been insufficient to achieve their victory. Thus instead of taking these events as proving the importance of technology, we can equally well take them to be proof of the need for unity among the Muslims. That disunity leads to loss is supported by the Quran and can form part of an Islamic worldview.

An Islamic worldview must give primacy to spiritual and moral factors over material ones. It is easily possible to trace

Muslim decline to decline in morals among Muslims. Similarly, moral factors such as concern for the poor can be traced as the source of the ascendance of the Europeans. Such analyses would be useful to develop within the perspective of an Islamic worldview. The issue of the relative priority of science and technology in a program of reform for the Islamic world is too complex to discuss in detail here. It will be treated in a separate paper dealing with priorities for Muslim education.

It should be obvious that this is a vast project, but one which is essential for the Ummah. Within the broad framework sketched above, there is room for substantial variations and even conflicts, just as within the Western worldview there is room for many competing and hostile ideologies (like Communism and Capitalism). The unity of the Islamic worldview lays giving primacy to Allah as the cause of all causes, and of giving moral and spiritual aspect a central position, and only secondary importance to material and physical aspects. Because a coherent worldview of this type has not yet been developed, Muslim children read texts which indoctrinate them into the European worldview. This can lead to loss of faith at worst, and many conflicting and contradictory notions at best. It is essential to infuse and Islamic worldview into an Islamic education.

To put matters in terms of an action plan, here is what we recommend: One of the biggest obstacles to developing an Islamic Worldview is the desire of Muslim intellectual to ensure that the West is included among the audience for their views. There is no doubt that there is a dynamic, strong and living intellectual tradition in the West. Currently, this is the touchstone for Muslim intellectuals. If a piece of writing is publishable in a Western Journal, then it is of high quality. If it is not, then it is of dubious quality. There is some merit to this point of view – Western journals have rigorous refereeing standards and garbage typically does not get by the refereeing process (although there are exceptions).

On the other hand, Eastern journals typically lack such

standards and therefore publications are of extremely uneven quality. Nonetheless, the only way forward is to develop our own media and discourse. It is impossible to develop a genuinely Islamic Worldview which has the approval of the West. We must learn to have faith in our own traditions and continue the deep and sophisticated dialogue and reflections initiated by our prominent but currently neglected intellectuals like Ibn-e- Khaldun, Ghazali, Shah Waliullah, as well as several more recent figures who have continued the work in these traditions while incorporating Western insights.

One of the most important objectives of Islam is to enable its followers to live an enlightened life. The *Quran* does not hide its preference for those who possess knowledge and those, whose faith is tempered by reason. Muslims correctly value those who have knowledge and *Ulema* have for centuries determined how Muslims understand Islam and the world. But over time Muslims have mistakenly began equating knowledge with a narrowly defined conception of religious knowledge, and scholars with again narrowly defined conception of scholarship. Thus ironically as the frontiers of knowledge expanded and human understanding of things and the scope of sciences expanded, – sometimes astronomically – the Muslim vision of what is knowledge and who is knowledgeable shrunk.

There is no doubt in my mind that the diminishing Muslim vision of knowledge and the knowledgeable is singularly responsible for the decline of creativity, dynamism, vitality and power of the Islamic civilization. Today, without doubt, the Muslim world lags behind all other civilizations in its production and consumption of knowledge. Today, most Muslims think of knowledge as limited to the familiarity with medieval Muslim understanding of law and jurispru-dence. Scholars are only those who "memorize" Quran and the traditions and are familiar with pedagogical and epistemological tools developed a thousand years ago. It is therefore not surprising that under the intellectual leadership of this class of scholars the *Ummah* has gone from one low to another lower low.

One area of knowledge that has been deeply neglected by Muslims is the arena of social sciences. Except for the Islamization of Knowledge project and the *American Journal of Islamic Social Sciences,* both initiatives launched by American Muslims in early 1980s, there has been very little attempt by Muslims to indegenize social sciences. Social sciences, unlike Islamic sciences, which are essentially normative paradigms, have an empirical focus. Social sciences are more interested in understanding and describing the world as it is rather than on postulating on how it ought to be.

Without being prejudicial about what is more important, we must realize that while medieval Islamic sciences do provide a view of how the world ought to be a thousand years ago they do not equip our jurist-scholars with the training and tools necessary to understand the world as it is. *Ulema's* discourses on how the world ought to be become meaningless and therefore ineffective because they are not grounded in contemporary realities. Very simply, if you do not understand where you are, even if you know where you have to go, you will go no where. Hence you need social sciences to understand where you are and put religious knowledge of where to go to effective use. To put it bluntly, without social sciences, traditional Islamic sciences are useless.

Role of Social Scientists

The most important function that social scientists can perform is providing our leaders and the attentive public with an empirical understanding of our existential conditions. Without an accurate analysis of where we are effective remedial policies cannot be articulated. Social scientists provide the in depth analysis necessary for informed decision making. The Quran in a beautiful passage praises those who reflect on the empirical realities of our world – contemplate the creation – in *Surah Al Imran*:

Verily in the creation of the heavens and the earth,

and the alternation of night and day - there are indeed signs

for men of understanding; Men who remember Allah,

standing, sitting, and lying down on their sides,

and contemplate the creation

of the heavens and the earth [Quran 3:190-191]

Some countries such as Japan, India and China have developed indegenized social scientists who use advanced analytical and research skills in the interest of their nations and provide the necessary information to make effective policy. The progress and growth and development of these nations are indicative of the success of their social scientists. The Muslim world, which often looks to "the *Ulema*" to ask all questions such as is it *halal* to eat gummy bears or if one can one marry two sisters simultaneously, and is it ok to join the WTO and is democracy a good idea, remains strikingly underdeveloped. While the *Ulema* are "trained" to answer the first two questions, contemporary reality is outside their domain. The success of non-Muslims and the failure of Muslims in worldly matters can be explained only through the knowledge deficit that plagues the Muslim community. The Quran once again is so clear on this issue:

Allah will raise up to (suitable) ranks (and degrees) those of you who believe and who have been granted knowledge. [Quran 58:11]

While comment on the faith of anyone can be understand that Allah has raised the West and the Far East to great heights and honor purely because of their commitment to freedom of thought and knowledge. The best universities and the most productive work in knowledge accumulation is taking place in the West and the Far East. Actually everywhere except in the Muslim World. Social scientists must not only be consulted but also encouraged to research, speak and write freely on the most important and pressing issues such as external and internal security, geopolitics, globalization, inter-faith politics, economics, social and public policy and short and long term planning. Other issues that they can enrich are normative discussions based on empirical experience of institutions and polities that are best suited for our times. Social sciences are now very diverse, very complex and very advanced. They deal with issues all across the board and their findings impact policy at all levels.

The *Ummah* today does not need *Ulema* who are incapable of knowing the world we live in, but rather social scientist that are also familiar with the *maqasid al Shariah* — the divine way – to help develop and govern our societies efficiently and effectively.

Islamic sciences that were developed - remember they were developed by human beings not revealed by God - were quite advanced for their time and help vitalize the Islamic world and make it a dominant and thriving civilization. However they have enjoyed little development in over a thousand years. In Islamic Madrassahs syllabi have not been revised in over 200 years! All good social scientists revise their curriculum every time they teach their courses. While Islamic sciences have languished, social sciences have advanced. While the former remains a dead tradition the latter is alive and growing. Social sciences have also added Islamic studies to their realm and have developed a more nuanced, more sophisticated and even empowering vision of Islam by critiquing and building upon traditional Islamic sciences.

Today it is easy to find Muslim social and humanities scholars who are also trained in traditions methods, who now empowered by new epistemologies and are doing wonderful research that if the *Ummah* were to embrace would resuscitate the community. Today the knowledge to revive and develop the Islamic Ummah is available. It is time the community recognizes that for centuries we have failed to become leaders of humanity and fulfill our mandate as Allah's vicegerents on earth (Quran 2:30) is because we have surrendered our vision, our faith and our reason to deadwood. Power is a function of knowledge.

Say: Are those equal, those who know and those who do not know? [Quran 39:9]

The *Ummah* is powerless because those who they consider as knowledgeable have failed for over 500 years to provide us with an empowering vision. American Muslims now live in times where the basic objectives and even values of the community are questioned. It is time American Muslim social scientists stepped up to the plate and addressed some of these issues. The community needs new vision and new direction. In academic journals and conferences Muslim social scientists have provided sophisticated analysis of our condition and also enlightening pathways for a better and more secure future for all. It is now up to the community leaders to connect the output of these scholars with the direction of the community. Scholars by nature are isolationists. They need seclusion to think research and write. It is not fair to expect them to come forward, some do like yours truly, but the community must also seek them and seek their guidance. The future belongs to those who have thought the deepest about it.

7

Conservative and Liberal Islamic Views of Science

Creationism is too often thought of as a conservative Christian preoccupation. In the United States, young-earth creationists insist that the universe and all life were created in six days about six thousand years ago. There is also the newer intelligent design movement, which is a potent source of pressure on science education. Christian-flavored antievolutionary thought has a worldwide constituency, surfacing in Canada, Britain, Australia, Africa, Russia, and elsewhere. Still, attempts to promote "creation science" and intelligent design as alternatives to mainstream science seem especially strong in the United States. Muslim populations, however, provide a counterexample to this picture.

Indeed, Islam has been the world religion that has proved most resistant to Darwinian evolution. Creationist distortions of science enjoy considerable support among modern Muslims. Among devout Muslim intellectuals, antievolutionary views are not fringe ideas but mainstream options. And Islamic versions of creationism have enjoyed official support to a degree that is the envy of American creationists. In many ways, the world's most successful creationists are those who rise up to defend Islam, not Christianity. Muslim thinkers first encountered evolution in the late nineteenth century, in the context of efforts to import Western knowledge. For example,

7

Conservative and Liberal Islamic Views of Science

Creationism, we often think, is a conservative Christian preoccupation. In the United States, young-earth creationists insist that the universe and all life were created in six days about six thousand years ago. There is also the newer intelligent design movement, which is a potent source of pressure on science education. Christian-flavored anti-evolu-tionary thought has a worldwide constituency, surfacing in Canada, Britain, Poland, Australia, Africa, Russia, and elsewhere. Still, attempts to promote "creation-science" and intelligent design as alternatives to mainstream science seem especially strong in the United States. Muslim populations, however, provide a counterexample to this picture.

Indeed, Islam has been the world religion that has proved most resistant to Darwinian evolution. Creationist distortions of science enjoy considerable support among modern Muslims. Among devout Muslim intellectuals, antievolutionary views are not fringe ideas but mainstream options. And Islamic versions of creationism have enjoyed official support to a degree that is the envy of American creationists. In many ways, the world's most successful creationists are those who rise up to defend Islam, not Christianity. Muslim thinkers first encountered evolution in the late nineteenth century, in the context of efforts to import Western knowledge. For example, both Arabs and Turks in the decaying Ottoman Empire looked toward Europe for the latest and the best of modern science, and when Darwinian ideas attracted attention, evolution became a matter for debate among Muslims.

A handful of intellectuals embraced evolution wholeheartedly. These, however, belonged to a very small, secularist, radically Western-oriented minority. Indeed, such intellectuals did not care much about biology; they took Darwinian ideas to be part of nineteenth-century materialism and celebrated evolution as a prime example of how science could overcome ossified religious ways of thinking. Most Muslim thinkers were more cautious. While positive toward technology and other forms of useful knowledge, they were also deeply concerned about limiting European influence on their local cultures.

Encountering Darwinian ideas as part of a materialist critique of supernatural beliefs, devout Muslims rejected evolution as an impious philosophy. Traditional religious scholars did not need to learn much to denounce the "Darwin hypothesis," but more reform-minded intellectuals also responded negatively. For example, Jamal al-Din al-Afghani, one of the leading figures in early Islamic modernism, had nothing but praise for science, and using European science to revive Islamic intellectual life was an important theme in his proposals for reform in Muslim lands. Nevertheless, he attacked evolution as an absurdity that was unacceptable to Muslims. So the initial reaction to Darwinian evolution among Muslim thinkers did not go further than a superficial response, whether in the form of enthusiasm among the very few or more widespread rejection.

Evolution did not penetrate into popular consciousness. And even those devout intellectuals who felt a need for a more modern apologetic for traditional beliefs rarely paid evolution much attention. Said Nursi, the most important religious thinker in early twentieth-century Turkey, was typical in this regard. Throughout his career, Nursi tried to develop a modern but orthodox Muslim response to Western intellectual influences, including Western science. Writing on what he saw as the materialist mistakes incorporated into science, Nursi included denunciations of evolutionary thinking. But his attacks on evolution never went into any great depth; he was more preoccupied with classical Muslim philosophical themes such as showing how natural causality was a deeply flawed concept.

Until recently, Muslim discomfort with evolution rarely went beyond assertions of incompatibility between Darwinian biology and traditional Islam. Muslim countries became exposed to secular political ideas and harbored westernizing intellectuals, but scientific matters such as evolution did not take center stage in heated debates about achieving culturally authentic forms of modernity. Public science education tended to focus on physical and applied science. And since evolution did not become a major theme in education, it did not provoke a conservative reaction.

With limited penetration of Darwinian ideas, there was no constituency for a creationist movement that went beyond religious affirmations of special creation and distrust of ideas with materialist connotations. In particular, conservative Muslims felt no need for a creationist pseudoscience proclaiming that science, when done properly, supported traditional beliefs about nature and its creator. This picture of somewhat passive resistance to evolution has, however, been changing.

In conditions where conservative Muslims have been strongly challenged by local westernizers or otherwise been exposed to modern scientific views of nature in public education, low-key resistance to evolution has had an opportunity to develop into affirmations of creationist pseudoscience. The example of Turkey is most illuminating, as Turkey has been the most Western-oriented among Muslim countries, and has recently taken the lead in Islamic creationism. The Turkish Revolution of the 1920s and 1930s established official secularism, removed overt religious influences on education, and inserted evolution into the curriculum.

This did not immediately lead to creationist activity; in any case, the Turkish state exerted much control over cultural life. Popular resistance to state-imposed secularization included distrust of evolution, but evolution remained a relatively small offense against religion in an educational system that promoted privatization of religious sentiment. Until recent decades, Turkey presented a picture of grudging but gradual secularization. There was little creationist literature of note, and anti-evolutionary activity was confined to the subculture of a strictly observant, self-consciously orthodox minority. Some popular religious movements explicitly opposed evolution; the most significant was the Nur movement inspired by the writings of Said Nursi.

In keeping with their modernizing, pro-technology outlook, adherents of the Nur movement were attracted to claims that modern science affirmed traditional Muslim beliefs. Evolution remained unacceptable, and literature inspired by the Nur movement regularly charged evolution with being nonscientific as well as offensive to true religion. Little of this, however, drew attention from the secular elites who dominated most public culture. In the 1970s, political Islam started to gain strength in Turkey as well as the rest of the Muslim world. Evolution became a minor culture war item, as a way for Islamists to demonstrate opposition to secular life without taking the risk of naming official secularism as a target. But creationism came into its own only in the mid 1980s, when in the aftermath of a short period of military dictatorship, religious conservatives gained control of the Turkish Ministry of Education.

These conservative Muslims thought evolutionary ideas were morally corrosive, yet they found themselves in an environment where science commanded significant cognitive authority. So they needed a way to suggest that evolution was a fraudulent, scientifically dubious idea. They found the resources they needed in American "scientific creationism," and invoked Christian creationists in a curious mirror image of the way Turkish secularists regularly relied on Western scientific authorities. While the Muslims downplayed some features of popular American creationism such as a young earth and flood geology, they adopted the bulk of the anti-evolutionary debating points developed by their Christian counterparts.

Indeed, the Ministry of Education had many instances of creation-science literature officially translated and made available to high school teachers and libraries. Since this mid-80s breakthrough, Turkish textbooks have often contained anti-Darwinian or explicitly creationist material. The creationist paragraphs have disappeared in the infrequent occasions when secularist parties have shared power and reappeared when Islamists returned to government. At present a moderate Islamist party sympathetic to creationist views holds power. This party won another overwhelming electoral victory in 2007, and so it looks like conservative Muslim concerns will continue to influence Turkish science and education policy for the foreseeable future.

The constituency for creationism is not traditionalists but modern people, even though creationists typically affirm conservative doctrines and traditional beliefs. It is precisely because many devout Muslims want to take their place in the modern world, where mastering technology is the key to success, that creationists fashion a pseudoscience that promises to harmonize science and their religious convictions. For example, the ever-popular Nur movement has been and continues to be instrumental in the develop-ment of Islamic creationism in Turkey. And social scientists have emphasized the modern character of the Nur movement. Such movements are especially notable for their enthusiasm for technology and embrace of capitalism. Nur adherents do not depart far from traditional doctrines, but their leadership structure and modes of religious partici-pation are decidedly non-traditional.

Due in part to the worldly success and influence of Nur and similar movements, many anti-evolutionary leaders and intellectuals are professionals; some are even academics. This, in fact, is an important difference between Islamic and Christian creationism. In Turkey and in other Muslim countries, anti-evolutionary views find plenty of elite support, including among academic theologians and scientists. In North America and Europe, the more sophisticated intelligent design variety of creationism exists on the fringes of intellectual life.

In the Muslim world, ideas similar to intelligent design tend to be respectable intellectual options. Indeed, intelligent design itself has begun to attract attention in Turkey. Many intelligent design books have been translated, and in 2007 the local government of Istanbul sponsored public meetings promoting intelligent design. The last 10 years has seen a deepening of the popular appeal of Turkish creationism. Moreover, Turkish creationism has attained an international influence. The central figure in this development is Harun Yahya, a pseudonym that serves as a brand name for an ubiquitous, well-funded, and media-intensive form of creationism. In content, there is nothing new in the Yahya material: scientifically negligible arguments and outright distortions often copied from Christian anti-evolution literature, presented with a conservative Muslim emphasis.

The range and production quality of this material, however, is impressive. Large numbers of glossy books, magazines, videos, Web sites, and public events make Yahya's simple, intuitively appealing creationism available to a large public. None of this material focuses on a conservative Muslim subculture; from its presentation style to its use of everyday language, Yahya material is designed to be marketed to ordinary, modern Muslims who need not be attracted to strictly observant varieties of Islam. Furthermore, Yahya material is artificially cheap, and is often distributed free of cost. Clearly the Yahya enterprise has considerable financial backing, though the source of these funds remains unknown.

Turkish scientists have tried to counter such popular creationism, but in the public arena, the creationists have clearly won the day. Building on their success in Turkey, the Yahya brand of creationists has more recently gone global. Today, Yahya publications are available in languages spoken by Muslim populations all over the world. Yahya books are prominently displayed in Islamic bookstores in London, used in classrooms in Pakistan, promoted by speaking tours in Indonesia. Very recently, as a publicity stunt, the Yahya organization mailed copies of a volume of a typically lavishly produced encyclopedia called *Atlas of Creation* to scientists and educators in Europe and North America, drawing media attention outside of Muslim circles.

We now have a global variety of Islamic creationism that goes beyond long-standing Muslim resistance to a Darwinian conception of life. Many modern Muslims are attracted to claims that Darwinian evolution is scientifically false, and that science, properly done, supports Quranic notions of special creation. Muslims hold a variety of views on evolution; Yahya-style creationists do not speak for all. Some Muslim thinkers accept evolution in the sense of descent with modification, provided that this evolution is explicitly divinely guided.

Even such comparative liberals, however, almost always reject the Darwinian, naturalistic view of evolution that is current in natural science. Human evolution meets with particularly strong rejection. Indeed, it is safe to say that most committed Muslims take naturalistic evolution to be religiously unacceptable. Most would consider the evolution of complex life forms through natural mechanisms alone, without the visible direction of a divine intelligence, to be an intellectual absurdity. The Harun Yahya material has no scholarly standing whatsoever. But more sophisticated anti-evolution views have wide currency among serious Muslim intellectuals, including very well-known Western-based scholars of Islam such as Seyyed Hossein Nasr.

Moreover, in the Muslim world, defenders of Darwinian

evolution suffer from an extra handicap due to their association with political secularism. Especially in the last few decades, secularism has been increasingly discredited as an alien cultural imposition, a tool of despotic regimes, and the ideology of westernized elites who have lost touch with the pious bulk of Muslim populations. In European history, the development of popular democracy included an anticlerical element, so that developments favoring science, secularism and democracy have often reinforced one another. In Muslim populations, however, anti-evolution sentiments usually belong to political moderates and democratic forces more than to stereotypical militants.

Indeed, the recent trend has been that in Muslim lands, more democracy has meant increased religious populism, less political secularism, and a tension between democracy and elite institutions such as science. We should expect that creationism will continue to enjoy a strong following in Muslim populations. The prospects for a Western-style accommodation between science and religion, where each have their separate cultural spheres, are doubtful. Culturally and politically, conservative interpretations of Islam are very strong, and conservative Muslims see little reason to back off from their ideal of religion at least distantly regulating all aspects of life. The notion that revelation must condition how we understand the world remains a dominant, though not exclusive, theme in Muslim intellectual life.

All this may change, as this is a time of experimentation and rapid religious change for Muslims. Political Islam, for example, may yet fail, especially in its promise to make Muslims equal players in the realm of technology-driven development. Conservative failure could create more space for theologically more liberal versions of Islam and for the autonomy of science. But at least in the short term, the Islamic world will continue to harbor very serious tensions between science and religion.

Several things began to come together in my thinking at the MLT Conference in Copenhagen. To be clear, it was not a result of the planning of the MLT, but a series of amorphous thoughts that started to click from meeting people at the conference. With the Progressive Faith Blog Con coming straight after, these ideas began gaining more clarity. Coincidentally, both the good folks at Progressive Islam and Von Aurum published pieces that further moved my thoughts forward. I had been planning on this post for some time, but as the adage goes "Man proposes, God disposes." After this rather long preamble, I'd like to explain to you why am a conservative-liberal Muslim (not progressive, as the correct antonym should be reactionary; and in my world view Islam by definition is progressive, it's just how we implement that message), and why I hope never have to use that label again.

At the beginning of the MLT, we were asked to describe ourselves as liberal or conservative based on how other people saw us. Most people when referencing others spoke of non-Muslims. I choose to reference other Muslims and their perception of me. As a Shi'ah, I said that most Muslims would automatically consider me liberal, to the extent that I would be considered heretical. There is the pernicious use of language that talks about Islam and Shi'ah Islam (or Muslims and Shi'ah Muslims), relegating the Shi'ah to not being true Muslims; making us aberrations to the true understanding of Islam. This approach was readily apparent in the panel on Pluralism, where individuals said they were Muslim when asked to describe what type of Muslim they were.

By simply stating "Muslim," the power relationship of majority Sunni interpretations is normalized and the Shi'ah are marginalized. Those who argue against unequal power relationships when it applies to their disempowered status are more than happy to exercise the same unequal power when they are in power. Even if the use of "Muslim" was more innocent, to indicate difference doesn't matter in this setting, I would argue that it helps the homogenizing influence of the Cult of Abd al-Wahhab, which wants sameness at all costs. In a panel on pluralism, difference should be acknowledged. In general, I think we as Muslims do not do enough to acknowledge difference. I'm suggesting it should be all we talk about, but it has to be stated.

We'll agree on 90% of everything related to the faith, but we need to know about the 10% as well. Our definitions are simple: if you accept that Hazrat Ali was the designated religious leader after Prophet Muhammad, you are Shi'ah. If you don't, you are Sunni. Not tough. The reality is that conservative has become a polite why of saying fundamentalist, or to indicate a degree of fundamentalism. There are of course real concerns with using the term fundamentalist to refer to Muslims. By that logic, and it is one I subscribe to, I am a fundamentalist/conservative. I believe that our common source text, the Quran, is our *raison d'être*. However, I do not believe that the text involves sameness. It is the word of God, and just as God is unknowable in His totality, so too is His word.

If all the trees of the earth were pens
And the oceans ink,
With many more oceans fro replenishing them,
The words of God could never be written.
Truly he is all-mighty and all-wise. (31:27)
He [God] has sent down this Book which contains
some verses that are categorical and basic to the Book,
and others allegorical.

But those who are twisted of mind look for [the] metaphorical verses,

to give them their own interpretation and deviate [from the truth.]

No one knows their meaning except God
and those firmly grounded in knowledge.

They attest "We believe in them as all of them are from the Lord."

Only those with wisdom understand. (3:7)
[Adapted from Ahmed Ali's translations.]

That level of knowledge is incomprehensible to us, and so the human endeavor is to make it comprehensible. In turn, that leads to the diversities in interpretations that we see in the Islamic tradition. Because of that lack of sameness, to be a conservative in respecting the text, does not mean that there is a conservative attitude in what I understand the text to mean. I am a believer that all the Abrahamic faiths are inherently progressive. The political idea of liberal and conservative is that they are ends of a spectrum in a particular system, and they are, in some capacity, interested in maintaining the system.

A progressive ideology is one that sees what could be better, and tries to make it so, even if it means upsetting the system. Its opposite, the reactionary ideology, wishes to prevent change in the system, fossilizing it at a particular moment, a move that is equally upsetting to a balanced, dynamic functioning system. Using these definitions, the Abrahamic revelations, and communities of followers, are all progressive. Judaism institutionalized the idea of radical monotheism; an idea so revolutionary that even 500 years after its introduction, an Egyptian pharaoh could still not introduce the idea to his people. Christianity brought us the radical idea of Love as an article and practice of faith. The Prophet Jesus spoke not only of the law, but of justice and temperament and humanity.

Prophet Muhammad was given a revelation that spoke briefly of law, but gave us the idea of a radical equality amongst people. From this perspective, I do not believe that the appellation of "progressive" is necessary; in fact, I think to use it is to cede power to the reactionary forces in our traditions that are becoming normative. Unfortunately, what is happening now is that the idea of political progressivism is being read back into faith discussions, so that politically progressive ideas are being forced onto faith communities to show that they are modern. As a result, particularly in the Islamic tradition, progressive Islam has come to mean leaving the text behind, or coming to a conclusion as to what "Islam" says and creating a forced reading of the text.

In this respect, progressive Muslims are similar to the cults of Bin Laden and Abd al-Wahhab; they are willing to leave behind the traditions of Islam to achieve their ends. Islam has existed for over 1400 years changing and adapting, and we have had our radical departures from tradition (think of the Mihna, or even Ghazali's appropriations of Fatimid thought for Sufi Sunni thinking), but these events have all engaged with the past. What the "progressives" and the cultists are doing now is breaking with the past and creating a new framework what is modeled on personal desires rather than intellectual vigor.

To me, both are contributing to the decline of Muslim thought, and thus to the decline of Muslim societies. In many respects the "progressives" are as reactionary as the cultists when it comes to dealing with modernity. Rather than reading progressivism into the text, we need to read it out of the text. With a document as revolutionary as the Quran, it should not be difficult. Although the dominant movement in Islam in recent times has been religious fundamentalism, there are a number of liberal movements within Islam which seek alternative ways to reconcile the Islamic faith with the modern world.

Islamic traditions have several sources: the Quran, the hadiths, and interpretations of both by scholars. Over the centuries, there has been a tendency towards funda-mentalism, with interpretations being regarded as immu-table, even those that consist of folk religion not directly traceable to the prophet Muhammad. Early shariah had a much more flexible character than is currently associated with Islamic jurisprudence, and many modern Muslim scholars believe that it should be renewed, and the classical jurists should lose their special status. This would require formulating a new fiqh suitable for the modern world, e.g. as proposed by advocates of the Islamization of knowledge, and would deal with the modern context.

This movement does not aim to challenge the funda-mentals of Islam; rather, it seeks to clear away misinterpretations and to free the way for the renewal of the previous status of the Islamic world as a center of modern thought and freedom. The claim that only liberalisation of the Islamic Shariah law can lead to distinguishing between tradition and Islam is countered by many Muslims by saying that 'fundamentalism' rejects the cultural inventions e.g. they will accept that men and women have God given rights and duties that no human can infringe on but it rejects riba (interest). Fundamentalism as referred to often means traditionalism which is a separate issue. A good example of a fundamentalist organisation is Hizb ut-Tahrir Hizb ut-Tahrir Web Site.

Liberal Movements within Islam

In modern times there have been a number of liberal movements within Islam (or 'interpretation-based Islam', also 'Progressive Islam'). These generally denote religious outlooks which depend mainly on ijtihad or re-inter-pretations of scriptures. Liberal Muslims interpret the Quran and Hadith from their personal perspective rather than the medievalist traditional Muslim point of view. Liberals generally claim that they are returning to the principals of the early Muslim community, arguing that the Medievalists have diverged from true Islam through their focus on the literal word rather than the ethical intent of scripture.

It should be noted that these are movements within Islam, rather than an attempt at schism. As such, they believe in the basic tenets of Islam, such as the Six Elements of Belief and the Five Pillars of Islam. They consider their views to be fully compatible with the teachings of Islam. Their main difference with more conservative Islamic opinion is in differences of interpretation of how to apply the core Islamic values to modern life.

Contemporary and Controversial Issues

Over the course of the 19th and 20th centuries, liberal Muslims have tended to reinterpret and reapply many aspects of their religion in accordance with their increasingly modern societies and outlooks on one hand and re-examining their traditions. This is particularly true of Muslims who now find themselves living in non-Muslim countries. Such people may describe themselves variously as liberal, progressive or reformist; but rather than implying a specific agenda, these terms tend to incorporate a broad spectrum of views which contest medievalist and traditional interpretations of Islam in many different ways.

Although there is no full consensus amongst liberal Muslims on their views, they tend to agree on some or all of the following beliefs:

- Most liberal Muslims oppose slavery and the associated practice of concubinage, or extra-marital sex between a man and his female slaves. This was not abolished during the time of Muhammad and is permitted in the Quran (although Islamic apologetics claim that the Quran does discourage slavery to and encourages its elimination, which was in it a progressive attitude at the time). In fact, liberals see this point as a notable example of how religion inevitably changes over time, and in fact most Muslims have accepted that Quranic laws which implicitly allow slavery are outdated.
- Human rights are a major concern for most liberals. Many Muslim majority countries have signed international human rights treaties, but the impact of these largely remains to be seen in local legal systems. The Quranic story of Adam is sometimes interpreted to support human rights. Prominant Muslim international lawyers such as Mohammad Zafrullah Khan claim that there is no contradiction between International Human Rights and Sharia.
- Feminism is likewise a major issue. For this reason, non-liberal Muslims are often critical of polygamy. Some liberal Muslims accept that women may lead group prayers, although this topic remains contraversial. It is also accepted by many liberal Muslims that a woman may lead the state,

and that women should not be segregated from men in society or in mosques, although the custom is for women to pray behind men. Some Muslim feminists are also opposed to the traditional requirements of the veil, claiming that any modest clothing is sufficiently Islamic for both men and women.

- Many liberal Muslims favor the idea of modern democracy with separation of church and state, and support secular governments. The existence or applicability of Islamic law is thus questioned by liberals. Their argument often involves variants of the Mu'tazili theory that the Quran is created by God for the particular circumstances of the early Muslim community, and reason must be used to apply it to new contexts.
- This means that the majority of liberal Muslims have dropped literal or traditional interpretations of the Quran in favour of readings which they find more easily adaptable to modern society. For example, some liberals may tolerate homosexuality even though conservatives forbid it. However, this topic remains highly controversial even amongst Muslim liberals.
- The reliability and applicability of Hadith literature is questioned by liberals, as much of traditional Islamic law derives from it.
- Most liberal Muslims consequently do not believe in the authority of traditional scholars to issue a fatwa, since they generally favour the individual's ability to interpret Islamic sacred texts on their own. Tolerance is another major issue. Liberal Muslims are generally open to interfaith dialogue and differences, particularly in the case of the Ahmadi and other controversies with Jews, Christians, Hindus, etc.
- Liberal Muslims also tend to oppose the idea of jihad as armed struggle, and tend to prefer ideals such as non-violence. The Quranic figure of Abel seems to support the idea that anyone who dies as a result of refusing to commit violence is forgiven of their sins.

- Liberal Muslims tend to be skeptical about the validity of Islamization of knowledge (including Islamic economics, Islamic science and Islamic philosophy) as separate from mainstream fields of enquiry. This is usually due to the often secular outlook of Muslim liberals, which makes them more disposed to trust mainstream secular scholarship. They may also regard the propagation of these fields as merely a propaganda move by Muslim conservatives.

Liberals are also less likely to treat narratives of Adam, Noah, Abraham, Jesus and other prophets of Islam in the Quran as historical fact, viewing them instead as moral stories meant to reinforce the ethical message of Islam. As such liberals are more accepting of secular history and ideas such as evolution which they claim the Quran supports. As a result, liberals are generally opposed to the idea of Islamic history. The world today seems to be divided along several axes.

The two most widely discussed here in the United States are the Liberal-Conservative divide and the Islamic-Western one. Bill O'Reilly's recent best seller, *Culture Warrior,* sets out a potentially more useful division between traditionalists and secular progressives. While O'Reilly's actual division appears less theoretically or conceptually rigorous than it ought to be to actually have the intended effect — to wit, to awaken Americans to the assault on its national existence by America's enemies from without and within- withal, the popular television and radio pundit's intent and effect is a good and valuable one. O'Reilly defines a traditionalist or "T-Warrior" as follows: (a) He believes the US is essentially a good country seeking to do well in the world.

While he admits to flaws and mistakes, he nonetheless unqualifiedly defends his country. (b) He believes in a "Judeo-Christian philosophy," which O'Reilly distinguishes from religion per se or theology. The traditionalist explicitly welcomes Muslims and "all religious beliefs and one with no religious beliefs" so long as they don't try to destroy the traditional founding beliefs of the country. When asked to define this "philosophy" or to describe "the traditional founding beliefs," it appears to be a belief in private property, limited government, and the Golden Rule.

A secular-progressive, what O'Reilly terms in shorthand an S-P, believes that this country is fundamentally flawed and that it must "progress" to a more "enlightened" plane of existence. Essentially, what O'Reilly is getting at with this notion is the Elite's hatred of America and Western nation-states simply and a desire to establish a kind of liberal, multi-cultural One World State. O'Reilly insists that not all liberals are S-Ps, although it would seem that the modern liberal-conservative divide is mostly at work. To get a better flavor of how O'Reilly applies his archetypes we have the advantage of his Traditional/S-P test as an application of the paradigm. Yes = S-P; No = T-Warrior:

1. Do you believe in "income redistribution" – that is, the government taxing affluent Americans at a higher proportional rate in order to fund entitlements to the less well off?
2. Do you believe the definition of marriage should include homosexuals?
3. Do you think suspected terrorists captured overseas are entitled to Geneva Convention protections – that is, the same rights that military people are afforded?
4. Do you believe that the USA, in general, is harmful to the world?
5. Are you against states legally mandating that parents be informed when their underage daughters have abortions?

O'Reilly contends his divide does not follow a conservative-liberal axis, and he suggests this is demonstrated by his including Senator Lieberman and former Presidents Kennedy and Clinton among the traditionalists. The advantage of O'Reilly's *Culture Warrior* analysis is in a language that begins to get at the real threat to our survival. The shortcoming of his paradigm is that it lacks any sustained integrity of thought or of application. Thus, on the plus side of the ledger, the secular and progressive adjectives go to the heart of what it means to deny national existence simply and America's greatness.

A secular person rejects the Judeo-Christian principles and understanding of the world that was the bedrock of this country's approach to the establishment of a nation, the ties that bound neighbors and fellow citizens as one people, and the foundation of its laws. The secular, however, is of the view that freedom of thought and action is what made this country great and that religion, certainly organized religion, and this includes the Judeo-Christian varieties, are all to be removed from any and all aspect of political or public life. Morality for this crowd is a wholly civil affair devoid of truth and determined by preferences.

A progressive, accordingly, embraces first and foremost science because it is the progress of the modern scientific age which informs his view that History now occupies the place of the Transcendent in man's affairs. Man is able to study his Beginning and his End with a certainty and clarity only science and the new age of scientific reason can supply. That is, man can know nothing and experience no truth of the Beginning or the Beyond not objectified by the methods of science. A man might have a belief or personal faith in some religious view of his world, but it is mere belief and lacks the certainty only science provides.

The progressive is certain that America's now ancient and primitive past, including the original meaning and intent of its Constitution, is to be advanced and rectified along a linear line, if not exponential curve, toward an existence that knows absolutely no distinction among men and things in the world not verified by science. This view incorporates by necessity a radical egalitarianism and move toward internationalism and the One World Order quite simply because science does not recognize nations or peoples as anything but artificial and socially constructed prejudices. (Libertarians also fit the S-P mold with but the amendment that no political entity is to be trusted, preferring instead some version or degree of anarchic capitalism; this preference is driven as much by their own peculiar version of secular progressivism as in the case of the big government liberals.)

What O'Reilly terms an S-P, we have referred to as the Elite. In truth, the S-P nomenclature is probably a better one. It is here that O'Reilly has really hit on something. But, the fundamental shortcoming of O'Reilly's analytical divide lies in the fact that he does not take it seriously. A more serious and precise approach to and understanding of the secular progressive would include most everyone today who adopts the science-certainty/democracy-uncertainty reciprocal – likely a majority of Americans.

For the modern, the mathematical certainty of science is a given. And, this mathematically driven certainty occupies the only sphere of human knowledge which can claim certainty. All else of man's affairs, including his political experience as a nation and people, is founded upon subjective belief which can only be governed through a procedure or method which embraces the notion of a radical uncertainty. We call that method democracy. In other words, there is no truth in human affairs, only the method of deciding between and among ever-shifting beliefs, attitudes, and preferences. And, because there can be no truth in democracy, the losing minorities in the voting process are granted "rights" so as to guarantee there to be no loser in a political world that knows neither truth nor order.

But this description of the secular progressive includes just about everyone. Many religious Americans will accept the conclusion that their religious faith is mere belief. Truth is only available to science in its mathematical method. While a man might accept a Christian faith, there is no truth in his faith beyond his own "belief" or "opinion." To stake out a position of a participatory truth of existence in a Judeo-Christian world would be to exile oneself to the land of religious fanaticism – a political fate worse than that suffered by those who publicly acclaim America's undoing. This is why O'Reilly's application of his own terms is so wishy-washy and why he has been accused, properly so, of creating an artificial divide. As it turns out, even O'Reilly is a secular-progressive.

A traditionalist, if he were truly a man of tradition, would reject the implication that undermined the most basic concepts underlying America's founding. Those concepts included the understanding that while representative government was a legitimate system of governance, it must be carefully guarded by restricting the political franchise to the men who represented a People. In other words, representation works if there is some unique and defined People to represent. If a country claims to represent everyone, all religions, cultures, races, creeds equally, then it represents no People only "all things to all people" everywhere. This is precisely the undoing of Peoplehood and of national existence.

So it was that at America's founding and for more than a century thereafter that only male, white, land owners voted. The only "popular" vote allowed at the national level, again of white males and predominantly Christians, was for the House of Representatives, the least important of the representative bodies. Local governments and their legislative enactments were very much tied to the dominant religious affiliation of the common folk. Marriage, relationships, work, commerce, and legal holidays were all subject to laws that reflected the local Christian understanding of the world. At the founding and for many years thereafter a majority of the states had established churches. Political power was local and ordered and meant to reflect this truth of existence met by one's participation in America's political order.

Today, all of this is gone. The constitutional republic has been replaced by an Open Society, multi-cultural democracy driven by daily polls and surveys and virulently opposed to any political recognition of America's Christian foundings. Men and women of all creeds, colors, and loyalties have been granted the franchise to participate in governance. The idea of an American People is no more or less than mere legal citizenship and even that limitation is under assault by the Open Borders crowd.

Today, to be a "traditionalist" in any true sense is either to be condemned as a fascist or racist. To avoid this condemnation, O'Reilly sets about to rather arbitrarily redefine a traditionalist into a 20th century traditionalist. What this means is that what O'Reilly calls an S-P is anyone who doesn't agree with O'Reilly's personal view of which secular and progressive changes are good and which are ba d. O'Reilly is popular precisely because he understands that most Americans today are S-Ps and if he can arbitrarily redefine the terminology so that a traditionalist amounts to a kind of blended post-Civil Rights era conservative, he can still capture quite a big market for his brand of patriotism. O'Reilly is a populist, not a traditionalist and not strictly speaking a conservative.

To translate Bill O'Reilly is to explain that he most certainly accepts the understanding that science is certain and that all else is mere belief. This is why he purposefully defines the Judeo-Christian worldview as a "secular" philosophy and not a religious understanding. He wants to provide his Judeo-Christian worldview with a form of modern scientific rationalist glow. This is also why he is not prepared to condemn Islam even though the evidence is clear that Islam, historical and traditional Islam, is an enemy of America and the West. And, this is why he would condemn a return to an America that had not "progressed" into the 20th Century and provided African-Americans and women the right to vote.

While he opposes same-sex marriage, he is not prepared to embrace the Judeo-Christian condemnation of homosexuality, and certainly not for purposes of establishing a political or legal framework which might punish such behavior. The list goes on. Notwithstanding the obvious shortcomings, O'Reilly's book, *Culture Warrior*, is a good start because it is a popular book written by a conservative-leaning populist. By creating the semantic divide between secular-progressives and traditionalists, he has allowed a broader discussion and critique of the real divide undoing America's national existence.

For that, we applaud his move beyond the Republican Democrat or conservative-liberal divisions that have been so much a part of American political discourse. Whether the S-P/T-warrior distinction will become a useful approach depends very much on the ability of thoughtful religious conservatives to push this discussion beyond the PC discussion allowed on network or cable television.

8

Islam's Reaction to the West and Modernization

Elsewhere in the Muslim world bigotry and prejudice thrive as never before. Under Muslim rule today religious minorities live a life of fear and suspicion. In Malaysia, for example, demolition of Hindu temples and shrines; the ban on the use of the word Allah by Christians in the Malay language Bible; interdictions on proselytization; and the forced "rehabilitation" of apostates are among some of the sweeping norms of the Muslim fervor. The Arab world fares no better. While sharing many of the above traits with their co-religionists, Jordan and Egypt actively prosecute converts from Islam as is the case with the revolutionary Islamic Republic of Iran. Some recent reports indicate that the prevailing atmosphere of extremism in the Arab world is forcing Christians to emigrate in large numbers from their Arab motherland.

Not to mention the fact that "Muslim anti-Semitism"—an oxymoron in its own historical context (because Arabs are Semites) is touching new heights. On the other side of the fence—as if the last sigh of the Moor—the edifice of multiculturalism is crumbling under the burden of bigotry. Newspapers and electronic media, particularly the blogosphere, are replete with distortions and a degenerated discourse on Islam. One cannot fail to miss the surge in Islamophobia. Not limited to America, it is fast spreading to Europe under the coinage of "Eurabia," a euphemism for the invasion of Europe by Saracens leading to white slavery under the sharia laws. In other theaters, the birth of several Islamophobes, whether of con or neo-con lineage, is reinforcing the view that Muslim bashing is synonymous with career advancement.

The anti-Muslim lobby prides in its permanent members as well as glorified ex-Muslims and for the latter, opting for "apostasy" is not without tangible rewards. A bonus awaits those like Ayaan Hirsi Ali who are media savvy, compared to the poor ones who are lynched by mobs, flogged, stoned to death or imprisoned. The events and ideas shaping these two worlds do not necessarily support Samuel Huntington's thesis of a clash of civilizations. A closer look reveals a parallel idea: The claim to moral "superiority" under the authority of modernity fails to make an impact. Whereas Muslims are alleged to be engaging in medieval practices in the 21st century, the West too is not shy of invoking medieval symbolism in the contemporary discourse. On that count, it becomes a level playing field.

The presidential parleys on the Crusades and "Islamic fascism" aside, what is missing in this war of ideas is self-criticism, introspection, and the courage to laugh at ourselves. The absence of these crucial ingredients is what is fanning the flames of this war, sometimes touted as the Fourth World War. Beyond the blamable rhetoric, both Muslims and non-Muslims need to transcend the pious historicity and examine their affairs in an ontological setting. That is a small opening into the wider world of self-criticism that so badly awaits the Muslim discourse. Muslims, for most of their acts, have invariably sought refuge in blaming the West for all their ills. Any Western criticism of practices such as wife beating, honour killing, rape, and other afflictions brings up an apoplectic response, often laced with violence. Salman Rushdie's Satanic Verses and the Danish cartoons offer classic examples of typical Muslim reaction.

Little noticed is the fact that while the perpetrators of the blasphemies are unharmed, Muslims themselves bear self-inflicted loss of life and property. Muslim social ills are then relegated to cultural deviations rather than things theologically inspired. As an act of intellectual subservience, Muslim media show a reactionary streak in hoisting the virtuous flag of self-criticism. Why, for instance, should the genesis of self-criticism owe a debt to 9/11? Why must the wholesale apologia be made just suited to the aftermath of terror attacks? And by what token of reciprocity do the Western media owe them a debt? While Muslims in the West are not only the beneficiaries but ardent claimants to the fruits of a civic and democratic society, Muslim media have rarely told the plight of non-Muslims in Muslim lands.

If history is any guide, the medieval period in the life of these two worlds was not all that hostile. There was Convivencia. It was a period of free flowering of intellect where the three Abrahamic faiths coexisted in a mutually beneficial manner. Above self-criticism, the courage to accept and offer constructive criticism was the hallmark of that society. It was a powerful transition in the history of human ideas that spanned nearly five centuries in medieval Spain, only to be ruined by Reconquista. Contrary to the fears expressed, Kosovo's status as the world's newest largely Muslim nation in the heart of Europe will have far-reaching implications for the world.

In the words of Ilmi Krasniqi, the Imam at one of the mosques in the town of Gnjilane: "Our Islam is 'lite'—like Coke Lite or Marlboro Light." Are the tolerant voices coming out of independent Kosovo a precursor to a new Convivencia? And positive notes too are being played on the Western front: In Britain, officials now prefer to replace "Islamic terrorism" with the term "violent extremism," while the European Organization for Security and Cooperation has admitted that the failure to agree on a shared terminology in the wake of the September 11 attacks was "a major mistake on our part."

Isn't it time for Muslims to rise above self-pity and self-piety and pave the way for mutual engagement on some substantive issues? Perhaps the first step on the path to Convivencia is to recognize the pivotal role of self-criticism and a commitment to make it a public-square event. Outshining the mundane press releases on assorted condemnation of violence in the name of Islam is the fertile land of intro-spection. Will Muslims have the courage to meet this moral challenge?

The eighteenth century, which is generally viewed as a lean period of Islamic history with reference to the political disintegration and socio-moral decline, happened to be the seed bed of the Islamic revivalism. During this century, various movements started in different parts of the Muslim world to regenerate the society. This continued during the nineteenth century. To arrest the decadence and infuse new vitality in a society in which they were convinced that religion must remain the focal point, the reformers advocated a return to the movements and masters of Islamic theology and philosophy.

The essential diagnosis arrived at by the leaders of these reform movements was that Muslims reached this stage because they ceased to be "pure" Muslims since the purity of pristine Islam has been compromised with un-Islamic accretions both in doctrine and practice. The eighteenth century revivalism attempted to rehabilitate the theory and practice of Islam by insuring its authenticity and workability in changing situations. The revivalists slashed much of law and theology and rejected Sufism in its popular and speculative form.

It was an attempt to ensure that the new orientation of the Muslim world view in the limits set by Hadith studies and Neo-sufism would not only maintain the continuity and Islamic authenticity but would be a meaningful answer in the changing situation in terms of socio-moral reconstruction. The revivalist efforts have gone a long way to liberate Islam from the numbing medieval influences. Their influence has been certainly salutary in activating creative forces and in this connection the term "Ijtihad" (independent judgment) has once again assumed great importance, at least in theory.

The spirit of socio-moral reconstruction reached its zenith in the movement of Mohammad ibn Abdul Wahab (1703-1792), in the Arabian peninsula, who stressed that Islam was not static but a dynamic religion which in itself contained forces that would enable the Muslims to seek scientific and technical knowledge to put them on a level with the advancing nations of the world. He condemned Sufism and saint-worship. He denied all acts implying polytheism and advocated a return to the original teachings of Islam as incorporated in the Quran and Hadith, with condemnation of all innovations (bid'ah).

His rejection of medieval authorities left enough room for right of independent analysis of the fundamentals of faith. Mohammad ibn Abdul Wahab's theology and jurispro-ducence is based on the reaching of Ibn Taymiyah and on the legal school of Imam Ahmad ibn Hanbal. In India, Shah Walihullah, [1703-1762] a contemporary of Abdul Wahab, was of the view that Islamic code of life was meant for all ages and for all peoples could prove true only if it had enough elasticity to provide an answer to the growing needs of a progressive civilization and the new problems which humanity would have to face from time to time.

The Muslim jurists in every age would therefore necessarily be called upon to exercise their judgement in reinterpreting and making new provisions in law, of course within the framework of the fundamentals of Shariah. He believed that it was the duty of Muslim scholars and Ulema of every age to exercise ijtihad and laments that the simple minded people of his time were too ignorant to attach due importance to it. Since the nineteenth century, the Muslim world has felt the impact of the West—first political and then cultural. Therefore, the main intellectual concern regarding the direction of the Muslim world, during the past two centuries, has been with the demands of modernity placed upon traditional societies.

The main thrust of modernism was the search for an acceptable formula to reconcile Islam with the secularized West. In this effort, modernists begin with internal criticism of the existing state of Muslims in history. They sought a return to the first principles of Islam to unburden it of all the unnecessary dogmas accumulated over the centuries, and face the challenge of the new world by being favourably disposed toward it. The modernist perspective was shaped in the milieu of colonial imperial expansion of European powers into the Muslim world, and at the peak of Europe's confidence of itself as the most highly evolved civilization. The reality of the 19th century Europe favorably influenced a great many Muslim intellectuals of the period.

The situation of Muslims in general was now the reverse of the one they occupied in the pre-Renaissance period, when Europe borrowed from the Islamic Arab Persian civilization. The most distressing reality for modernists was the state of decay of the Muslim world when compared to the dynamism of the European. The primary concern for the first generation of modernist thinkers was the need to reorient the direction of Muslim history, to reinterpret Islam in the context of modern science and learning, to put a brake on further decay of the Muslim world. The intellectual challenge for modernists was to convince Muslims that the demands of both Islam and the West "were not incompatible with each other."

The five most prominent modernists during the latter half of the 19th century were: Sayed Ahmad Khan and Sayed Amir Ali in India, Jamal alDin al Afghani in Iran, Namik Kemal in Turkey and Muhammad Abduh in Egypt. They insisted on returning to the undiluted first principles of Islam through a new reading of the Quran which would show that the new science based on the principles of observation and experimentation was Quranic in its impulse.

They recommended the revitalization of ijtihad (independent reasoning) in Muslim thinking and practice, and called for the rejection of taqlid (imitation), the submission to the authority of classical jurists in interpreting the Quran and the Sunnah. Technological modernity intrinsic to western civilization, it is said, allows ultimately no alternative to Muslims or anyone clinging to pre-technical values. According to Daniel Pipes, "worldly success requires modernization; modernization requires Westernization; westernization requires secularism; secularism must be preceded by a willingness to emulate the West."

The development gap made continuously wider by technological modernity places Muslims on the lower side of the gap, and presents them with the most difficult of all historical questions: can a traditional society achieve industrial development by importing technology which undermines its cultural heritage, opens a breach in its tradition and undermines its world view? However, very few Muslims believe that the appropriation of modern technology would necessitate a change in ideological commitment.

The idea that science and Islam are compatible is put forward in one form or another in the construction of all Muslim ideologues of the nineteenth and twentieth centuries. Jamal al-Din al-Afghani (1839-1897), the pioneer of pan-Islamism, was convinced that nothing but science and technology could eliminate economic and cultural backwardness. Afghani objected to dividing science into European and Muslim. He said modern science as universal, transcending nations, cultures and religion. Afghani criticised the Muslim scholars for not seeing it that way by saying: "The strangest thing of all is that our ulema these days have divided science into two parts. One they call Muslim science, and one European science. Because of this they forbid others to teach some of the useful sciences."

Afghani was indignant that natural science was left out of the curriculum of Muslim educational establishments. He said: 'Those who imagine that they are saving religion by imposing a ban on some sciences and knowledge are enemies of religion.' In an article, 'The Benefits of Study and Education", Afghani said that the misery in the Eastern countries was due to their ignoring "the noble and important role of the scientists". Afghani himself set a very high value on the public mission of the scientist.

In December 1870, speaking at a conference on the progress of science and the crafts held in the New Istanbul University, Dar ul-funun, he described the scientist's work as missionary. He compared the scientist with a prophet, saying that prophecy is a craft (sanat) like medicine, philosophy, mathematics, and so on. The sole difference was that the prophet's verity was the fruit of inspiration, whereas scientific verity was the fruit of reason. Whilst expounding the virtues and indispensability of science, Afghani was also at pains to stress that science needed another "science" which is more comprehensive which would enable man to know how to apply each field in its proper place.

This field of knowledge is falsifa (philosophy) or hikam (wisdom) and only it can show man the human prerequisites (values such as what is more important, more fair, more just etc.) Afghani says: "It is philosophy that shows the man the proper road and makes man understandable to man." To Afghani, Islam is a scientific religion and by this he did not mean to circumscribe Islam within mere science either. He says: "Since it is known that religion is unquestionably the source of man's welfare, therefore if it is placed on firm foundations and sound bases, that religion will naturally become the complete source of total happiness and perfect tranquillity.

Above all it will be the cause of material and moral progress. It will elevate the banner of civilization among its followers. It will cause those who are religious to attain all intellectual and spiritual perfection and to achieve good fortune in this world and the next." He did not advocate a merely negative Islamic reaction against the West. He believed that the Muslim belief is a powerful political force. He called for a revitalization of Islam which would permit the Muslim world to absorb modern science. Afghani continued the cosmopolitan tradition of Islamic intellectuals in the course of a migrant life which took him from his native Iran to India, Afghanistan, Turkey, Egypt, France Russia and elsewhere.

In the late nineteenth century, Sir Syed Ahmad Khan from India and Sheikh Muhammad Abduh from Egypt recommended reformation of Islamic society along similar lines though from slightly different perspectives. Syed Ahmad Khan was in favor of showing that modern science and technology were in conformity with the articles of Islamic faith. Muhammad Abduh' rulings as the Chief Mufti of Egypt, were influenced by the principle of public interest (maslaha). He observed: "If a ruling has become the cause of harm which it did not cause before, then we must change it according to the prevailing conditions."

Traditional Islam, Sheikh Mohammad Abduh argued, faced serious challenge by the modern, rational and scientific thought. But he did not believe that the faith of Islam in its pure and permanent core of norms clashed with science. Instead he asserted that the faith and scientific reason operate at different levels. The real Islam, he maintained: "had simple doctrinal structure: it consisted of certain beliefs about the greatest questions of human life, and certain general principles of human conduct. To enable us to reach these beliefs and embody them in our lives both reason and revelation are essential. They neither possess separate spheres nor conflict with each other in the same sphere..."

Sheikh Mohammad Abduh's aim was to interpret the Islamic law in such a way as to free it from the traditional interpretations and prove that Islam and modern Western civilization were compatible. Abduh was convinced of the supremacy of human reason. Religion merely supplements and aids reason. Reason sits in judgment on religion. Islam is, above all, the religion of reason and all its doctrines can be logically and rationally demonstrated.

Sheikh Abduh was thus the chief exponent of what has been termed as the "Two-Book" school of thought which, though it basically holds the unity of God inseparable from the unity of truth, recognizes two open ways to it: the way of revelation and that of natural science. He contended that since

God's purpose in marking His revelation was to promote human welfare, a true interpretation of the Quran and the Sunnah should essentially be the one which best fulfils this purpose. He himself took the lead in this direction.

As the Chief Mufti of Egypt, he issued fatwas ranging from the questions of law to those of social morality and employed the same measure of innovation and rationality in his interpretations, assessments and judgements. In matters of Islamic law, which governed Muslim family relationships, ritual duties, and personal conduct, Abduh tried to break through the rigidities of scholastic interpretation and to promote considerations of equity, welfare, and common sense, even if this occasionally meant disregarding the literal texts of the Quran.

Abduh's, rationalism is directed against inert traditional thinking and blind observance of the medieval interpretation of Islam. Also it is designed to vindicate and defend religion, to adapt it to the new times, and to reconcile it with science. It would be a mistake to think, however, that Abduh and other Muslim reformers confine themselves exclusively to justifying and modernizing religion.

Despite the narrowness of their concepts they are sincerely interested in eliminating the obstacles to the development of science and technology essential for the revival of the Muslim peoples and for economic and cultural progress. What they want, however, is to use scientific achievements without heed of the world outlook implicit in science. Abduh deplored the blind acceptance of traditional doctrines and customs and asserted that a return to the pristine faith of the earliest age of Islam not only would restore the Muslims' spiritual vitality but would provide an enlightened criterion for the assimilation of modern scientific culture.

The pioneer of Indian Muslim reform, Sir Sayyed Ahmad Khan, basically subscribed to the same ideas of Islamic reform as Sheikh Abduh. Both agreed to the point of necessity to harmonize Islam with modern science and rationalism. Sir Sayyed, however, viewed revelation by the criterion of its conformity to Nature. To him, Islam was the religion of most akin to Nature. Reason and 'conformity to Nature' according to Sir Sayyed was the essence of Islam.

His main argument was that the Quran was the word of God and the nature was the work of God; a disparity between the two was unthinkable. According to him, Wahy (revelation) and reason are identical. The latter operates in man's scientific investigations as much as in his concept of deity, his distinction between good and evil, his views on divine judgment and retribution, and his belief in life after death. For him reason alone is the right instrument of judging truth.

Although Sir Sayyed Ahmad Khan accepts the term Wahy but does not attach to it any special significance; it is mere inspiration in a most highly developed state: prophethood, in other words, was a natural faculty, and not a gift through the grace of God as the orthodox Muslims believes. As a corollary he puts forward the view that revelation was not something external brought to a prophet by an angel, as was generally believed, but a natural phenomenon like other human faculties.

Sir Sayyed Ahmad Khan rejects the Fiqh totally. He says that in the past religiously mined scholars thought that, as far as possible, every thing should be done with the support of some religious authority. Therefore, when any problem arose, they searched for some religious sanction and with the help of far-fetched arguments and interpretations; they placed it under some religious ruling or subjected it to some general principle laid down by themselves. The sayings and arguments of those religious scholars began to be collected and assumed the shape of Fiqh and books relating to the principles of Fiqh.

Sir Sayyed Ahmad Khan lays stress on the fact that every age should have a living Mujtahid whom all the problems should be referred to. He says that it is a great error on the part of the Ahlussnah Wal Jama'aah to hold the opinon that Ijtihad has come to an end and Mujtahids have become non-existent. This doctrine has done immense harm to the Muslims and should now be abandoned. We should develop a spirit of enquiry and research. Life in every age brings new problems and new needs. If we do not have living Mujtahids then how can we ask the dead Mujtahids of their needs and problems which had no existence.

Sir Sayyed Ahmad Khan goes on to stress that worldly affairs should not be dragged into the province of religion, because what is religious is unchangeable, while worldly matters keep on changing. The Quran, he adds, contains less than five hundred verses bearing on worldly affairs. In any case, the fact that the Quran mentions a few worldly matters constitutes no argument that worldly affairs are included in the religion. Sir Sayyed Ahmad Khan had sought to show that Islam was no barrier to scientific inquiry and social progress. He was the first thinker, after the 1857 Muslim revolt against the British colonialists, to realize this pathetic condition of the Muslims.

He attributed this condition to three causes:

1. The superstitious beliefs and practices that had entered Indian Islam.
2. Lack of emphasis on the assimilative and universal character of Islam, and
3. The aversion of the Muslims to Western education.

Against the opposition of the Ulama, who declared him as a heretic, Sayyed Ahmad Khan established the Anglo-Muhammadan College at Aligarh, the nucleus of the Muslim University of Aligarh, which created a new Muslim generation who believed in Islam and also favored modern trends. In his series of articles published in the "Tahzibul Akhlaq" and public speeches, he boldly spoke against the general and indiscriminate practice of polygamy, for modification of the doctrine of riba (interest) and against some punishments like stoning to death and cutting off of hands. He also explained the phenomenon of revelation and restricted Quran and Sunnah to devotional matters. In his opinion religious injunctions relating to social, economic and cultural matters were applicable to primitive societies.

Rashid Rida, a Syrian scholar and the disciple of Mohammad Abduh, also argues in favour of reasoning when he says that the Quran taught its followers to ask for arguments and our virtuous ancestors followed the same course. Rashid Rida emphasizes the need for going back to the spirit of Islamic laws and for knowledge of the principles on which they are founded. He says that many people know what is lawful and what is unlawful but they do not know why a particular act has been declared unlawful.

To act on laws it is necessary to understand the reasons lying behind them and to know what purposes or general interests, they serve. Today people know Ahkam (injunctions) without knowing the Hikmah (wisdom) behind them. Yet it was essentially the knowledge of Hikma behind the laws which enabled the companions of the prophet to rule over large territories and administer them in the best interests of the people.

Rashid Rida pleads for Ijtihad by stressing that Islam as a religion is based on reason and the Islamic Sharia is founded on the basis of Ijtihad. Without Ijtihad, it is difficult to claim that Islam is an eternal religion. Therefore, if any person stands in the way of Ijtihad or tries to prevent it, he is really undermining the basis of Islam and its Sharia and destroying its distinctiveness from other religions. "What a heinous crime is being committed, then, by these ignorant persons who call themselves the Ulema of Islam."

Rashid Rida says that Islam had given us perfect liberty to order the affairs of our life. Barring a few restrictions laid down in the Quran and the Sunnah, the entire field of human affairs was left open, only it was stipulated that matters would be decided through shura or consultations. But we put ourselves under unnecessary restrictions which were not sanctioned by religion and it was thought in later ages, that in defending these artificial restrictions, we are defending our religion. This circumscribed our freedom of action and disabled us from marching with times or borrowing useful institutions and laws from other nations.

He believed that the backwardness of the Muslim countries resulted from a neglect of the true principles of Islam. He believed that these principles could be found in the teachings of the Prophet Mohammed and in the practices of the first generation of Muslims, before corruption began to spread among the religious practices of the faithful. He was convinced that Islam, as a body of teachings correctly understood, contained all the principles necessary for happiness in this world and the hereafter, and that positive effort to improve the material basis of the community was the essence of Islam.

Zia Gokalp, who has been considered as the most influential spiritual founder of Turkish nationalism, affirmed that Islam had been equipped with an adequate framework to accommodate and adapt to morphological changes in time and space. He says that the injunctions of the Quran (nass or text) stay eternal and unchangeable while 'urf' or the collective ideas and ijma – the consensus of the scholars – allow enough room for the dogma to adapt itself to changing necessities of life.

According to Gokalp, the Islamic law has a two-fold source: the traditional Shariah and the Social Shariah.

The Social Shariah is continually changing in accordance with social evolution. The stagnation of the world of Islam is due to the failure of the Muslims to relate the 'nass' to the 'urf' by means of ijtihad. Gokalp has no doubt that Islam is the only religion that exhorts change. He found Quranic sanction for the secular authorities to assume legislative functions in Islam in the verse: 'Obey God and the Prophet, and those in authority among you.' Those 'in authority' are surely to exercise their authority in the secular-mundane sphere.

For this differentiation, he demanded the transfer of the judiciary functions of the Sheikh al Islam to the legislature and urged that the office of Sheikh al Islam should be more of a scholar, devoid of political authority. Another of his demands was the abolition of the Ministry of Awkaf and a ban on the various Dervish orders who had misused the pious endowments for self-perpetuation and the propagation of their exaggerated belief in fatalism. Gokalp also advocated the modernization of Muslim family life and urged the complete abandonment of purdah and the unqualified recognition of equality of the sexes.

Ziya Gokalp was among the earliest public figures in Turkey to champion a purely secular state which was later established by Mustafa Kemal. "In the first place, in a modern state, the right to legislate and to administer directly belongs to the people. No office, no tradition and no other right can restrict and limit this right. In the second place, all members of the modern nation, regardless of their religious affiliation, are regarded as equal to reach other in every respect. In short, all provisions existing in our laws that are contrary to liberty, equality and justice and all traces of theocracy and clericalism should be completely eliminated."

The same struggle at an intellectual level was pursued by Muhammad Iqbal during the 1930s in the Indian subcontinent. Iqbal's greatest contribution lay in his attempts to understand the nature and thrust of global forces as manifested in Western cultural and intellectual dominance. His response was both intellectual and institutional. He argued that, "the claim of present generations of Muslim liberals to interpret the foundational legal principles, in the light of their own experience and the altered conditions of modern life is perfectly justified.

The teachings of the Quran that life is a process of progressive creation necessitates that each generation, guided but unhampered by the work of its predecessors, should be permitted to solve its own problems. A false reverence of past history and its artificial resurrection constitute no remedy for a people's decay. The verdict of history is that worn out ideas& nbsp; have never risen to power among a people who have worn them out."Iqbal believed that there are two spheres of Islam; one is "ibadaat" which is based on the religious obligations (arkan-i- deen) - these do not require any change; the other sphere is that of "muamelaat" (social dealings) which is subject to the law of change.

He says: "The Shariah values (ahkam) resulting from this application (for example, rules referring to penalties for crimes) are in a sense specific to that people; and since their observance is not an end itself they cannot be strictly enforced in future generations."

Iqbal thought that both the institutions of ijma (overall consensus of the community) and ijtihad (creative judgment) could be lodged in a Muslim assembly. If such an assembly were to develop its own knowledge and expertise in Islamic law, there was no need for the ulama to exercise their veto on the deliberations of the assembly. "The primary source of the law of Islam is the Quran. The Quran however, is not the legal code. Its main purpose is to awaken in man the higher consciousness of his relation with God and the universe. The principle of movement in Islam is ijtihad - effort to form an independent opinion.

The transfer of power of ijtihad to a Muslim legislative assembly which, in view of the growth of the opposing sects is the only possible form ijma can take in modern times; will secure contributions to legal discussions from laymen who happen to possess a keen insight into affairs. The closing of the door of ijtihad is a pure fiction suggested partly by the crystallization of legal thought in Islam and partly by intellectual laziness which, especially in the period of spiritual decay turns great thinkers into idols."

Iqbal pleaded that equipped with penetrative through and fresh experience the world of Islam should courageously proceed to the work of reconstruction before them. But he was aware that this work of reconstruction has a far more serious aspect than mere adjustment in modern conditions life. He was of the view that "humanity needs three things today - a spiritual interpretation of the universe, spiritual emancipation of the individual, and basic principles of a universal import directing the evolution of human society on a spiritual basis.

Modern Europe, has no doubt, built idealistic systems on these lines, but experience shows that truth revealed through pure reason is incapable of bringing that fire of living conviction which personal revelation alone can bring. This is the reason why pure thought has so little influenced men while religion has always elevated individuals, and transformed whole societies."

Sayyed Amir Ali, an eminent Indian scholar, was of the view that the plight that has fallen on the Mu to the universality of the Master's teachings, unassisted by his spirit and devoid of his inspiration, have adapted his utterances to their own limited notions of human needs and human progress. They mixed up the temporary with the permanent, the universal with the particular. In the Western world, the Reformation was ushered in by the Renaissance and the progress of Europe commenced when it threw off the shackles of Ecclesiasticism. In Islam also, enlightenment must precede reform and before there can be a renovation of religious life, the mind must first escape from the bondage, centuries of literal interpretation and the doctrine of conformity have imposed upon it."

Sayyed Amir Ali called for reformation in Islam. He advocated the philosophy of Mutazilites by saying "Under them rationalism acquired a predominance such as it has not gained perhaps even in modern times in European countries. The idea of these philosophers was the same as has gained ground in modern times owing to the extension of natural science. But they were, in fact, the exponents of the doctrine of Ta'lil or agnosticism. It appears, therefore that the Islam of Muhammad contains nothing in itself which bars the progress or the intellectual development of humanity."

Sayyed Amir Ali believes that the ordinances and injunctions of the prophet were of a temporary nature and that the prophet never intended them to be eternally binding on the Muslims. The prophet relied more on moral persuasion. "...to suppose that the greatest Reformer the world has ever produced, the greatest upholder of the sovereignty of reason, ever contemplated that those injunctions which were called forth by the passing necessities of a semicivilised people should become immutable, is doing an injustice to the Prophet of Islam," he suggested. Sayyed Amir Ali accuses the jurists and theologians of having misinterpreted the message of Islam to satisfy their own whimsicalities or the capricious dictates of the Caliphs and Sultans whose obsequious servants they were.

Bibliography

Armstrong, Karen. *Islam: A Short History.* New York: Modern Library, revised ed., 2002.

Awde, Nicholas, trans. and ed. *Women in Islam: An Anthology from the Qur'an and Hadîths.* New York: Palgrave Macmillan, 2000.

Burrell, D. *Knowing the Unknowable God: Ibn Sina, Maimonides, Aquinas* (Notre Dame: 1986).

Cook, Michael. *The Koran: A Very Short Introduction.* Oxford, UK: Oxford University Press, 2000.

Corbin, H. *History of Islamic Philosophy*, trans. L. Sherrard. London, 1993.

Craig, E. (ed.), *Routledge Encyclopedia of Philosophy.* London, 1998.

Davidson, H.A. *Proofs for Eternity, Creation and the Existence of God in Medieval Islamic and Jewish Philosophy.* Oxford, 1987.

Elias, Jamal J. *Islam.* Upper Saddle River, NJ: Prentice Hall, 1999.

Esposito, John L. and John Obert Voll. *Makers of Contemporary Islam.* UK, Oxford University Press, 2001.

Esposito, John L. *Islam: The Straight Path.* New York, Oxford University Press, 3rd ed., 1998.

Esposito, John L. *The Oxford Encyclopedia of the Modern Islamic World*, 4 Vols. UK, Oxford University Press, 1995.

Fakhry, M. *A History of Islamic Philosophy* , 2nd ed. New York, 1983.

Gutas, D. *Greek Philosophers in the Arabic Tradition.* Aldershot, 2000.

Hodgson, Marshall G.S. *The Venture of Islam,* 3 Vols. Chicago, IL: University of Chicago Press, 1974.

Hourani, G. (ed.), *Essays on Islamic Philosophy and Science.* Albany, 1978.

Hyman, A. and Walsh, J.J. *Philosophy in the Middle Ages.* Indianapolis,1973.

Murata, Sachiko and William C. Chittick. *The Vision of Islam.* New York: Paragon House, 1994.

Nasr, S.H. and Leaman, O. (eds.), *History of Islamic Philosophy* , 2 vols. London , 1996.

Nasr, Seyyed Hossein. *Ideals and Realities of Islam.* London: Allen & Unwin, 1966.

Nasr, Seyyed Hossein. *Islam: Religion, History, and Civilization.* San Francisco, CA: Harper San Francisco, 2002.

Nasr, Seyyed Hossein. *Islamic Spirituality I: Foundations.* New York: Crossroad, 1987.

Nasr, Seyyed Hossein. *Islamic Spirituality II: Manifestations.* New York: Crossroad, 1991.

Nasr, Seyyed Hossein. *The Heart of Islam: Enduring Values for Humanity.* San Francisco, CA, Harper San Francisco, 2002.

Newby, Gordon D. *A Concise Encyclopedia of Islam.* Oxford, UK, Oneworld, 2002.

Peters, F.E. *A Reader on Classical Islam.* Princeton, NJ: Princeton University Press, 1994.

Qadir , C.A. *Philosophy and Science in the Islamic World.* London, 1990.

Rahman, Fazlur. *Islam.* Chicago, IL: University of Chicago

Press, 2nd ed., 1979.

Rosenthal, F. *Greek Philosophy in the Arab World.* Aldershot, 1990.

Ruthven, Malise. *Islam in the World.* New York: Oxford University Press, 2nd ed., 2000.

Savory, R.M., ed. *Introduction to Islamic Civilization.* Cambridge, UK: Cambridge University Press, 1976.

Schimmel, Annemarie. *Islam: An Introduction.* Albany, NY: State University of New York Press, 1992.

Schulze, Reinhard. *A Modern History of the Islamic World.* Washington Square, NY: New York University Press, 2000.

Stern, S.M., Hourani, H. and Brown, V. (eds.), *Islamic Philosophy and the Classical Tradition.* Oxford, 1972.

Tayob, Abdulkader. *Islam: A Short Introduction.* Oxford, England: Oneworld, 1999. University of Chicago Press, 1986.

Waines, David. *An Introduction to Islam.* Cambridge, UK: Cambridge University Press, 1995.

Watt, M.W. Islamic Philosophy and Theology. Edinburgh, 1962, revised ed. 1985.

Wolfson, H.A. *Studies in the History of Philosophy and Religion* , ed. I. Twersky, G.H. Williams, in 2 vols. Cambridge, MA, 1973, 1977.

Wolfson, H.A. *The Philosophy of the Kalam.* Cambridge, MA, 1976.

Ziai, H. "Islamic Philosophy," in *The Oxford Companion to Philosophy,* ed. T. Honderich. Oxford , 1955.

INDEX